THUCYDIDES

ATHENS AND CORCYRA

THUCYDIDES

ATHENS AND CORCYRA

Strategy and Tactics in the Peloponnesian War

JOHN WILSON

Bristol Classical Press

This impression 2003
This edition published in 1987 by
Bristol Classical Press
an imprint of
Gerald Duckworth & Co. Ltd.
90-93 Cowcross Street, London EC1M 6BF
Tel: 020 7490 7300
Fax: 020 7490 0080
inquiries@duckworth-publishers.co.uk
www.ducknet.co.uk

© by John Wilson 1987

A catalogue record for this book is available
from the British Library

ISBN 0 86292 196 1

CONTENTS

PREFACE

My chief aim in this book hardly requires explanation or defence:
it is to shed more light on certain events in Corcyrean history, as
described by Thucydides, in relation to Athenian strategy during
the Peloponnesian War, particularly in the period 433-25 B.C.
Part 1 deals with the Epidamnos and Sybota campaigns (435-33);
Part 2 with the Corcyrean *stasis* (civil war) (427-25), together
with important tailpieces which fall outside that period. On any
account, the subject-matter has received much less its due share of
attention from historians: much less, certainly, than Thucydides
himself gives it (52 chapters: see Appendix). Indeed it is fair
to say that north-west Greece in general (not just Corcyra) has
usually been seen as historically and strategically peripheral,
just as - perhaps partly because - it appears geographically
peripheral to the main centres of Greek power towards the east and
south. Hence many important problems have passed unnoticed, and
solutions to other problems too casually adopted. I hope to show
the reader that my topic is central to the strategy of the
Peloponnesian War as a whole.

The first task for any serious scholarship here must surely be to
establish the facts: that is, the historical, topographical and
tactical details of what actually happened, together with the immediate causes and explanations. This can only be done by pressing the
text of Thucydides as hard as possible: and the larger part of
this book is concerned with the detailed analysis necessary for
this purpose. I write for the general reader who may be interested
in what is by any standards an exciting piece of history, as well
as for scholars; but I do not want to retrace ground already covered by other authors, and shall confine myself almost entirely to
dealing with new problems and shedding new light on old ones. I
hope thereby to produce a fuller and more coherent narrative of the actual events than we now possess.

However, certain features emerge from this analysis which (in my
judgement) appear important for a better understanding of Athenian
strategy in the Peloponnesian War, and of the crucial part which
Corcyra played in it. Here, inevitably, we bump up against wider
considerations of strategy, politics and other more general matters,
which must inevitably be regarded as more controversial - or, at
least, controversial at a more theoretical level. Rather than con-
fuse these issues with my main aim - to establish the detailed facts -,
I have relegated them to an Appendix, which I hope will be of interest if only because it makes use of the insights achieved by a more
detailed grasp of the facts themselves.

For convenience, I have printed the relevant passages of Thucydides
at the beginning of each Part of the book (and also one from Diodorus),
together with my own translation (which aims at clarity rather than
aesthetic merit); this should enable the reader to grasp the general
picture, and also saves repeating parts of the text in those (very
many) cases where historical fact turns upon a correct interpretation of the Greek.

I have not thought it right to mention by name all those past and
present Thucydidean scholars whose remarks are at any point rele-
vent; the constant references would make a complex topic impossible

to lay out with any clarity or concision. I make an exception
in the case of Gomme, whose commentary rates as a standard work
and is readily available to all readers, and in one or two other
cases (notably Hammond, perhaps our leading authority on north-
west Greece); but my hope is to avoid, as far as possible, re-
producing the hand-to-hand combats of scholarship. This has been
the easier in that scholars have given little or no attention to
many of the topics here treated.

For the same reason I have not considered it desirable, for the
purposes of this book, to offer the reader anything like a full
bibliography and set of references: a herculean task in view of
the immense amount that has been written on Thucydides and on the
Peloponnesian War. It seemed more sensible to list only those
(comparatively few) authors who are mentioned in the text, together with a brief selection of other works which are either
directly relevant or useful for grasping the general background.
Nearly all important references are given in Gomme's commentary
(I include its continuation by Andrewes and Dover). For the
reader who wishes to put our topic into a wider perspective there
are several excellent general histories, which I have listed; for
the reader who wishes rather to devote himself to detailed analysis
and research, either into our topic or any similar one, I should
recomment close and repeated reading of Thucydides rather than,
or at least before, any other author ancient or modern.

So far as ancient authors are concerned, I shall take it for
granted that Thucydides is by far the most important source for
our topic (indeed for details of tactics and topography he is
our only source); and also that he was a sufficiently conscientious,
reliable and well-informed writer for his words to stand up to very
close analysis. Most of that is, I imagine, common ground: that
this kind of close analysis does in fact justify our high opinion
of him I have tried to show elsewhere (Wilson 1979) and hope again
to show here. Nearly all scholars have been far too quick to convict him of mistakes or misinformation, or to convict the received
text of inaccuracy. There is, however, one event - the second
Corcyrean *stasis* in 410 - for which we have to rely on other and
less trustworthy reportage: fortunately it does no more than shed
a sidelight on our main topic, and the reliability of our evidence
is discussed briefly in the main text. Apart from this, I shall
mention secondary sources (notably Diodorus) only when they have
some claim to credibility.

Familiarity with good maps, and in some cases personal inspection
of the terrain, is virtually essential. There are few if any wholly
accurate maps (none on a large enough scale); as a basis for the
maps at the end of this book I have used the outlines of existing
maps but with certain relevant features redrawn from my own observation during the summers of 1977-79. There are some hydrographical
problems concerning the exact shoreline and sea-depths in some
places: unfortunately, according to most scientists, without defini-
tive solutions, but fortunately not of much historical significance.
The same is true of weather and wind conditions.

Finally I should point out in advance that I intend nothing like
a complete coverage of the period, even so far as Corcyra is concerned; nor yet a complete commentary on the Thucydides text. My
topic is tolerably circumscribed by the notions of strategy and

tactics. Other cognate matters are of course relevant: particularly, perhaps, further investigation of the Corcyrean economy and Corinthian trade, and some discussion of the home politics behind Athenian decisions (or lack of them), might have been added. Both these, however, are extremely speculative and uncertain topics, already covered more fully and competently by other authors than I could have done (see for instance Ste. Croix (1972)). I confine myself largely to the more pedestrian, but to my mind equally exciting, task of trying to determine what actually happened in as much detail as possible.

The paucity of scholarly writing on my topic does not mean, of course, that I have not learned a great deal from others: particularly from Gomme, Hammond and Ste. Croix; if I mention their views chiefly to disagree with them, that is because they have given us something worth taking seriously: indeed anyone writing on Thucydides must stand on their shoulders, however heavily. I am also much indebted to many individuals who have spent time and trouble on the manuscript of this book: especially Professor H.L. Westlake, and to Thomas Wiedemann, both of whose comments and criticisms have been particularly detailed and illuminating.

Proper Names

Where names may be familiar to readers, I have kept the standard forms (Athens, Corinth, Corcyra, Diodorus, Thucydides, etc.): elsewhere I have endeavoured to keep as close to the classical Greek spellings as possible. There are of course many borderline cases, and I trust that readers will forgive apparent inconsistencies.

References

For convenience I have incorporated references to other authors in the main text. References to modern authors - there are comparatively few - are given thus: Gomme (1956, p.43), or without the date when there is no ambiguity about the work in question. Full details of these works, with some others, will be found in the short bibliography. References to Thucydides and other ancient authors are given in the usual way: e.g. I.36.2.

Text and Translation

For the main narrative in Thucydides, I have printed the Oxford Classical Text as its stands: problems about variant readings (not many) are discussed in the main text, along with problems of translation and interpretation. The same goes for the short passage from Diodorus, where I have used the text of the Loeb edition (1950, reprinted 1962).

All this is translated in full, page by page; the reader without any knowledge of Greek should find it easy to refer to this translation when particular passages are discussed in the main text (where I have not always repeated the translation). Where passages outside this main narrative are discussed in the text, I have given an accompanying translation.

Technical Terms in Greek

There are a few transliterations of Greek words, which (like most ancient historians) I have used for convenience: e.g. *stasis*, *oligoi*, *demos*. Brief translations of these are given for the reader without Greek when the terms are first used; he should be warned, however, that there is often no exact English equivalent. (The sense of the terms is often deeply embedded, so to speak, in the history itself: which is why historians continue to use them.)

PART I

EPIDAMNOS AND SYBOTA (435-433 B.C.)

The relevant passages, given below, are I.24-31 and I.44-55.
I have not included the speeches of the Corcyrean and
Corinthian ambassadors (I.32-43). It is both more conveni-
ent and more reliable to deal with those few passages in
these speeches which are relevant to our concern under different headings, where they may be placed alongside evidence from Thucydides speaking in his own person rather
than reporting (or inventing) someone else's speech: for
instance, the Corcyrean arguments of 36.2-3, to which
Thucydides gives the Athenian reaction in 44.2-3. The
historicity of Thucydidean speeches in general is widely
questioned; and though I myself would go a good deal
further towards accepting it than many scholars, I do not
want to build on questionable assumptions.

24 Ἐπίδαμνός ἐστι πόλις ἐν δεξιᾷ ἐσπλέοντι ἐς
τὸν Ἰόνιον κόλπον· προσοικοῦσι δ' αὐτὴν Ταυλάντιοι
2 βάρβαροι, Ἰλλυρικὸν ἔθνος. ταύτην ἀπώκισαν μὲν
Κερκυραῖοι, οἰκιστὴς δ' ἐγένετο Φαλίος Ἐρατοκλείδου
Κορίνθιος γένος τῶν ἀφ' Ἡρακλέους, κατὰ δὴ τὸν
παλαιὸν νόμον ἐκ τῆς μητροπόλεως κατακληθείς.
ξυνῴκισαν δὲ καὶ Κορινθίων τινὲς καὶ τοῦ ἄλλου
3 Δωρικοῦ γένους. προελθόντος δὲ τοῦ χρόνου ἐγένετο
ἡ τῶν Ἐπιδαμνίων δύναμις μεγάλη καὶ πολυάνθρωπος·
4 στασιάσαντες δὲ ἐν ἀλλήλοις ἔτη πολλά, ὡς λέγεται,
ἀπὸ πολέμου τινὸς τῶν προσοίκων βαρβάρων ἐφθάρησαν
5 καὶ τῆς δυνάμεως τῆς πολλῆς ἐστερήθησαν. τὰ δὲ
τελευταῖα πρὸ τοῦδε τοῦ πολέμου ὁ δῆμος αὐτῶν
ἐξεδίωξε τοὺς δυνατούς, οἱ δὲ ἐπελθόντες μετὰ
τῶν βαρβάρων ἐλῄζοντο τοὺς ἐν τῇ πόλει κατά τε
6 γῆν καὶ κατὰ θάλασσαν. οἱ δὲ ἐν τῇ πόλει ὄντες
Ἐπιδάμνιοι ἐπειδὴ ἐπιέζοντο, πέμπουσιν ἐς τὴν
Κέρκυραν πρέσβεις ὡς μητρόπολιν οὖσαν, δεόμενοι
μὴ σφᾶς περιορᾶν φθειρομένους, ἀλλὰ τούς τε
φεύγοντας ξυναλλάξαι σφίσι καὶ τὸν τῶν βαρβάρων
7 πόλεμον καταλῦσαι. ταῦτα δὲ ἱκέται καθεζόμενοι ἐς
τὸ Ἥραιον ἐδέοντο. οἱ δὲ Κερκυραῖοι τὴν ἱκετείαν
οὐκ ἐδέξαντο, ἀλλ' ἀπράκτους ἀπέπεμψαν.

25 Γνόντες δὲ οἱ Ἐπιδάμνιοι οὐδεμίαν σφίσιν ἀπὸ
Κερκύρας τιμωρίαν οὖσαν ἐν ἀπόρῳ εἴχοντο θέσθαι
τὸ παρόν, καὶ πέμψαντες ἐς Δελφοὺς τὸν θεὸν
ἐπήροντο εἰ παραδοῖεν Κορινθίοις τὴν πόλιν ὡς
οἰκισταῖς καὶ τιμωρίαν τινὰ πειρῷντ' ἀπ' αὐτῶν
ποιεῖσθαι. ὁ δ' αὐτοῖς ἀνεῖλε παραδοῦναι καὶ
2 ἡγεμόνας ποιεῖσθαι. ἐλθόντες δὲ οἱ Ἐπιδάμνιοι ἐς
τὴν Κόρινθον κατὰ τὸ μαντεῖον παρέδοσαν τὴν ἀποικίαν,
τόν τε οἰκιστὴν ἀποδεικνύντες σφῶν ἐκ Κορίνθου ὄντα
καὶ τὸ χρηστήριον δηλοῦντες, ἐδέοντό τε μὴ σφᾶς
3 περιορᾶν φθειρομένους, ἀλλ' ἐπαμῦναι. Κορίνθιοι
δὲ κατά τε τὸ δίκαιον ὑπεδέξαντο τὴν τιμωρίαν,

2

24. The city of Epidamnos is on the right-hand side as one sails into the Ionian Gulf; the country near it is inhabited by an Illyrian race of barbarians, the Taulantioi. It was colonised by Corcyra; and the founder was Phalios son of Eratocleides, a Corinthian from the family of the Heraclids, invited from the mother-city in accordance with the ancient custom. Among the colonists were also some Corinthians and others of the Dorian race. As time went on the Epidamnians became powerful and numerous: and then (it is said) for many years there was political strife amongst them, and a war with the neighbouring barbarians, which ruined them and deprived them of most of their power. Finally, just before the Peloponnesian War, the *demos* (popular party) exiled the more powerful citizens, who then went over to the barbarians and with them made raids against those in the city by land and sea. When the Epidamnians in the city found themselves in these difficulties, they sent delegates to Corcyra (as their mother-city), asking the Corcyreans not to be indifferent to the fact that they were being destroyed, but to make some agreement between the exiles and themselves, and to stop the war with the barbarians. The delegates made these requests by taking up a position as suppliants in the temple of Hera. But the Corcyreans did not accept their supplication: they sent the delegates away without their having achieved anything.

25. When the Epidamnians realised that Corcyra would give them no support, they were at a loss how to deal with the situation; so they sent to Delphi to ask the god if they should hand their city over to the Corinthians (as their official founders) and try to get some support from them. The god answered that they should hand it over, and accept Corinth as their leader. So the Epidamnians went to Corinth and handed over their colony, as the oracle had told them: they pointed out that their original founder was a Corinthian, explained what the oracle had said, and asked the Corinthians not to be indifferent to their destruction but to succour them.

The Corinthians agreed to come to their assistance,

νομίζοντες οὐχ ἧσσον ἑαυτων εἶναι τὴν ἀποικίαν
ἢ Κερκυραίων, ἅμα δὲ καὶ μίσει τῶν Κερκυραίων,
4 ὅτι αὐτῶν παρημέλουν ὄντες ἄποικοι· οὔτε γὰρ ἐν
πανηγύρεσι ταῖς κοιναῖς διδόντες γέρα τὰ νομιζό-
μενα οὔτε Κορινθίῳ ἀνδρὶ προκαταρχόμενοι τῶν ἱερῶν
ὥσπερ αἱ ἄλλαι ἀποικίαι, περιφρονοῦντες δὲ αὐτοὺς
καὶ χρημάτων δυνάμει ὄντες κατ' ἐκεῖνον τὸν
χρόνον ὁμοῖα τοῖς Ἑλλήνων πλουσιωτάτοις καὶ
τῇ ἐς πόλεμον παρασκευῇ δυνατώτεροι, ναυτικῷ δὲ
καὶ πολὺ προύχειν ἔστιν ὅτε ἐπαιρόμενοι καὶ κατὰ
τὴν Φαιάκων προενοίκησιν τῆς Κερκύρας κλέος
ἐχόντων τὰ περὶ τὰς ναῦς (ᾗ καὶ μᾶλλον ἐξηρτύοντο
τὸ ναυτικὸν καὶ ἧσαν οὐκ ἀδύνατοι· τριήρεις γὰρ
εἴκοσι καὶ ἑκατὸν ὑπῆρχον αὐτοῖς ὅτε ἤρχοντο
26 πολεμεῖν), πάντων οὖν τούτων ἐγκλήματα ἔχοντες οἱ
Κορίνθιοι ἔπεμπον ἐς τὴν Ἐπίδαμνον ἄσμενοι τὴν
ὠφελίαν, οἰκήτορά τε τὸν βουλόμενον ἰέναι κελεύοντες
2 καὶ Ἀμπρακιωτῶν καὶ Λευκαδίων καὶ ἑαυτῶν φρουρούς.
ἐπορεύθησαν δὲ πεζῇ ἐς Ἀπολλωνίαν, Κορινθίων
οὖσαν ἀποικίαν, δέει τῶν Κερκυραίων μὴ κωλύωνται
ὑπ' αὐτῶν κατὰ θάλασσαν περαιούμενοι.

3   Κερκυραῖοι δὲ ἐπειδὴ ᾔσθοντο τούς τε οἰκήτορας
καὶ φρουροὺς ἥκοντας ἐς τὴν Ἐπίδαμνον τήν τε
ἀποικίαν Κορινθίοις δεδομένην, ἐχαλέπαινον· καὶ
πλεύσαντες εὐθὺς πέντε καὶ εἴκοσι ναυσὶ καὶ ὕστερον
ἑτέρῳ στόλῳ τούς τε φεύγοντας ἐκέλευον κατ' ἐπήρειαν
δέχεσθαι αὐτούς (ἦλθον γὰρ ἐς τὴν Κέρκυραν οἱ τῶν
Ἐπιδαμνίων φυγάδες, τάφους τε ἀποδεικνύντες καὶ
ξυγγένειαν, ἣν προϊσχόμενοι ἐδέοντο σφᾶς κατάγειν)
τούς τε φρουροὺς οὓς Κορίνθιοι ἔπεμψαν καὶ τοὺς
4 οἰκήτορας ἀποπέμπειν. οἱ δὲ Ἐπιδάμνιοι οὐδὲν
αὐτῶν ὑπήκουσαν, ἀλλὰ στρατεύουσιν ἐπ' αὐτοὺς οἱ
Κερκυραῖοι τεσσαράκοντα ναυσὶ μετὰ τῶν φυγάδων ὡς
κατάξοντες, καὶ τοὺς Ἰλλυριοὺς προσλαβόντες.
5 προσκαθεζόμενοι δὲ τὴν πόλιν προεῖπον Ἐπιδαμνίων
τε τὸν βουλόμενον καὶ τοὺς ξένους ἀπαθεῖς ἀπιέναι·

both because it was only right and proper (they took the view that
it was their colony as much as the Corcyreans'), and out of hatred
for the Corcyreans, because they showed them no respect although they
were colonists of Corinth. For the Corcyreans did not give the
Corinthians the customary privileges in the common festivals, nor
special honours in their sacrifices, as was the usual practice in
other colonies. Indeed the Corcyreans despised them, both in virtue of their financial resources (being at that time as rich as the
richest of the Greeks) and on the grounds that their military strength
was greater. In particular they sometimes boasted of their naval
superiority and of the Phaiacians having lived in their land previously, who were famous for their nautical prowess. (Because of this
they did in fact pay even greater attention to their navy, and it
was far from weak: they had 120 triremes when the war began.)
26. Anyway, the Corinthians held all this against them, and gladly
sent Epidamnos help: they offered anyone who wanted to go the chance
of being a settler there, and arranged a garrison of Ambracians,
Leucadians, and their own men. They went by foot to Apollonia, a
Corinthian colony, for fear that if they travelled by sea they might
be impeded by the Corcyreans.

When the Corcyreans realised that the settlers and garrison had
reached Epidamnos, and that the colony had been given over to the
Corinthians, they were furious. They sailed there at once with twenty-
five ships, afterwards increased by an additional squadron; then they
ordered them in violent language to take back the exiles (for the
Epidamnian exiles had come to Corcyra, and asked the Corcyreans to
reinstate them pointing to the tombs of their ancestors and appealing
to their kinship), and to send away again the garrison-force which
Corinth had sent, together with the settlers too. The Epidamnians
rejected all these demands; so the Corcyreans attacked them with
forty ships and the exiles whom they wanted to reinstate: they also had
the help of the Illyrians. They took up positions in front of the
city and made a declaration that anyone of the Epidamnians who wished,
and any foreigners, could leave the city with being harmed:

5

εἰ δὲ μή, ὡς πολεμίοις χρήσεσθαι. ὡς δ᾽ οὐκ
ἐπείθοντο, οἱ μὲν Κερκυραῖοι (ἔστι δ᾽ ἰσθμὸς τὸ
χωρίον) ἐπολιόρκουν τὴν πόλιν, Κορίνθιοι δ᾽,
27 ὡς αὐτοῖς ἐκ τῆς Ἐπιδάμνου ἦλθον ἄγγελοι ὅτι
πολιορκοῦνται, παρεσκευάζοντο στρατείαν, καὶ ἅμα
ἀποικίαν ἐς τὴν Ἐπίδαμνον ἐκήρυσσον ἐπὶ τῇ ἴσῃ
καὶ ὁμοίᾳ τὸν βουλόμενον ἰέναι· εἰ δέ τις τὸ
παραυτίκα μὲν μὴ ἐθέλει ξυμπλεῖν, μετέχειν δὲ
βούλεται τῆς ἀποικίας, πεντήκοντα δραχμὰς κατα-
θέντα Κορινθίας μένειν. ἦσαν δὲ καὶ οἱ πλέοντες
2 πολλοὶ καὶ οἱ τἀργύριον καταβάλλοντες. ἐδεήθησαν
δὲ καὶ τῶν Μεγαρέων ναυσὶ σφᾶς ξυμπροπέμψαι,
εἰ ἄρα κωλύοιντο ὑπὸ Κερκυραίων πλεῖν· οἱ δὲ
παρεσκευάζοντο αὐτοῖς ὀκτὼ ναυσὶ ξυμπλεῖν, καὶ
Παλῆς Κεφαλλήνων τέσσαρσιν. καὶ Ἐπιδαυρίων
ἐδεήθησαν, οἳ παρέσχον πέντε, Ἑρμιονῆς δὲ μίαν
καὶ Τροιζήνιοι δύο, Λευκάδιοι δὲ δέκα καὶ
Ἀμπρακιῶται ὀκτώ. Θηβαίους δὲ χρήματα ᾔτησαν καὶ
Φλειασίους, Ἠλείους δὲ ναῦς τε κενὰς καὶ χρήματα.
αὐτῶν δὲ Κορινθίων νῆες παρεσκευάζοντο τριάκοντα
καὶ τρισχίλιοι ὁπλῖται.
28   Ἐπειδὴ δὲ ἐπύθοντο οἱ Κερκυραῖοι τὴν παρασκευήν,
ἐλθόντες ἐς Κόρινθον μετὰ Λακεδαιμονίων καὶ Σικυωνίων
πρέσβεων, οὓς παρέλαβον, ἐκέλευον Κορινθίους τοὺς
ἐν Ἐπιδάμνῳ φρουρούς τε καὶ οἰκήτορας ἀπάγειν,
2 ὡς οὐ μετὸν αὐτοῖς Ἐπιδάμνου. εἰ δέ τι ἀντι-
ποιοῦνται, δίκας ἤθελον δοῦναι ἐν Πελοποννήσῳ
παρὰ πόλεσιν αἷς ἂν ἀμφότεροι ξυμβῶσιν· ὁποτέρων
δ᾽ ἂν δικασθῇ εἶναι τὴν ἀποικίαν, τούτους κρατεῖν.
ἤθελον δὲ καὶ τῷ ἐν Δελφοῖς μαντείῳ ἐπιτρέψαι.
3 πόλεμον δὲ οὐκ εἴων ποιεῖν· εἰ δὲ μή, καὶ αὐτοὶ
ἀναγκασθήσεσθαι ἔφασαν, ἐκείνων βιαζομένων,
φίλους ποιεῖσθαι οὓς οὐ βούλονται ἑτέρους τῶν νῦν
4 ὄντων μᾶλλον ὠφελίας ἕνεκα. οἱ δὲ Κορίνθιοι
ἀπεκρίναντο αὐτοῖς, ἢν τάς τε ναῦς καὶ τοὺς βαρβάρους
ἀπὸ Ἐπιδάμνου ἀπαγάγωσι, βουλεύσεσθαι· πρότερον

6

if they did not, they would treat them as enemies. As they were not persuaded to do this, the Corcyreans laid siege to the city (it is situated on an isthmus); 27. and the Corinthians, when news came from Epidamnos that the city was being besieged, prepared an expedition. At the same time they advertised that colonial rights, fair for all and the same for all, would be available at Epidamnos for anyone who wanted to go: or if a person did not wish to sail with them immediately, but wanted a share in the colony, he could stay at home and pay fifty Corinthian drachmas. Many took up this offer and sailed, and many also put down the money. They asked the Megarians to help by sending ships with them as an escort, in case their voyage was impeded by the Corcyreans: the Megarians contributed eight ships to the convoy, and the men of Pale in Cephallenia contributed four. They asked the Epidaurians too, who provided five: those of Hermione gave one, the Troizenians two, the Leucadians ten and the Ambracians eight. The Thebans and Phleiasians were asked for money, and the Eleans for hulls and money. Thirty ships came from the Corinthians themselves, and 3,000 hoplites.

28.   When the Corcyreans learned of this preparation, they went to Corinth, taking with them representatives from Sparta and Sicyon, and told the Corinthians to remove the garrison and settlers in Epidamnos, as Corinth had no rights there. If Corinth had a counter-claim to make, they were willing to accept arbitration in the Peloponnese by whatever cities both sides agreed upon: and to whichever of the two cities the colony was adjudged to belong, that city should control it. They were also willing to hand the matter over to the Delphic oracle. They were trying to prevent a conflict: but if they failed, and the Corinthians used force, they too (they said) would be forced to acquire other friends different from those they now had, more for the sake of practical help, though they did not really want to do so. The Corinthians answered that the matter might be considered if Corcyra removed her fleet and the barbarian army from Epidamnos.   But before

δ' οὐ καλῶς ἔχειν τοὺς μὲν πολιορκεῖσθαι, αὐτοὺς
5 δὲ δικάζεσθαι. Κερκυραῖοι δὲ ἀντέλεγον, ἢν καὶ
ἐκεῖνοι τοὺς ἐν Ἐπιδάμνῳ ἀπαγάγωσι, ποιήσειν
ταῦτα· ἑτοῖμοι δὲ εἶναι καὶ ὥστε ἀμφοτέρους μένειν
κατὰ χώραν, σπονδὰς δὲ ποιήσασθαι ἕως ἂν ἡ δίκη
29 γένηται. Κορίνθιοι δὲ οὐδὲν τούτων ὑπήκουον, ἀλλ'
ἐπειδὴ πλήρεις αὐτοῖς ἦσαν αἱ νῆες καὶ οἱ ξύμμαχοι
παρῆσαν, προπέμψαντες κήρυκα πρότερον πόλεμον
προεροῦντα Κερκυραίοις, ἄραντες ἑβδομήκοντα ναυσὶ
καὶ πέντε δισχιλίοις τε ὁπλίταις ἔπλεον ἐπὶ τὴν
Ἐπίδαμνον Κερκυραίοις ἐναντία πολεμήσοντες·
2 ἐστρατήγει δὲ τῶν μὲν νεῶν Ἀριστεὺς ὁ Πελλίχου
καὶ Καλλικράτης ὁ Καλλίου καὶ Τιμάνωρ ὁ Τιμάνθους,
τοῦ δὲ πεζοῦ Ἀρχέτιμός τε ὁ Εὐρυτίμου καὶ
3 Ἰσαρχίδας ὁ Ἰσάρχου. ἐπειδὴ δ' ἐγένοντο ἐν
Ἀκτίῳ τῆς Ἀνακτορίας γῆς, οὗ τὸ ἱερὸν τοῦ
Ἀπόλλωνός ἐστιν, ἐπὶ τῷ στόματι τοῦ Ἀμπρακικοῦ
κόλπου, οἱ Κερκυραῖοι κήρυκά τε προύπεμψαν αὐτοῖς
ἐν ἀκατίῳ ἀπεροῦντα μὴ πλεῖν ἐπὶ σφᾶς καὶ τὰς ναῦς
ἅμα ἐπλήρουν, ζευξαντές τε τὰς παλαιὰς ὥστε
πλωΐμους εἶναι καὶ τὰς ἄλλας ἐπισκευάσαντες.
4 ὡς δὲ ὁ κῆρύξ τε ἀπήγγειλεν οὐδὲν εἰρηναῖον παρὰ
τῶν Κορινθίων καὶ αἱ νῆες αὐτοῖς ἐπεπλήρωντο
οὖσαι ὀγδοήκοντα (τεσσαράκοντα γὰρ Ἐπίδαμνον
ἐπολιόρκουν), ἀνταναγαγόμενοι καὶ παραταξάμενοι
5 ἐναυμάχησαν· καὶ ἐνίκησαν οἱ Κερκυραῖοι παρὰ πολὺ
καὶ ναῦς πέντε καὶ δέκα διέφθειραν τῶν Κορινθίων.
τῇ δὲ αὐτῇ ἡμέρᾳ αὐτοῖς ξυνέβη καὶ τοὺς τὴν
Ἐπίδαμνον πολιορκοῦντας παραστήσασθαι ὁμολογίᾳ
ὥστε τοὺς μὲν ἐπήλυδας ἀποδόσθαι, Κορινθίους δὲ
30 δήσαντας ἔχειν ἕως ἂν ἄλλο τι δόξῃ. μετὰ δὲ τὴν
ναυμαχίαν οἱ Κερκυραῖοι τροπαῖον στήσαντες ἐπὶ τῇ
Λευκίμμῃ τῆς Κερκυραίας ἀκρωτηρίῳ τοὺς μὲν ἄλλους
οὓς ἔλαβον αἰχμαλώτους ἀπέκτειναν, Κορινθίους δὲ
δήσαντες εἶχον. ὕστερον δέ, ἐπειδὴ οἱ Κορίνθιοι
2 καὶ οἱ ξύμμαχοι ἡσσημένοι ταῖς ναυσὶν ἀνεχώρησαν

that happened, it was inappropriate: the two parties would be going
to arbitration while the Epidamnians were still being besieged! The
Corcyreans replied that they would do that if the Corinthians also
took away their people from Epidamnos: alternatively, they were willing for both sides to remain where they were, and to make a truce
till the result of the arbitration was settled.   29.   The
Corinthians rejected all of this: when their ships were manned and
their allies present, they first sent out a herald to declare war
on the Corcyreans, and then set sail with seventy-five ships and
2,000 hoplites, making for Epidamnos in order to fight the Corcyreans
face to face.   Their admirals were Aristeus son of Pellichas,
Callicrates son of Callias, and Timanor son of Timanthes: the commanders of the land forces were Archetimos son of Eurytimos and
Isarchidas son of Isarchos.

When they were at Actium in Anactorian territory, where the
temple of Apollo is, at the mouth of the Ambracian Gulf, the Corcyreans sent out a herald to them in a light boat ordering them not to
sail against Corcyra; and at the same time they manned their ships,
reinforcing the cross-beams in the old ships so as to make them seaworthy and fitting out the others also.   When their herald reported
that the Corinthians had said nothing tending towards peace, and their
ships were manned - there were eighty of them, forty being engaged
in the siege of Epidamnos - they put out to sea against the Corinthians, formed line, and fought a battle.   It was an overall victory
for the Corcyreans, who disabled fifteen Corinthian ships; and on the
same day it happened that the besiegers of Epidamnos forced the city
to make terms - the agreement was that all the foreigners should be
sold as slaves, except for the Corinthians who were to be kept under
guard and held until a further decision was made.   30.   After the
sea-fight the Corcyreans set up a trophy on Cape Leukimme (part of
Corcyra): the other prisoners whom they had taken they killed, but
they put the Corinthians under guard and held them.

Afterward, when the Corinthians and their allies, now defeated,
had taken their ships

ἐπ’ οἴκου, τῆς θαλάσσης ἀπάσης ἐκράτουν τῆς κατ’
ἐκεῖνα τὰ χωρία οἱ Κερκυραῖοι, καὶ πλεύσαντες ἐς
Λευκάδα τὴν Κορινθίων ἀποικίαν τῆς γῆς ἔτεμον
καὶ Κυλλήνην τὸ Ἠλείων ἐπίνειον ἐνέπρησαν, ὅτι
3 ναῦς καὶ χρήματα παρέσχον Κορινθίοις. τοῦ τε
χρόνου τὸν πλεῖστον μετὰ τὴν ναυμαχίαν ἐπεκράτουν
τῆς θαλάσσης καὶ τοὺς τῶν Κορινθίων ξυμμάχους
ἐπιπλέοντες ἔφθειρον, μέχρι οὗ Κορίνθιοι περιιόντι τῷ θέρει πέμψαντες ναῦς καὶ στρατίαν, ἐπεὶ
σφῶν οἱ ξύμμαχοι ἐπόνουν, ἐστρατοπεδεύοντο ἐπὶ
Ἀκτίῳ καὶ περὶ τὸ Χειμέριον τῆς Θεσπρωτίδος
φυλακῆς ἕνεκα τῆς τε Λευκάδος καὶ τῶν ἄλλων
4 πόλεων ὅσαι σφίσι φίλιαι ἦσαν. ἀντεστρατοπεδεύοντο
δὲ καὶ οἱ Κερκυραῖοι ἐπὶ τῇ Λευκίμμῃ ναυσί τε καὶ
πεζῷ. ἐπέπλεον δὲ οὐδέτεροι ἀλλήλοις, ἀλλὰ τὸ
θέρος τοῦτο ἀντικαθεζόμενοι χειμῶνος ἤδη ἀνεχώρησαν ἐπ’ οἴκου ἑκάτεροι.
31 Τὸν δ’ ἐνιαυτὸν πάντα τὸν μετὰ τὴν ναυμαχίαν
καὶ τὸν ὕστερον οἱ Κορίνθιοι ὀργῇ φέροντες τὸν
πρὸς Κερκυραίους πόλεμον ἐναυπηγοῦντο καὶ παρεσκευάζοντο τὰ κράτιστα νεῶν στόλον, ἔκ τε αὐτῆς
Πελοποννήσου ἀγείροντες καὶ τῆς ἄλλης Ἑλλάδος
2 ἐρέτας, μισθῷ πείθοντες. πυνθανόμενοι δὲ οἱ
Κερκυραῖοι τὴν παρασκευὴν αὐτῶν ἐφοβοῦντο, καὶ
(ἦσαν γὰρ οὐδενὸς Ἑλλήνων ἔνσπονδοι οὐδὲ ἐσεγ-
ράψαντο ἑαυτοὺς οὔτε ἐς τὰς Ἀθηναίων σπονδὰς
οὔτε ἐς τὰς Λακεδαιμονίων) ἔδοξεν αὐτοῖς ἐλθοῦσιν
ὡς τοὺς Ἀθηναίους ξυμμάχους γενέσθαι καὶ ὠφελίαν
3 τινὰ πειρᾶσθαι ἀπ’ αὐτῶν εὑρίσκεσθαι. οἱ δὲ
Κορίνθιοι πυθόμενοι ταῦτα ἦλθον καὶ αὐτοὶ ἐς τὰς
Ἀθήνας πρεσβευσόμενοι, ὅπως μὴ σφίσι πρὸς τῷ
Κερκυραίων ναυτικῷ καὶ τὸ αὐτῶν προσγενόμενον
ἐμπόδιον γένηται θέσθαι τὸν πόλεμον ᾗ βούλονται.

home, the Corcyreans had control of all the sea in that area; they
sailed against the Corinthian colony of Leucas and ravaged the land,
and burned Cyllene (the dockyard of the Eleans) because they had
given ships and money to the Corinthians. For a long time after
the sea-fight they kept control of the sea, and conducted damaging
naval expeditions against the allies of Corinth; until at the beginning of the next summer the Corinthians sent out ships and an
army, since their allies were in trouble. They made camp at Actium
and round Cheimerion in Thesprotia, as a protection for Leucas and
the other cities that were friendly to them. The Corcyreans encamped opposite them at Leukimme, with ships and troops. Neither
side sailed against each other, but for that summer they held their
positions facing each other, and when winter came both sides went
home.

31.   For the whole year after the sea-fight, and the year after that,
the Corinthians were angry about the war against Corcyra; so they
built ships and prepared as powerful a nautical armada as possible,
collecting rowers from the Peloponnese and the rest of Greece by
offering them pay. The Corcyreans learned of this armada and were
frightened; they had no agreement with any state in Greece, and their
names had not been put down in the treaty either on the Athenian
or the Spartan side; so they thought it best to go to the Athenians
and become their allies, to see if they could get any support from
them. When the Corinthians heard of this they too sent a diplomatic
mission to Athens, for fear that Athenian naval forces might be added
to the Corcyrean navy, which would stop the war from going as they
wished it to go.

44 Άθηναῖοι δὲ ἀκούσαντες ἀμφοτέρων, γενομένης
καὶ δὶς ἐκκλησίας, τῇ μὲν προτέρᾳ οὐχ ἧσσον τῶν
Κορινθίων ἀπεδέξαντο τοὺς λόγους, ἐν δὲ τῇ
ὑστεραίᾳ μετέγνωσαν Κερκυραίοις ξυμμαχίαν μὲν
μὴ ποιήσασθαι ὥστε τοὺς αὐτοὺς ἐχθροὺς καὶ
φίλους νομίζειν (εἰ γὰρ ἐπὶ Κόρινθον ἐκέλευον
σφίσιν οἱ Κερκυραῖοι ξυμπλεῖν, ἐλύοντ' ἂν αὐτοῖς
αἱ πρὸς Πελοποννησίους σπονδαί), ἐπιμαχίαν δ'
ἐποιήσαντο τῇ ἀλλήλων βοηθεῖν, ἐάν τις ἐπὶ
Κέρκυραν [ῃ ἢ Ἀθήνας ἢ τοὺς τούτων ξυμμάχους.

2 ἐδόκει γὰρ ὁ πρὸς Πελοποννησίους πόλεμος καὶ ὣς
ἔσεσθαι αὐτοῖς, καὶ τὴν Κέρκυραν ἐβούλοντο μὴ
προέσθαι τοῖς Κορινθίοις ναυτικὸν ἔχουσαν
τοσοῦτον, ξυγκρούειν δὲ ὅτι μάλιστα αὐτοὺς ἀλλήλοις, ἵνα ἀσθενεστέροις οὖσιν, ἤν τι δέῃ, Κορινθίοις
τε καὶ τοῖς ἄλλοις ναυτικὸν ἔχουσιν ἐς πόλεμον
καθιστῶνται. ἅμα δὲ τῆς τε Ἰταλίας καὶ Σικελίας
καλῶς ἐφαίνετο αὐτοῖς ἡ νῆσος ἐν παράπλῳ κεῖσθαι.

45 Τοιαύτῃ μὲν γνώμῃ οἱ Ἀθηναῖοι τοὺς Κερκυραίους
προσεδέξαντο, καὶ τῶν Κορινθίων ἀπελθόντων οὐ
πολὺ ὕστερον δέκα ναῦς αὐτοῖς ἀπέστειλαν βοηθούς·

2 ἐστρατήγει δὲ αὐτῶν Λακεδαιμόνιός τε ὁ Κίμωνος
καὶ Διότιμος ὁ Στρομβίχου καὶ Πρωτέας ὁ Ἐπικλέους.

3 προεῖπον δὲ αὐτοῖς μὴ ναυμαχεῖν Κορινθίοις, ἢν
μὴ ἐπὶ Κέρκυραν πλέωσι καὶ μέλλωσιν ἀποβαίνειν
ἢ ἐς τῶν ἐκείνων τι χωρίων· οὕτω δὲ κωλύειν κατὰ
δύναμιν. προεῖπον δὲ ταῦτα τοῦ μὴ λύειν ἕνεκα

46 τὰς σπονδάς. αἱ μὲν δὴ νῆες ἀφικνοῦνται ἐς τὴν
Κέρκυραν, οἱ δὲ Κορίνθιοι, ἐπειδὴ αὐτοῖς παρεσκεύαστο, ἔπλεον ἐπὶ τὴν Κέρκυραν ναυσὶ πεντήκοντα καὶ ἑκατόν. ἦσαν δὲ Ἠλείων μὲν δέκα,
Μεγαρέων δὲ δώδεκα καὶ Λευκαδίων δέκα, Ἀμπρακιωτῶν δὲ ἑπτὰ καὶ εἴκοσι καὶ Ἀνακτορίων μία,

2 αὐτῶν δὲ Κορινθίων ἐνενήκοντα· στρατηγοὶ δὲ τούτων
ἦσαν μὲν καὶ κατὰ πόλεις ἑκάστων, Κορινθίων δὲ

44. The Athenians listened to both sides, and discussed the matter
at two assemblies. At the first, they inclined rather to accept the
Corinthians' arguments; but at the next they changed their minds.
They decided not to make a full alliance with the Corcyreans (count-
ing Corcyra's friends and enemies as their own), for if the Corcyreans
then told them to sail with them against Corinth, the Athenians'
treaty with the Peloponnesians would be thereby broken; but rather
to make a defensive alliance to help each other in the event of
an attack on Corcyra or Athens or any of their allies. For they
thought that war with the Peloponnesians would come anyway; and they
did not want to sacrifice Corcyra to the Corinthians, since she had
such a large fleet. They preferred that the two states should battle
against each other as much as possible and thereby be weakened: in
that way they themselves (if they had to fight) would be in a stronger
military position vis-à-vis the Corinthians and other naval powers.
Also the island of Corcyra seemed to them to be excellently situated
for the coastal voyage from or to Italy and Sicily.

45. With all this in mind the Athenians accepted the Corcyrean
proposal. The Corinthians went away, and not long afterwards the
Athenians sent ten ships to help Corcyra. Their commanders were
Lacedaimonios the sone of Cimon, Diotimos the son of Strombichos,
and Proteas the son of Epicles. They had instructions not to fight
a sea-battle with the Corinthians unless they sailed against
Corcyra and intended to make a landing there, or on any part of
Corcyrean territory - if the Corinthians did that, they were to
stop them so far as they were able. These instructions were given
to avoid breaking the treaty.

46. The ships reached Corcyra; and the Corinthians, when they had
made everything ready, sailed against Corcyra with 150 ships. There
were ten Eleans, twelve Megarians, ten Leucadians, twenty-seven
Ambracians, one from Anaktorion, and ninety of the Corinthians
themselves. Each of the allied groups had commanders from its own
city; the Corinthians

3   Ξενοκλείδης ὁ Εὐθυκλέους πέμπτος αὐτός. ἐπειδὴ δὲ
    προσέμειξαν τῇ κατὰ Κέρκυραν ἠπείρῳ ἀπὸ Λευκάδος
    πλέοντες, ὁρμίζονται ἐς Χειμέριον τῆς Θεσπρωτίδος
4   γῆς. ἔστι δὲ λιμήν, καὶ πόλις ὑπὲρ αὐτοῦ κεῖται
    ἀπὸ θαλάσσης ἐν τῇ Ἐλαιάτιδι τῆς Θεσπρωτίδος
    Ἐφύρη. ἐξίησι δὲ παρ' αὐτὴν Ἀχερουσία λίμνη
    ἐς θάλασσαν· διὰ δὲ τῆς Θεσπρωτίδος Ἀχέρων
    ποταμὸς ῥέων ἐσβάλλει ἐς αὐτήν, ἀφ' οὗ καὶ τὴν
    ἐπωνυμίαν ἔχει. ῥεῖ δὲ καὶ Θύαμις ποταμός, ὁρίζων
    τὴν Θεσπρωτίδα καὶ Κεστρίνην, ὧν ἐντὸς ἡ ἄκρα
5   ἀνέχει τὸ Χειμέριον. οἱ μὲν οὖν Κορίνθιοι τῆς
    ἠπείρου ἐνταῦθα ὁρμίζονταί τε καὶ στρατόπεδον
47 ἐποιήσαντο. οἱ δὲ Κερκυραῖοι ὡς ᾔσθοντο αὐτοὺς
    προσπλέοντας, πληρώσαντες δέκα καὶ ἑκατὸν ναῦς,
    ὧν ἦρχε Μικιάδης καὶ Αἰσιμίδης καὶ Εὐρύβατος,
    ἐστρατοπεδεύσαντο ἐν μιᾷ τῶν νήσων αἳ καλοῦνται
2   Σύβοτα· καὶ αἱ Ἀττικαὶ δέκα παρῆσαν. ἐπὶ δὲ τῇ
    Λευκίμμῃ αὐτοῖς τῷ ἀκρωτηρίῳ ὁ πεζὸς ἦν καὶ
3   Ζακυνθίων χίλιοι ὁπλῖται βεβοηθηκότες. ἦσαν δὲ
    καὶ τοῖς Κορινθίοις ἐν τῇ ἠπείρῳ πολλοὶ τῶν βαρ-
    βάρων παραβεβοηθηκότες· οἱ γὰρ ταύτῃ ἠπειρῶται
    αἰεί ποτε αὐτοῖς φίλοι εἰσίν.
48   Ἐπειδὴ δὲ παρεσκεύαστο τοῖς Κορινθίοις,
    λαβόντες τριῶν ἡμερῶν σιτία ἀνήγοντο ὡς ἐπὶ
2   ναυμαχίαν ἀπὸ τοῦ Χειμερίου νυκτός, καὶ ἅμα ἕῳ
    πλέοντες καθορῶσι τὰς τῶν Κερκυραίων ναῦς μετε-
3   ώρους τε καὶ ἐπὶ σφᾶς πλεούσας. ὡς δὲ κατεῖδον
    ἀλλήλους, ἀντιπαρετάσσοντο, ἐπὶ μὲν τὸ δεξιὸν
    κέρας Κερκυραίων αἱ Ἀττικαὶ νῆες, τὸ δὲ ἄλλο
    αὐτοὶ ἐπεῖχον τρία τέλη ποιήσαντες τῶν νεῶν, ὧν
4   ἦρχε <τῶν> τριῶν στρατηγῶν ἑκάστου εἷς. οὕτω
    μὲν Κερκυραῖοι ἐτάξαντο, Κορινθίοις δὲ τὸ μὲν
    δεξιὸν κέρας αἱ Μεγαρίδες νῆες εἶχον καὶ αἱ
    Ἀμπρακιώτιδες, κατὰ δὲ τὸ μέσον οἱ ἄλλοι ξύμμαχοι
    ὡς ἕκαστοι· εὐώνυμον δὲ κέρας αὐτοὶ οἱ Κορίνθιοι
    ταῖς ἄριστα τῶν νεῶν πλεούσαις κατὰ τοὺς Ἀθηναίους

had Xenocleides the son of Euthycles and four others.

They sailed from Leucas; and when they reached the mainland opposite to Corcyra, they anchored at Cheimerion in the territory of
Thesprotis. Now there is a harbour, and a city sited above it,
away from the sea, in the Elaiatian district of Thesprotis - the
city of Ephyre, past which the waters of the Acherousian Lake
flow to the sea (the river Acheron flows through Thesprotis and
empties into the lake, from which the lake has its name); and
there is also the river Thyamis flowing in these parts, which
forms the boundary between Thesprotis and Kestrine. Between these
two points there juts out the promontory of Cheimerion. This, then,
was the place on the mainland where the Corinthians came to anchor
and made camp. 47. When the Corcyreans perceived that they were
sailing against them, they manned 110 ships, their admirals being
Mikiades, Aisimides and Eurybatos: they then made camp in one of
the islands called Sybota. The ten ships from Attica were with
them, and their army was at Cape Leukimme, with 1,000 hoplites of
the Zacynthians who had reinforced them. The Corinthians also had
reinforcements, large numbers of the barbarians, on the mainland:
for the inhabitants there were and had always been friendly to them.
48. When the Corinthians had made their preparations, they took
food for three days and embarked by night for Cheimerion, ready
for a sea-fight. At dawn, while they were sailing on, they saw
the Corcyrean ships at sea and sailing towards them. When both
sides saw each other, they arranged themselves against each other
for battle. The ships from Attica were on the right wing, and the
Corcyreans occupied the rest of the line, having divided their ships
into three squadrons, of which each of the admirals led one. That
was how the Corcyreans were organised: the Corinthians had the ships
from Megara and Ambracia on their right wing, in the middle their
other allies in groups, and themselves occupied the left with the
ships that sailed best, over against the Athenians

49 καὶ τὸ δεξιὸν τῶν Κερκυραίων εἶχον. ξυμμείξαντες
δέ, ἐπειδὴ τὰ σημεῖα ἑκατέροις ἤρθη, ἐναυμάχουν,
πολλοὺς μὲν ὁπλίτας ἔχοντες ἀμφότεροι ἐπὶ τῶν
καταστρωμάτων, πολλοὺς δὲ τοξότας τε καὶ ἀκοντιστάς,
τῷ παλαιῷ τρόπῳ ἀπειρότερον ἔτι παρεσκευασμένοι.
2 ἦν τε ἡ ναυμαχία καρτερά, τῇ μὲν τέχνῃ οὐχ
ὁμοίως, πεζομαχίᾳ δὲ τὸ πλέον προσφερὴς οὖσα.
3 ἐπειδὴ γὰρ προσβάλοιεν ἀλλήλοις, οὐ ῥᾳδίως ἀπελύοντο
ὑπό τε τοῦ πλήθους καὶ ὄχλου τῶν νεῶν, καὶ μᾶλλόν
τι πιστεύοντες τοῖς ἐπὶ τοῦ καταστρώματος
ὁπλίταις ἐς τὴν νίκην, οἳ καταστάντες ἐμάχοντο
ἡσυχαζουσῶν τῶν νεῶν· διέκπλοι δ' οὐκ ἦσαν,
ἀλλὰ θυμῷ καὶ ῥώμῃ τὸ πλέον ἐναυμάχουν ἢ ἐπιστήμῃ.
4 πανταχῇ μὲν οὖν πολὺς θόρυβος καὶ ταραχώδης ἦν
ἡ ναυμαχία, ἐν ᾗ αἱ Ἀττικαὶ νῆες παραγιγνόμεναι
τοῖς Κερκυραίοις, εἴ πῃ πιέζοιντο, φόβον μὲν
παρεῖχον τοῖς ἐναντίοις, μάχης δὲ οὐκ ἦρχον δεδιότες
5 οἱ στρατηγοὶ τὴν πρόρρησιν τῶν Ἀθηναίων. μάλιστα
δὲ τὸ δεξιὸν κέρας τῶν Κορινθίων ἐπόνει· οἱ γὰρ
Κερκυραῖοι εἴκοσι ναυσὶν αὐτοὺς τρεψάμενοι καὶ
καταδιώξαντες σποράδας ἐς τὴν ἤπειρον καὶ μέχρι
τοῦ στρατοπέδου πλεύσαντες αὐτῶν καὶ ἐπεκβάντες
ἐνέπρησάν τε τὰς σκηνὰς ἐρήμους καὶ τὰ χρήματα
6 διήρπασαν. ταύτῃ μὲν οὖν οἱ Κορίνθιοι καὶ οἱ
ξύμμαχοι ἡσσῶντο [τε] καὶ οἱ Κερκυραῖοι ἐπε-
κράτουν· ᾗ δὲ αὐτοὶ ἦσαν οἱ Κορίνθιοι, ἐπὶ τῷ
εὐωνύμῳ, πολὺ ἐνίκων, τοῖς Κερκυραίοις τῶν
εἴκοσι νεῶν ἀπὸ ἐλάσσονος πλήθους ἐκ τῆς διώξεως
7 οὐ παρουσῶν. οἱ δὲ Ἀθηναῖοι ὁρῶντες τοὺς
Κερκυραίους πιεζομένους μᾶλλον ἤδη ἀπροφασίστως
ἐπεκούρουν, τὸ μὲν πρῶτον ἀπεχόμενοι ὥστε μὴ
ἐμβάλλειν τινί· ἐπειδὴ δὲ ἡ τροπὴ ἐγίγνετο λαμπρῶς
καὶ ἐνέκειντο οἱ Κορίνθιοι, τότε δὴ ἔργου πᾶς
εἴχετο ἤδη καὶ διεκέκριτο οὐδὲν ἔτι, ἀλλὰ ξυνέπεσεν
ἐς τοῦτο ἀνάγκης ὥστε ἐπιχειρῆσαι ἀλλήλοις τοὺς
Κορινθίους καὶ Ἀθηναίους.

16

and the Corcyrean right wing.

49.   After the signals had been hoisted on both sides they joined
battle and fought. Both sides had many hoplites on deck, together
with many archers and javelin-throwers, being somewhat unskilled
and still organised in the old-fashioned manner. The fighting was
hard, though their skill did not match it: in general it was like an
infantry battle. For when the ships came up against each other,
they could not easily get clear, because there were many ships all
close together; and they trusted for victory mostly to the hoplites
on deck, who stood and fought while the ships did nothing. There
were no break-throughs of the line: this sea-fight was a matter
of courage and strength rather than science. The battle was a
confused one, and there was a good deal of shouting everywhere.
The ships from Attica came to help the Corcyreans if they were hard
pressed at any point, and frightened the enemy; but their admirals
were afraid to take the initiative in fighting, because of the
instructions the Athenians had given them.

The right wing of the Corinthians was in particular difficulty;
for the Corcyreans with twenty ships routed them, and pursued them
(as they scattered) to the mainland. They sailed as far as the
Corinthian camp, disembarked, burned the empty tents and plundered
the valuables. Here, then, the Corinthians and their allies were
defeated, and the Corcyreans victorious; but where the Corinthians
themselves were, on the left of the allied line, they were winning
easily: the Corcyrean fleet was smaller as a whole, and the twenty
ships had not returned from the pursuit. The Athenians, seeing the
Corcyreans being crushed, were already beginning to help them more
openly. At first they had kept their distance so as not to attack
any ship; but when it was clear that the Corcyreans were being
routed, and the Corinthians pressing on them, then everyone joined
in the battle and no distinctions were made: the situation reached
a point where, from necessity, the Corinthians and Athenians were
actually fighting each other.

50   Τῆς δὲ τροπῆς γενομένης οἱ Κορίνθιοι τὰ σκάφη
μὲν οὐχ εἷλκον ἀναδούμενοι τῶν νεῶν ἃς καταδύσειαν,
πρὸς δὲ τοὺς ἀνθρώπους ἐτράποντο φονεύειν διεκπλέοντες μᾶλλον ἢ ζωγρεῖν, τούς τε αὐτῶν φίλους,
οὐκ ᾐσθημένοι ὅτι ἥσσηντο οἱ ἐπὶ τῷ δεξιῷ κέρᾳ,
2   ἀγνοοῦντες ἔκτεινον. πολλῶν γὰρ νεῶν οὐσῶν
ἀμφοτέρων καὶ ἐπὶ πολὺ τῆς θαλάσσης ἐπεχουσῶν,
ἐπειδὴ ξυνέμειξαν ἀλλήλοις, οὐ ῥᾳδίως τὴν διάγνωσιν
ἐποιοῦντο ὁποῖοι ἐκράτουν ἢ ἐκρατοῦντο· ναυμαχία γὰρ αὕτη Ἕλλησι πρὸς Ἕλληνας νεῶν πλήθει
μεγίστη δὴ τῶν πρὸ αὐτῆς γεγένηται. ἐπειδὴ δὲ κατε-
3   διώξαν τοὺς Κερκυραίους οἱ Κορίνθιοι ἐς τὴν γῆν,
πρὸς τὰ ναυάγια καὶ τοὺς νεκροὺς τοὺς σφετέρους
ἐτράποντο, καὶ τῶν πλείστων ἐκράτησαν ὥστε προσ-
κομίσαι πρὸς τὰ Σύβοτα, οἱ αὐτοῖς ὁ κατὰ γῆν
στρατὸς τῶν βαρβάρων προσεβεβοηθήκει· ἔστι δὲ τὰ
Σύβοτα τῆς Θεσπρωτίδος λιμὴν ἔρημος. τοῦτο
δὲ ποιήσαντες αὖθις ἀθροισθέντες ἐπέπλεον τοῖς
4   Κερκυραίοις. οἱ δὲ ταῖς πλωίμοις καὶ ὅσαι ἦσαν
λοιπαὶ μετὰ τῶν Ἀττικῶν νεῶν καὶ αὐτοὶ ἀντεπέπλεον, δείσαντες μὴ ἐς τὴν γῆν σφῶν πειρῶσιν
5   ἀποβαίνειν. ἤδη δὲ ἦν ὀψὲ καὶ ἐπεπαιάνιστο
αὐτοῖς ὡς ἐς ἐπίπλουν, καὶ οἱ Κορίνθιοι ἐξαπίνης
πρύμναν ἐκρούοντο κατιδόντες εἴκοσι ναῦς Ἀθηναίων
προσπλεούσας, ἃς ὕστερον τῶν δέκα βοηθοὺς ἐκέπεμψαν
οἱ Ἀθηναῖοι, δείσαντες, ὅπερ ἐγένετο, μὴ νικηθῶσιν
οἱ Κερκυραῖοι καὶ αἱ σφέτεραι δέκα νῆες ὀλίγαι
51   ἀμύνειν ὦσιν. ταύτας οὖν προϊδόντες οἱ Κορίνθιοι
καὶ ὑποτοπήσαντες ἀπ᾽ Ἀθηνῶν εἶναι οὐχ ὅσας
2   ἑώρων ἀλλὰ πλείους ὑπανεχώρουν. τοῖς δὲ
Κερκυραίοις ἐπέπλεον γὰρ μᾶλλον ἐκ τοῦ ἀφανοῦς οὐχ
ἑωρῶντο, καὶ ἐθαύμαζον τοὺς Κορινθίους πρύμναν
κρουομένους, πρίν τινες ἰδόντες εἶπον ὅτι νῆες
ἐκεῖναι ἐπιπλέουσιν. τότε δὲ καὶ αὐτοὶ ἀνεχώρουν·
ξυνεσκόταζε γὰρ ἤδη, καὶ οἱ Κορίνθιοι ἀποτραπό-
μενοι τὴν διάλυσιν ἐποιήσαντο. οὕτω μὲν ἡ ἀπαλλαγὴ

50.   After the rout, the Corinthians did not attach ropes to the
hulls of the ships they had sunk and take them in tow, but turned
their attention to the men, killing rather than taking prisoners
as they sailed through the battle lines; and they killed some of
their own men in ignorance, not having perceived that those on their
right wing had been defeated. For both combatants had many ships,
and they covered a wide area of sea; so that when they were joined
in battle together, they could not easily judge who were the victors
and who the vanquished. For this was the greatest sea-fight, in
terms of ship-numbers, that had happened hitherto between Greek
states.

When the Corinthians had pursued the Corcyreans to the land, they
turned their attention to the wrecks and to their own dead, and
managed to get hold of most of them: they brought them to Sybota,
where the land army of their barbarian allies had come up in support. (Sybota is an uninhabited harbour in Thesprotian territory.)
Having done this, they collected their fleet together again and
sailed against the Corcyreans. The latter themselves sailed out
against the Corinthians with all their seaworthy ships, and all
others not hitherto used, and with the ships from Attica also:
they were afraid that the Corinthians might try to land on their
territory.

It was already late and both sides had sung the paean as for an
attack: then suddenly the Corinthians backed water. They had seen
twenty Athenian ships sailing towards them, ships which the Athenians
had sent out after they sent the original ten, for fear that (as
actually happened) the Corcyreans would be beaten and their own ten
ships would be insufficient support.   51.   The Corinthians saw
these ships and suspected that they were Athenians, and that there
were more of them coming than the twenty they saw. So they retreated.
The Corcyreans did not see them, for they were coming from a direction
in which they could be less easily seen; so they were amazed at the
Corinthians backing water, until eventually some did see them, and
shouted that there were ships out there sailing towards them. Then
they themselves retreated; for it was already getting dark, and the
Corinthians turned away and broke off the battle. In this way,
then, they separated

ἐγένετο ἀλλήλων, καὶ ἡ ναυμαχία ἐτελεύτα ἐς
4 νύκτα. τοῖς δὲ Κερκυραίοις στρατοπεδευομένοις
ἐπὶ τῇ Λευκίμμῃ αἱ εἴκοσι νῆες αἱ ἐκ τῶν Ἀθηνῶν
αὗται, ὧν ἦρχε Γλαύκων τε ὁ Λεάγρου καὶ †Ἀνδοκίδης
ὁ Λεωγόρου†, διὰ τῶν νεκρῶν καὶ ναυαγίων προσ-
κομισθεῖσαι κατέπλεον ἐς τὸ στρατόπεδον οὐ πολλῷ
5 ὕστερον ἢ ὤφθησαν. οἱ δὲ Κερκυραῖοι (ἦν γὰρ
νύξ) ἐφοβήθησαν μὴ πολέμιαι ὦσιν, ἔπειτα δὲ
ἔγνωσαν· καὶ ὡρμίσαντο.
52 Τῇ δὲ ὑστεραίᾳ ἀναγαγόμεναι αἵ τε Ἀττικαὶ
τριάκοντα νῆες καὶ τῶν Κερκυραίων ὅσαι πλώιμοι
ἦσαν ἐπέπλευσαν ἐπὶ τὸν ἐν τοῖς Συβότοις λιμένα,
ἐν ᾧ οἱ Κορίνθιοι ὥρμουν, βουλόμενοι εἰδέναι εἰ
2 ναυμαχήσουσιν. οἱ δὲ τὰς μὲν ναῦς ἄραντες ἀπὸ
τῆς γῆς καὶ παραταξάμενοι μετεώρους ἡσύχαζον,
ναυμαχίας οὐ διανοούμενοι ἄρχειν ἑκόντες ὁρῶντες
προσγεγενημένας τε ναῦς ἐκ τῶν Ἀθηνῶν ἀκραιφνεῖς
καὶ σφίσι πολλὰ τὰ ἄπορα ξυμβεβηκότα, αἰχμαλώτων
τε περὶ φυλακῆς οὓς ἐν ταῖς ναυσὶν εἶχον, καὶ
ἐπισκευὴν οὐκ οὖσαν τῶν νεῶν ἐν χωρίῳ ἐρήμῳ· τοῦ
3 δὲ οἴκαδε πλοῦ μᾶλλον διεσκόπουν ὅπῃ κομισθήσονται,
δεδιότες μὴ οἱ Ἀθηναῖοι νομίσαντες λελύσθαι τὰς
σπονδάς, διότι ἐς χεῖρας ἦλθον, οὐκ ἐῶσι σφᾶς
53 ἀποπλεῖν. ἔδοξεν οὖν αὐτοῖς ἄνδρας ἐς κελήτιον
ἐσβιβάσαντας ἄνευ κηρυκείου προσπέμψαι τοῖς
Ἀθηναίοις καὶ πεῖραν ποιήσασθαι. πέμψαντές τε
2 ἔλεγον τοιάδε. 'ἀδικεῖτε, ὦ ἄνδρες Ἀθηναῖοι,
πολέμου ἄρχοντες καὶ σπονδὰς λύοντες· ἡμῖν γὰρ
πολεμίους τοὺς ἡμετέρους τιμωρουμένοις ἐμποδὼν
ἵστασθε ὅπλα ἀνταιρόμενοι. εἰ δ' ὑμῖν γνώμη
ἐστὶ κωλύειν τε ἡμᾶς ἐπὶ Κέρκυραν ἢ ἄλλοσε εἴ ποι
βουλόμεθα πλεῖν καὶ τὰς σπονδὰς λύετε, ἡμᾶς
τούσδε πρώτους λαβόντες χρήσασθε ὡς πολεμίοις.'
3 οἱ μὲν δὴ τοιαῦτα εἶπον· τῶν δὲ Κερκυραίων τὸ μὲν
στρατόπεδον ὅσον ἐπήκουσεν ἀνεβόησεν εὐθὺς λαβεῖν
τε αὐτοὺς καὶ ἀποκτεῖναι, οἱ δὲ Ἀθηναῖοι τοιάδε
4 ἀπεκρίναντο. 'οὔτε ἄρχομεν πολέμου, ὦ ἄνδρες

from each other, and the sea-fight ended with the coming of night.
The twenty ships from Athens, whose admirals were Glaucon the son
of Leagros and Andocides the son of Leogoras, travelled through
the wrecks and corpses and reached the Corcyrean camp at Leukimme
not long after they were sighted. The Corcyreans (for it was now
night) were frightened in case they should be hostile, but then
recognised them: and they came to anchor.

52.   Next day the thirty Attic ships and all the seaworthy Corcyrean
ships put to sea and sailed towards the harbour at Sybota in which
the Corinthians were at anchor, wanting to know if they would fight
by sea. The Corinthians had put out from shore, and formed their ships
into a line in the open sea; and they were staying quiet, having no
intention of starting a fight if they could help it. For they realised
that the ships from Athens which had come up in support were undamaged; and that they had many difficulties of their own, to do with
guarding the prisoners whom they held in their ships, and with the
lack of any facilities for repairing their ships in that uninhabited
locality. In fact they were more concerned with considering how they
could return home; they were afraid that the Athenians might suppose
the treaty to have been broken because they had fought each other, and
might not allow them to sail away.   53.   So they decided to put
some men into a boat, without any herald's staff, send them to the
Athenians, and try the situation out. They sent these men, then, and
spoke along the following lines:

> 'Athenians, you are acting unfairly in starting a war and
> breaking the treaty. We are here to enforce justice on
> our enemies, and you have taken up arms and are standing
> in our way. If your intention is to stop us sailing
> against Corcyra or anywhere else we want to sail against,
> and to break the treaty, then begin by taking us here
> prisoner and treat us as you would treat enemies.'

That was the substance of what they said; and those of the Corcyrean
forces who heard shouted immediately that they should take them
prisoner and kill them. But the Athenians answered along the following
lines:

> 'We are not starting a war, Peloponnesians,

Πελοποννήσιοι, οὔτε τὰς σπονδὰς λύομεν, Κερκυραίοις
δὲ τοῖσδε ξυμμάχοις οὖσι βοηθοὶ ἤλθομεν. εἰ μὲν
οὖν ἄλλοσέ ποι βούλεσθε πλεῖν, οὐ κωλύομεν· εἰ
δὲ ἐπὶ Κέρκυραν πλευσεῖσθε ἢ ἐς τῶν ἐκείνων τι
χωρίων, οὐ περιοψόμεθα κατὰ τὸ δυνατόν.'

54 Τοιαῦτα τῶν Ἀθηναίων ἀποκριναμένων οἱ μὲν
Κορίνθιοι τόν τε πλοῦν τὸν ἐπ' οἴκου παρεσκευάζοντο
καὶ τροπαῖον ἔστησαν ἐν τοῖς ἐν τῇ ἠπείρῳ Συβότοις·
οἱ δὲ Κερκυραῖοι τά τε ναυάγια καὶ νεκροὺς ἀνείλοντο
τὰ κατὰ σφᾶς ἐξενεχθέντα ὑπό τε τοῦ ῥοῦ καὶ ἀνέμου,
ὃς γενόμενος τῆς νυκτὸς διεσκέδασεν αὐτὰ πανταχῇ,
καὶ τροπαῖον ἀντέστησαν ἐν τοῖς ἐν τῇ νήσῳ
2 Συβότοις ὡς νενικηκότες. γνώμῃ δὲ τοιᾷδε ἑκάτεροι
τὴν νίκην προσεποιήσαντο· Κορίνθιοι μὲν κρατήσαντες
τῇ ναυμαχίᾳ μέχρινυκτός, ὥστε καὶ ναυάγια πλεῖστα
καὶ νεκροὺς προσκομίσασθαι, καὶ ἄνδρας ἔχοντες
αἰχμαλώτους οὐκ ἐλάσσους χιλίων ναῦς τε κατα-
δύσαντες περὶ ἑβδομήκοντα ἔστησαν τροπαῖοι·
Κερκυραῖοι δὲ τριάκοντα ναῦς μάλιστα διαφθείραντες, καὶ ἐπειδὴ Ἀθηναῖοι ἦλθον, ἀνελόμενοι τὰ
κατὰ σφᾶς αὐτοὺς ναυάγια καὶ νεκρούς, καὶ ὅτι αὐτοῖς
τῇ τε προτεραίᾳ πρύμναν κρουόμενοι ὑπεχώρησαν οἱ
Κορίνθιοι ἰδόντες τὰς Ἀττικὰς ναῦς, καὶ ἐπειδὴ
ἦλθον οἱ Ἀθηναῖοι, οὐκ ἀντεπέπλεον ἐκ τῶν Συβότων,
55 διὰ ταῦτα τροπαῖον ἔστησαν. οὕτω μὲν ἑκάτεροι
νικᾶν ἠξίουν· οἱ δὲ Κορίνθιοι ἀποπλέοντες ἐπ'
οἴκου Ἀνακτόριον, ὃ ἐστιν ἐπὶ τῷ στόματι τοῦ
Ἀμπρακικοῦ κόλπου, εἷλον ἀπάτῃ (ἦν δὲ κοινὸν
Κερκυραίων καὶ ἐκείνων) καὶ καταστήσαντες ἐν αὐτῷ
Κορινθίους οἰκήτορας ἀνεχώρησαν ἐπ' οἴκου, καὶ
τῶν Κερκυραίων ὀκτακοσίους μὲν οἳ ἦσαν δοῦλοι
ἀπέδοντο, πεντήκοντα δὲ καὶ διακοσίους δήσαντες
ἐφύλασσον καὶ ἐν θεραπείᾳ εἶχον πολλῇ, ὅπως
αὐτοῖς τὴν Κέρκυραν ἀναχωρήσαντες προσποιήσειαν·
ἐτύγχανον δὲ καὶ δυνάμει αὐτῶν οἱ πλείους πρῶτοι
2 ὄντες τῆς πόλεως. ἡ μὲν οὖν Κέρκυρα οὕτω περιγίγ-
νεται τῷ πολέμῳ τῶν Κορινθίων, καὶ αἱ νῆες τῶν
Ἀθηναίων ἀνεχώρησαν ἐξ αὐτῆς·

nor breaking the treaty; we have come to support the
Corcyreans here who are our allies. Now if you want to
sail anywhere else, we will not stop you; but if you sail
against Corcyra or any part of the Corcyreans' territory,
we shall do our best to prevent you.'

54. The Athenians answered to that effect: the Corinthians prepared
to sail home, and set up a trophy at Sybota on the mainland. The
Corcyreans gathered up those of the wrecks and corpses that had been
carried towards them by the current and the wind, which had arisen
in the night and scattered them in different directions; and they
set up a trophy in their turn on the island Sybota. The reasoning
behind each side claiming victory was this: the Corinthians had
been victorious in the sea-fight until nightfall, had collected
most of the wrecks and corpses, held not less than 1,000 prisoners,
and had sunk about seventy ships, so they set up their trophy; the
Corcyreans had disabled about thirty ships, and had gathered up the
wrecks and corpses in their area after the Athenians came: the
Corinthians had backed water in face of them on the day before when
they saw the Attic ships coming, and when the Athenians had arrived,
they did not sail out from Sybota against them - for these reasons
they set up their trophy. Thus both sides claimed the victory.

On their way back the Corinthians took Anaktorion, which is on
the mouth of the Ambracian Gulf, by treachery (it was a city held
in common by them and the Corcyreans): they settled Corinthian
colonists in it and then sailed back home. 800 of the Corcyrean
prisoners, who were slaves, they sold: 250 they put in restraint
and under guard, taking good care of them. Their intention was
that these prisoners should return to Corcyra and win Corcyra
over for them; for most of them were in fact amongst the most
powerful citizens of Corcyra.

In this way then Corcyra survived the war against the Corinthians;
and the Athenian ships left Corcyra and went home.

A. The Epidamnos Affair

Thucydides' account of this is condensed, when compared with his
treatment of the Sybota campaign: but there are some points of
interest and difficulty which deserve treatment both in their own
right and as connected with later developments. The most important of these concern the motivation of the various parties.

(1)   That of the Epidamnian democrats is tolerably clear: it is the
need for survival. We may guess that their nearest neighbour,
Apollonia, was either unable or unwilling to assist: so they naturally turn first to Corcyra, both as being sufficiently powerful to
help effectively and as being the μητρόπολις ('mother city',
24.6). When this fails, they are at a loss (ἐν ἀπόρῳ, 25.1),
presumably because there is no other state near by who would be an
obvious candidate for help. So they turn, via the Delphic oracle,
to Corinth, in a remoter sense also their μητρόπολις. We may,
however, reasonably ask why they could not have settled their own
affairs, at least with the exiled *oligoi*: for they could hardly
have regarded it as an ideal situation to invite intervention
from foreign powers, which would (and did) itself threaten their
independence - and they actually made over (παρέδοσαν, 25.2)
their city to Corinth, which must imply resigning such independence.
The answer is likely to be that the hostile Illyrians were a very
serious threat, able (with the help of the exiles) actually to
destroy the city (φθειρομένους, 25.2): it must have seemed preferable to the democrats to hand it over to Corinth, even though
the Corinthians might not have favoured the democratic cause. The
remarkable strength of the Illyrians may well have been an important factor in Corcyra's capture of the town (26.4). We have to
remember throughout that Epidamnos was in an extremely remote area
and probably more vulnerable to barbarian pressure than most
colonies.
    Nor is it surprising that the Epidamnians do not accede to the
Corcyreans' abusive demands in 26.3. For, first, it was one thing
to welcome Corcyra as a (neutral) mediator and saviour of the city,
quite another to welcome her as an enemy apparently backing the
exiles; and secondly, the presence of the Corinthian and allied
settlers and troops may have made it very difficult for any
Epidamnians who still wanted Corcyrean intervention to get their
way, or even to raise the matter publicly. Precisely by taking
the side of the exiles and associating with the Illyrians, Corcyra
had cast herself in a hostile role. We may say, with hindsight,
that the Epidamnians might have been wise to cooperate with Corcyra,
since Corcyra had the power to force the city to make terms; but
no doubt they expected more Corinthian help.

(2)   The Corcyrean position is, I think, equally clear, though
somewhat more surprising. It is in fact based on an isolationist
policy partly stated in 32.4: clearly a deliberate policy (ἑκούσιοι),
and with a reason: τὸ μὴ ἐν ἀλλοτρίᾳ ξυμμαχίᾳ τῇ τοῦ πέλας
γνώμῃ ξυνκινδυνεύειν - 'not to share risks induced by another
state's policies by getting involved in a foreign alliance'. Not

only alliances were avoided, however, but - more importantly - any
imperialist expansion. The Corcyreans held territory across the
straits (III.85.2) and perhaps elsewhere (see Hammond 1967), as
implied by τῶν ἐκείνων τι χωρίων (I.45.3, 53.4). But they did
not, as far as we know, permanently subjugate any towns or form
even the nucleus of an empire. Given their remarkable strength,
they could certainly have done so; and it is striking that they
chose this policy. Presumably they were more interested in wealth
than territorial power: and certainly they seem to have done very
well out of their isolationism, as we can see from 25.4 (even
though this may contain some exaggeration). It is interesting that
their isolationist policy generated such prosperity even though
they were surrounded - one might have thought, hemmed in - by
Corinthian colonies. But not all these would have been more pro-
Corinithian than pro-Corcyrean, any more than Epidamnos was:
though those to the south of Corcyra (notably Leucas and Ambracia)
always took the Corinthian side. Apollonia was clearly at this
time pro-Corinthian: of near-by Oricum, originally an Eretrian
foundation, we know little in this period. Conceivably a substantial part of Corcyra's wealth was amassed by straightforward
piracy - a major form of economic activity at this time, and a
tempting one for any state with a powerful navy: but if so, it is
surprising that Thucydides does not report the Corinthians as rais-
ing objections to it. In any case, it is clear that Corinthian
influence in this area was not overwhelming.

According to the Corinthians, part of Corcyra's good fortune was
διὰ τὸ ἥκιστα ἐπὶ τοὺς πέλας ἐκπλέοντας μάλιστα τοὺς
ἄλλους ἀνάγκῃ καταίροντας δέχεσθαι (37.3): translation below.
δέχεσθαι is not, I think, 'a curious word to use when the speaker
means, practically, "robbing"' (Gomme, p.173): it means simply 'take
in', 'entertain', or 'harbour'. The sense must be 'because they only
rarely make voyages to their neighbours, but very often give anchorage to ships from other states which are forced to put into port
there'. But why are they forced? Not, surely, for strictly geographical reasons: ships on the north-south route to and from the
Adriatic could simply skip Corcyra; and merchantmen at least (if
not triremes) to and from Italy and Sicily could do the same,
sailing straight from Italy to Leucas or the Corinthian gulf. It
is more likely that Corcyra had established herself as an important
emporium or centre of exchange in that area. She had no need to
send ships ἐπὶ τοὺς πέλας, either because her imports were brought
to her by others or because her economy was basically self-sufficient.

In any case, her interests were not primarily territorial: isolationism suited her well. It is thus intelligible that she turned
down the original Epidamnian request, having no desire to take
Epidamnos over and no direct interest in its rise or fall. But in-
directly the political situation was of course highly relevant to
Corcyra, inasmuch as Corinth might decide to strengthen her political
grip on the area, which would at least threaten Corcyrean interests.
There had been a long history of conflict between the two states,
and a consequent tradition of anti-Corinthian feeling at Corcyra
(I.13.4). Thus as soon as Corinth reinforced Epidamnos, the
Corcyrean attitude - hitherto apparently quite uncaring - changed

dramatically. Their violent language (κατ᾽ ἐπήρειαν, 26.3) displayed the anger and hatred they felt at the Corinthian intervention.

(3)   Corinthian motives are more obscure. But so far as the acceptance of the Epidamnian invitation was concerned, Thucydides says nothing about economic motives: even the remarks he later puts into the mouth of the Corinthian ambassador (I.27), about Corcyra's geographical position giving her a legal independence which she used unjustly, have only marginal reference to economics - his point is simply that disputed cases of all kinds were settled by Corcyrean decision alone, whereas they should be subject to international law or convention. Nothing is said by Thucydides about Corcyra (or Corinth) threatening the other's trade-routes or markets in any direct way. All the emphasis is on points of politics or honour: whether this or that colony 'belonged' to or 'respected' the mother-city, or the mother-city deserved a general right to command (ἡγεμόνες εἶναι, 'to be the leaders', 38.2). Thucydides says straightforwardly that the Corinthians acted 'out of hate of the Corcyreans, because the Corcyreans took no notice of them even though they were Corinthian colonists' (μίσει τῶν Κερκυραίων ὅτι αὐτῶν παρημέλουν ὄντες ἄποικοι, 25.3). Similarly the 'complaints' they have against Corcyra (ἐγκλήματα, 25.4) are not in any sense economic.

It is not so clear, however, just what practical objectives Corinth had in mind. The motives mentioned in 25.3ff. do not themselves imply that she wanted actually to conquer Corcyra, or even to engage the Corcyreans in any military action; it would be of some political value, valuable also in terms of prestige, and certainly a good way of snubbing the Corcyreans if Corinth merely rescued Epidamnos and reinforced it with her own or allied settlers. The fact that this party went by land to avoid being intercepted by the Corcyrean fleet shows that the Corinthians feared a head-on conflict. But when Corcyra reacted violently, the Corinthians found themselves obliged to follow up their move: if they had abandoned their own people (together with the allied Ambracians and Leucadians) to Corcyrean force, their prestige would have suffered irreparable damage. I do not suggest that they were particularly reluctant to follow up their reinforcement of Epidamnos; they may well have seized gladly on the excuse to justify a war against Corcyra. But this closely connected chain of events cannot fairly be described as (in the words of one author) 'insane aggression' (Ste. Croix, 1972). The original aggression, it might be justly thought, was the Corcyrean attack on Epidamnos.

After the Corcyrean attack, it is a somewhat different story. For reasons given above, the Corinthians had to fight. But there is still no reason to believe that they were out to conquer or totally subdue Corcyra (a considerable undertaking). Hence they declared war, but were sailing not for Corcyra but for Epidamnos (ἐπὶ τὴν Ἐπίδαμνον, 29.1). They hoped, in all probability, to reach Epidamnos, inflict a defeat on the blockading forces, and make the town secure. The Corcyreans, however, seem to have regarded the expedition (as well they might) in the light of a full-scale attack on Corcyra: they may even have entertained some concept of Corcyrean territorial waters, since they sent a herald as far south as Actium (29.3).

(4)   There is one further body of opinion to consider: the views
of certain neutrals. In 28 the Corcyreans make every possible
concession, and were supported by official representatives (πρέσβεων,
28.1) from Sparta and Sicyon. One of their suggestions was arbitration by agreed Peloponnesian cities, and we may reasonably suppose Peloponnesian opinion to have been in Corcyra's favour. Another
was arbitration from Delphi. This is remarkable in view of the
oracle's original advice that Epidamnos should bring in Corinth:
the Corcyreans must have had reason to believe that, despite this
advice, Delphi would not support Corinth to the point of war. These
neutrals, whose interest in Epidamnos *per se* was no doubt minimal,
must have been chiefly anxious to avoid a war: the important passage
is 28.3, where the Corcyreans make a thinly-veiled threat to seek
alliance from Athens. Such a move would (and did) bring the possibility of a major war much closer, and it is not surprising that
neutral opinion was against Corinth.

A closer look at 28.3 tells us quite a lot about the motivation
of the various parties. The Corcyreans say that if the Corinthians
force them into it, they will be compelled φίλους ποιεῖσθαι οὕς
οὐ βούλονται ἑτέρους τῶν νῦν ὄντων μᾶλλον ὠφελίας ἕνεκα.
This seems to mean (I interrupt the translation to show the problems):
'to make friends that they [the Corcyreans? the Corinthians? the
Peloponnesians generally?] do not want (*sc.* to make or be made),
different from their (*sc.* the Corcyreans') present friends [but who
are these?], and make them more for the sake of the help they can
give [than for what?]'. Bearing in mind that the discussion took
place with Spartan and Sicyonian representatives present, we may
best interpret this as meant for the ears of the Peloponnesian
neutrals as much as of the Corinthians. The Corcyreans' 'present
friends', τῶν νῦν ὄντων, cannot at this juncture very well refer
to Corinth (still less Athens): it must refer to some kind of friendship with the Peloponnese more generally (as in the Corcyrean vote
just before the *stasis* of 427: they were to be Πελοποηηνσίοις
φίλοι ὥσπερ καὶ πρότερον, 'friendly to the Peloponnesians as
before', III.70.2). We cannot be sure on what this friendship was
based: the Dorian blood which the Corcyreans had in common with many
Peloponnesian states (including Sparta) may have counted for something: probably more important were traditional ties of trade and
proximity. If we take the passage as an indirect appeal to these
'present friends', the subject of οὐ βούλονται, 'they do not
want', is best taken as the Corcyreans (as all editors do take it,
though as far as I can see without considering the alternative).
To say 'friends that you Peloponnesians don't want us to make' is
too brutal in substance, and the change of subject too harsh in the
Greek: the Corcyreans say rather 'friends that we really don't want
to make, but if our existing Peloponnesian friends don't actually
help us, we shall have to': that is, they will have to choose their
friends by the criterion of what help they can give rather than
(perhaps) the criterion of blood-ties or traditional good relation-
ships.
There is a little more to be squeezed out of οὐ βούλονται.
If we take this coyly or diplomatically (so to speak), we interpret
the Corcyreans as saying 'Of course we don't really want to make
such friends, but ...': and we may then believe that the Corcyreans

had in reality no objection to bringing in the Athenians (if they could), but pretended otherwise for diplomatic reasons. The alternative is to take it more straightforwardly and seriously: 'friends we really don't want to make'. That alternative seems to me preferable for a number of reasons. First, it reads more naturally in a sentence which, though intended to have diplomatic force, nevertheless sets out its points in a quite straightforward and utilitarian way. Secondly, it helps to account for a number of facts which would otherwise appear somewhat strange: (1) that Corcyra only approached Athens before the second expedition, though there would have been plenty of time for her to do so before the first; (2) that the (unforced) vote in III.70.2 suggests a continued tradition of friendship to the Peloponnese rather than to Athens; and (3) that despite her protestations to the Athenians (in the speech of the Corcyrean delegates, I.32ff.) Corcyra in fact gave Athens very little help. Thirdly, there are tolerably obvious reasons why Corcyra did not want Athenian intervention: it was by just such intervention that Athens had subjected many of the Aegean states, and Athens had a known interest both in north-west Greece (I.111, II.30, 102) and in the western Greeks (I.36,44; III.86; Gomme, p.198, 365-66).

Corcyra's foreign policy, then, though isolationist, was orientated more towards the Peloponnese than elsewhere. That probably counted fairly heavily in favour of the pro-Spartan party at Corcyra before the *stasis* in 427, and the vote in III.70.2 should come as no surprise. At least the Peloponnese left Corcyra independent, free to trade and grow rich: or would do so, if Corinthian aggression could be checked. In order to have it checked, Corcyra appealed naturally in the first place to the Peloponnesians themselves; she also bent over backwards to suggest all possible methods of avoiding war. In fact the appeal failed - not, surely, because the Spartans, Sicyonians and other Peloponnesian states were not sympathetic, but because not even Sparta was in any position to alienate Corinth. If a war came - and Thucydides certainly writes as if it were commonly regarded as imminent - Sparta needed Corinth and the Corinthians' naval power firmly on her side. At most the Spartan delegates attempted mild dissuasion: they were not able to say 'Drop this war against Corcyra, or else ...', for there was no realistic 'or else' that Sparta could deploy - particularly since that war was essentially a naval one, in which Sparta could produce no visible threats or impediments, as Athens attempted to do by the presence of her ten ships at Sybota. It is, nevertheless, an interesting sidelight on Sparta's impotence (or incompetence) that she totally failed to achieve a diplomatic solution: she was unable to prevent the clash between the Corcyrean and Corinthian fleets, and unable to prevent Athenian intervention.

Some more specifically strategic and tactical comments are also in order.

(1)   It is interesting, and relevant to the route of the Corinthians' first expedition, that the Corcyreans received no prior intelligence of the Corinthians' intentions to send a force overland to Epidamnos: the first thing they knew was that it had arrived (26.3). In view of the considerable distance between Corinth and Apollonia, that is

remarkable: particularly since the Corinthians had to pick up Leucadians and Ambracians on the way.

Once the Corinthians got as far as Apollonia, there was not much chance of news reaching Corcyra before the Corinthians reached Epidamnos (see map): presumably the Corinthians would have embarked at once, and the distance from Apollonia is shorter to Epidamnos than to Corcyra. An overland march from Ambracia might also have been unlikely to result in news: the route lay through territory inhabited partly at least by tribes friendly to Corinth (47.3). But it is very hard to believe, in view of Corcyra's interests further south, that someone from somewhere in the Leucas-Ambracia area - perhaps from Anaktorion, co-founded by Corcyra and Corinth - would not have given news which could come by sea to Corcyra much faster than the Corinthians and their allies could have marched overland.

That would be particularly improbable if, as most suppose, the expedition started from Corinth by sea and continued by sea via Leucas to Ambracia. Such a naval expedition, in however small numbers, could hardly have failed to excite local interest. It is, in any case, not unlikely that the Corcyreans had some sort of information service. On the other hand, the improbability is much lessened if the whole route as far as Apollonia was covered by land. Gomme brusquely says (*ad loc.*): 'not all the way by land, but by sea (within friendly waters) as far as Leukas and the Amprakiot Gulf, thence by land ...', but what Thucydides actually says is ἐπορεύθησαν πεζῇ ἐς Ἀπολλωνίαν (26.2), 'they went on foot to Apollonia'. This is not of course conclusive, since part of the subject of ἐπορεύθησαν is no doubt the Leucadians and Ambracians, who did in fact cover all the distance they had to cover on foot; but it is at least possible that the Corinthians did as well.

(2) Epidamnos' position - on an isthmus - was of crucial importance: it meant both that the city was vulnerable to sea power, and that a substantial fleet was necessary to reduce it. The Corcyrean ships prevented both any escape and any imports of food. For the same reason the Corinthians required a substantial fleet to relieve the city; their hoplites, though they might have been able to defend the walls indefinitely, could hardly have kept a supply route open with any security in the teeth of the Illyrian army, which was supported by the exiled *oligoi* from Epidamnos and by whatever land forces Corcyra brought there. (In fact we know little or nothing about numbers of troops: even the figures of 2,000 and 3,000 hoplites on the Corinthian side are untrustworthy.)

The city was not actually captured, but forced to make terms (ὁμολογίᾳ, 29.5). Probably this was because supplies had been cut off. A considerable time elapsed between the opening of the siege and the seafight, when the city capitulated; whether or not we accept that both these latter events occurred actually on the same day (a common and commonly false idea in Greek history, to which even Thucydides may not have been immune), we must accept a rough simultaneity. There was enough time for news to reach Corinth, for the Corinthians to advertise for volunteers and for the volunteers to respond, for the various allied cities to man and equip their triremes, in fact for all that happens in 28-29 - several weeks at

the least, long enough for any but a very well-stocked city to be
starved out if caught unawares. The terms were reasonable enough,
not significantly harsher than the Corcyreans had originally demanded: in essence, the removal of Corinthian and other foreign
elements. The Corcyreans kept the Corinthians presumably either
because they thought them useful political bargaining-pieces, or
because they would be ransomed for more money than they would
fetch by being sold as slaves.

(3)   It is a great pity that Thucydides tells us practically nothing
about the sea-fight. Probably (for tactical reasons mentioned below)
it took place in or near the southern channel between Corcyra and the
mainland, near to Cape Leukimme, where the Corcyreans put up a
trophy. We need to keep in mind the fact that the Corcyrean navy,
presumably using slave-rowers as at Sybota, could gain a decisive
victory without any significant numerical superiority.
     The prisoners whom the Corcyreans killed after the sea-fight
(30.1) must be only those captured in the sea-fight. The repeti-
tion (particularly of δήσαντας ἔχειν) would otherwise be intoler-
able, and the whole passage (from 29.5) muddled. Thucydides tells
us quite simply what happened after the surrender of Epidamnos, and
then what happened after the sea-fight. In any case, the story is
that the events occurred on the same day, and the likelikhood is
that both groups of prisoners were dealt with independently on
the spot, rather than that no action was taken before the Corcyreans
at Epidamnos had joined up with the Corcyreans in the sea-fight.
Gomme excuses the Corcyreans (p.165): 'the killing of the prisoners
was an act of justice, because the states to which they belonged
were not at war with Kerkyra'. But we do not know the exact terms
of the Corinthians' declaration of war (29.1) - it may have been in
the name of 'the Corinthians and their allies', or something like
that. If not, and if such 'acts of justice' were an accepted convention, the states that contributed ships to the Corinthian armada
might well have been less enthusiastic. It is more likely that the
Corcyreans were just bloodthirsty, as when they demand the killing
of the Corinthian embassy in 53.3 (where there is no question of con-
ventional justice); or else out to deter the cities friendly to Corinth from giving any further support.

(4)   There are two problems in 30.2-4:
(a) The first concerns the timing. I follow Gomme (p.165) in inter-
preting περιόντι τῷ θερέι (30.3), or reading if necessary
περιιόντι τῷ θερέι, as '"in the summer as it came round", i.e.
early next summer'; but the main reasons are not, as Gomme claims,
primarily linguistic - it would not be impossible to interpret
'in the remainder of that summer'. But this latter interpretation
would make nonsense of τὸ θέρος τοῦτο in 30.4. Thucydides says
here that 'for that summer' the Corinthians and Corcyreans encamped
opposite each other at Actium and Leukimme respectively; and this
can hardly refer to the summer of 435, which was taken up with the
Epidamnos affair, the sea-fight, and the Corcyrean reprisals. It
must refer to the summer of 434; which also gives the Corinthians a
more adequate amount of time to organise a proper defence.
     However, this does throw the meaning of τοῦ χρόνου τὸν πλεῖστον

(30.3) into some question. On the other interpretation of τὸ θέρος τοῦτο it would mean 'for most of the time (sc. the time occupied by that campaigning season, 435)': that is, the Corcyreans are in control for most of the summer, until at the end of it the Corinthians react. On what I have argued to be the better interpretation, the difficulty is that it is hard to see just *what period* of 'time' Thucydides means. He cannot mean most of the time between the sea-fight (probably to be dated in midsummer or later in 435) and Sybota, because that is false: the Corcyreans were in control for half the campaigning season of 435, but not at all in 434 and up to the time of Sybota in 433. He might perhaps mean 'for most of the time before the Corinthians organised their defences': that would imply that the Corcyreans were not always in control even for the rest of the first summer (435), which is surely unlikely – there is no reason to think that any Corinthian or allied forces challenged Corcyrean control until later: that is, until they organised the defences that Thucydides describes. We have, I think, to translate simply 'for much of the time', or 'for a good deal of time', which is acceptable Greek. That allows us to leave 'the time' vague: Thucydides means simply that there was a longish period during which the Corcyreans were in control - i.e. for the remainder of the campaigning season of 435, and perhaps during the winter also, until the Corinthian reaction at the beginning of the summer of 434.

(b) The second problem is how the Corinthians apparently managed to deter the Corcyreans simply by setting up bases at Actium and Cheimerion. Hammond says breezily that 'The post at Actium safeguarded the Ambraciote Gulf and Leucas town'; but the difficulty is to see how any such posts, however well sited, could have prevented the powerful and victorious Corcyrean fleet from raiding. The Corinthians sent ships as well as troops (ναῦς καὶ στρατιάν, 30.3); but the mere existence of a war fleet in the area, unless in sufficient numbers, could not have done the job. Nor could an army, unless very large and cleverly dispersed, have prevented sea-borne raids. (Compare Sparta's difficulties, IV.55).

The Corcyreans had a fleet of 120 ships, and could certainly have used at least fifty of them without undue effort (as they did when they helped the Athenians in 431). The remarkably small Corinthian contribution to the sea-fight - only thirty ships - may well not have represented anything like Corinth's full naval strength: though her need to engage later in a large-scale programme of shipbuilding (31.1) suggests, at least, that it represented a substantial proportion. But in any case, even if Corinth and her allies had enough ships available to counter anything that the Corcyreans could deploy - surely at least 100 - it would have been difficult and expensive to keep such a fleet throughout the whole campaigning season of 434, anchored and ready for action, at Actium and Cheimerion. At Actium, indeed, there would have been a supply-base and perhaps other naval facilities; but at Cheimerion the locale is much more remote and much more dangerously near to Corcyra. There is no difficulty in the Corcyrean fleet encamping at Leukimme, on their home ground and with easy supply; but is is wholly incredible that Corinth kept a large fleet on active service in these places for so long.

The answer must be, what is quite consistent with our general view

of Corcyrean motivation, that the Corcyreans did not want war and
had no imperialistic ambitions. They exercised reprisals, not without some justice, against Corinth's allies for the month or two of
the summer that remained after Leukimme; thereafter they were content
to remain on the defensive. As always, their chief purpose was to
remain independent and unthreatened, and perhaps they did not wish
to deploy a large fleet against the Corinthian contingents at
Actium and Cheimerion: though they remained on guard at Leukimme,
in case of a stronger Corinthian attack.

B. Corinthian Objectives after Leukimme

Before the battle near Leukimme in 435, as we have seen, the Corinthians apparently had no plans to conquer Corcyra. After it there
is a change. The Corinthians now wanted to bring Corcyra to heel:
not just (though of course this was desirable) to protect their
allies who were suffering Corcyrean reprisals (30.3), nor simply
(though this was essential) to defeat Corcyra in military engagements. The Corcyreans feared, at least, that Corinth would actually
conquer Corcyra: they saw themselves as unable to survive by their
own power alone, ἀδύνατοι ὄντες τῇ οἰκείᾳ μόνον δυνάμει
περιγενέσθαι (32.5). A complete Corinthian conquest would be
necessary to take over Corcyra's navy, a danger which was taken seriously (44.2). The Corinthians saw, or claimed to see, the Corcyreans
as 'rebellious' subjects (ἀφισταμένους, 40.4), on the analogy of
Samos' rebellion from Athens, and wished to bring them back to obedience.

These seem to be the facts, at least as Thucydides reports them;
but they may still make us wonder why it was, at this stage, so
important for Corinth to bring Corcyra to heel. It is hard to believe
that the motivation was entirely psychological, a matter of offended
matriarchal honour: particularly since Corcyra was a tough nut to
crack. The Corinthians had been badly mauled in 435: Epidamnos itself had been surrendered and was now not easily recoverable. Yet
the Corinthians thought it worth while to make a considerable effort
(surely involving substantial sacrifices) over the next two years
(31.1), in order to build up an armada powerful enough to have a
reasonable chance of victory. It was not necessary to do this simply
in order to protect their allies: 30.3-4 makes it clear that, even
if the Corinthian guard-posts at Cheimerion and Actium were not sufficient to deter any further Corcyrean reprisals, nevertheless the
Corcyreans were unlikely to cause any more serious trouble.

The answer must lie in the parallel which the Corinthians drew
with the Athenian empire (40.4-6). The Corinthians did not too much
mind the independence of Corcyra per se: they had, after all, made no
attempt to challenge it in the recent past. So long as Corcyra
stayed out of inter-state politics in the north-west, the Corinthians
could tolerate their economic prosperity and their military strength.
But it was essential for Corinth to keep the loyalty of her many
allies in that area, or at the very least their neutrality; and if
Corcyra had successfully challenged this in the case of Epidamnos,
other examples might follow (particularly after the blow to Corinthian
prestige: Corinthian prisoners had been taken at Epidamnos, and

Corinthians ships sunk at Leukimme). This also accounts for the
intransigence of the Corinthians in the face of the apparently
reasonable Corcyrean proposals in 28-29.1: to accept arbitration
from Peloponnesian cities or from Delphi, or that both sides should
withdraw from Epidamnos and discuss the matter, or that they should
at least make an armistice. For all these offers tacitly ceded
some rights of intervention and negotiation to Corcyra: something
the Corinthians could not allow, any more than Athens could allow
third-party intervention between herself and rebellious subjects
in her empire. Of course the parallel is by no means exact; but
the friendliness of the Corinthian colonies and trading-cities in
the north-west was as important to Corinth as the obedience of her
subject-states was to Athens. That is (if the term be pressed)
in part an 'economic' matter; but it was in a more direct sense
a political one. In particular, Corinth may have seen it as
necessary or desirable to control or safeguard the route to and
from Italy and Sicily, and seen the conquest of Corcyra as
essential for that purpose.

There is a further question about the Corinthians' ability to
achieve their objective. Corcyra was an exceptionally, large, fer-
tile, rich and powerful state, with the second strongest navy in
Greece. How could Corinth imagine that complete conquest would
be possible? Did she, indeed, hope not only to defeat Corcyra
in a sea-fight, but also to land and maintain enough troops to
conduct a successful siege of the city? In 427 Brasidas advised
that the Spartan-led fleet of 53 ships should make an attempt on
the city (III.79.3); but that was when the Corcyreans were in a
state of almost total chaos because of their civil war, and
Brasidas was a bold man. We are not even told that the Corinthians
took any large force of hoplites with them on this occasion, as they
had on the earlier expedition to Epidamnos, though they had considerable support from the barbarians on the mainland (I.47.3): did
they still hope to capture Corcyra?
  The answer to these questions must be 'yes': and certainly the
Corcyreans feared they would make a landing (50.4). Unless we at-
tribute grotesque misjudgement to the Corinthians, the implication
must be that Corcyra was much more vulnerable than her wealth and
naval strength would suggest. This would be true if, as there is
good reason to believe on other grounds (see below), there were
comparatively few Corcyreans in the hoplite class, and if the fleet
were manned largely by slaves. Provided the Corinthians could
inflict a severe naval defeat - thereby, perhaps, killing or in-
capacitating many of the hoplite class, who would be serving as
epibatai - they had some hope of success. This peculiarity of the
Corcyrean state has important implications for the kind of help
it could have given to Athens (unpaid rowers, but a *demos* apparently
not much committed to naval service and relying on the *oligoi* to
man any kind of fleet: see III.80).
  There is some conflict here, though more apparent than real,
with 25.4, where the Corcyreans are described as περιφρονοῦντες
αὐτοὺς καὶ χρημάτων δυνάμει ὄντες κατ' ἐκεῖνον τὸν χρόνον
ὁμοῖα τοῖς Ἑλλήνων πλουσιωτάτοις καὶ τῇ ἐς πόλεμον
παρασκευῇ δυνατώτεροι. Of course this may represent the views,

34

not of Corcyreans in general, but of the rich Corcyreans only;
nevertheless the claim to military power, if not the claim to wealth,
must refer to the Corcyrean state as a whole - the rich Corcyreans
could not make war on their own. Gomme says (*ad loc.*) that τῇ ἐς
πόλεμον παρασκευῇ δυνατώτεροι suggests that Corcyra 'was more
powerful in this respect than any Greek state, which is clearly
wrong', and implies that she was more powerful than Corinth. But,
first, the remarks which immediately follow about the Corcyrean
navy (ναυτικῷ δὲ καὶ ... πολεμεῖν) suggest that Thucydides
is contrasting the (possibly exaggerated) Corcyrean view of
Corcyra's strength with the actual facts: they were immensely proud
of their navy, and were in fact οὐκ ἀδύνατοι, having 120 triremes.
So it is plausible to translate along the lines of 'The Corcyreans
despised them, on the grounds that they were ...', rather than
'... because in fact they were ...'. Secondly, and perhaps more to
the point, a judicious punctuation can make it clear that the
Corcyreans are comparing themselves in military strength only with
Corinth. If we bracket, as it were, ὄντες ... πλουσιωτάτοις,
we may translate along the lines of: 'They thought themselves
superior both in terms of financial power (being at that time
as rich as the richest of any other Greeks), and in terms of their
military strength', or 'They despised them because they actually
were superior both ...': the former translation representing the
Corcyrean view, and the latter the actual facts.

It may seem as if Corcyra's inferiority to Corinth (both on paper,
as it were, and in the event) makes the latter interpretation impossible. But the facts are not so clear. On paper the inferiority of
the Corinthian fleet may be thought to outweigh any other military
advantages Corinth had over Corcyra; and in the event the Corcyreans
were defeated not by the Corinthians alone, but by a fleet two-
fifths of which came from Corinth's allies. I prefer the former interpretation chiefly because it sits better with the ensuing passage
about the Corcyrean navy.

C. Allies

Corcyra's only support (apart from Athens), that we know of, appears
to have come from Zacynthos: the Corcyrean army at Leukimme was reinforced by 1,000 hoplites from there. Zacynthos was (and remained)
friendly to Athens, and it is possible that Athenian pressure was
responsible for this very substantial support, perhaps particularly
necessary in view of Corcyra's weakness in hoplites. Alternatively,
the Zacynthians may have felt that they themselves might be the next
target for Corinthian aggression. Certainly their geographical
position might suggest this: their nearest neighbours, Cephallenia
(or at least the city of Pale) and Elis, were both hostile; the
former had contributed to the first Corinthian expedition, the latter
to both expeditions. No other state helped Corcyra: some confirmation of her isolationist policy. An (unsuccessful) attempt by the
Peloponnesians was in fact made on Zacynthos in 430, on a very large
scale (II.66).

The Corinthian allies present some points of interest. The respective ship-contributions for the two expeditions are as follows:

State	First expedition	Second expedition
Corinth	30	90
Leucas	10	10
Elis	7 hulls?	10
Epidauros	5	-
Hermione	1	-
Troezen	2	-
Ambracia	8	27
Anaktorion	-	1
Pale	4	-
Megara	8	12
	75	150

Some tentative inductions are possible. Corinth, as we know (31.1), did everything possible after 435 to increase the efficiency of her own navy, and succeeded in producing at least sixty new vessels (perhaps more, since some on the first expedition may have been among the fifteen disabled: 29.5). Leucas and Elis had been targets for Corcyrean reprisals after the first expedition; if this had any effect, it was apparently to make them continue the struggle with equal or greater ship-numbers. It is remarkable that Epidauros, Hermione and Troizen contributed at all, evidence perhaps of Corinthian pressure or financial support: less remarkable that the defeat of the first expedition dissuaded them from contributing to the second - Corcyra was not of direct concern to them, and they were a good deal further away than most of the other states (and the only ones on the wrong side of the Isthmus of Corinth). The Ambracian figures are striking and testify to the power that Ambracia could deploy when necessary: the geographical position of this state, like Anaktorion, gave it perhaps a strong incentive to check Corcyrean naval power. Pale may have had enough after the first expedition and their friendship to Corinth was clearly not very secure: Athens won the whole island over without having to fight a battle in 431, and a Corinthian expedition failed to make any impression on it in the winter of that year (II.30 and 33). Megara, interestingly enough, was willing to provide half as many ships again for the second expedition: evidence, perhaps, of either her unusual dependence on Corinth and/or her hatred of Athens at this time. We do not know, unfortunately, just whose ships were disabled in the first expedition among the fifteen mentioned by Thucydides: he says τῶν Κορινθίων (I.29.5), but that is likely to mean 'of the Corinthian-led force' rather than 'of the (specifically) Corinthian contingent'; for it would be a remarkable coincidence if all fifteen, out of a total of seventy-five, were from the thirty Corinthians. But no doubt what ships were sunk affected their states' contribution to the second expedition.

Gomme (p.178) offers two suggestions for the 'absence of contingents from Epidauros, Hermione, Troizen and Kephallenia in this second fleet': (1) 'doubtless because it was more likely to provoke a war with Athens', and (2) 'perhaps Sparta too had used some pressure'. The latter is weak, because the only 'Spartan pressure' we are told of concerns the first (Epidamnos) expedition, not the Sybota one

(28.1); and though either is of course possible as a motive, neither seems to cover all the requisite ground. Megara at least seems immune from (1), and the increased contributions from that state and from Elis tell against (2). If we are to generalise, geographical position together with pro-Corinthian feeling seems the best criterion: that will account for the continued or increased support of Leucas, Elis, Ambracia and Anaktorion; and Megara had a port on the Corinthian gulf. Cities on the Saronic Gulf understandably lapsed: and Pale's allegiance was doubtful.

D. Topography

1. Cheimerion

The major difficulty in Thucydides' account, described by Gomme (p.195) as 'the principle error in Thucydides', has always been thought to concern the location of the Corinthian base at Cheimerion. Nearly all editors, apparently relying on what Thucydides say in 46.4 (see below), confidently place it twenty miles away from Sybota, somewhere near the mouth of the Acheron (see map). But this is clearly inconsistent with what he says in 46.3: ἐπειδὴ δὲ προσέμειξαν τῇ κατὰ Κέρκυραν ἠπείρῳ ... ὁρμίζονται ἐς Χειμέριον ... Here προσέμειξαν must bear its normal sense of 'join with' or 'come up to': and this makes the location impossible, since Corcyra is not even visible from many places in this area, and is in any case far too far away from the area in general. We require a location a good deal farther north.

(a) It is clear that Χειμέριον names a promontory which juts out (ἡ ἄκρα ἀνέχει τὸ Χειμέριον), and I shall argue that we have no reason to think that it names a bay, harbour, camp or anything else. Hence, unsurprisingly, he says earlier that the Corinthians encamped περὶ τὸ Χειμέριον (30.3): and when they ὁρμίζονται ἐς Χειμέριον (46.3), and ἀνήγοντο ἀπὸ τοῦ Χειμερίου (48.1) he must mean something like 'the Cheimerion area'. I do not, of course, deny that the Corinthian fleet used some kind of harbour or anchorage; but what we have first to look for is a promontory, and this alone makes it hard to believe in a locale very close to the mouth of the Acheron, where no obvious promontory exists. The nearest would be a mile or two ESE of the modern Parga: and that is already too far from the Acheron mouth (six miles as the crow flies and about double that distance if we follow the coastline).

(b) Most editors have, more or less unconsciously, assumed Χειμέριον to name a bay because they have taken it as the subject of ἔστι δὲ λιμήν. As Poppo says (ad loc.): 'they want τὸ Χειμέριον to be the subject, so that the harbour Chimerium may be distinguished from the promontory. And Classen rightly thinks that Thucydides means the harbour Chimerium, by reason of the very words ὁρμίζονται ἐς'. Hence Forbes (ad loc.): 'We may rewrite the passage thus: "Chimerium, where the Corinthians stationed themselves, is a roadstead near the town of Ephyre ..."'; and Gomme (ad loc.): 'Cheimerion has been identified with a small bay ...' (my italics). Bloomfield (ad loc.) slightly improves on this by translating 'there is here a port'; but to make sense of the passage we have to go a good deal further.

Hammond's footnote on this passage reads: 'Jowett translates "Cheimerion is a harbour", and adds a footnote "or 'here there is a harbour'"; I prefer the former translation'. This destroys his own case, otherwise correctly and convincingly presented, for the Corinthian harbour being the bay of the Paramythia stream or Arila Bay. For on either translation the remainder of the sentence must run '... and *above it*, away from the sea, lies a city, Ephyre ...'. But Ephyre did not lie ὑπὲρ αὐτοῦ, if αὐτοῦ refers to the Paramythia or Arila bays; and in the remainder of the passage Thucydides shows that he is tolerably clear about where Ephyre was. Hammond says that 'the Acheron valley plain, beside which Ephyre probably lay, was served by the ports on the coast, whether Cheimerion, Glykys Limen or in modern times Parga'; but this is not sufficiently convincing, as a glance at the map will show. Not only is the distance to the Acheron Plain from the Paramythia bay (Hammond's candidate for the supposed harbour called 'Cheimerion') too great, but the mountains make communications very difficult. This is less true of the modern Parga and still less of Hagios Ioannes bay; but the only really plausible candidate for the harbour 'above' (ὑπὲρ) which the city lies is Glykys Limen. Strabo makes this geographical point quite clear when he says that Ephyre lies above (ὑπέρκειται) the gulf in which Glykys Limen is (vii.7.5). Nor is it clear that either Arila or the Paramythia bay would count as a λιμήν; both are open to winds from many quarters, not least the prevailing north-westerlies. Elsewhere it seems that Thucydides distinguishes between a λιμήν and a ὅρμος: the latter meaning more loosely 'a place to anchor', the former implying a good deal more protection.

Hammond grasps the point that here 'Thucydides introduces a digression', but does not drive it home. The digression begins with ἔστι δὲ λιμήν: this and the other topographical information - Ephyre, the Acherousian lake and the river Acheron - marks one boundary, the southern: and the other (northern) boundary is marked by the sentence ῥεῖ δὲ καὶ Θυαμις ... Κεστρίνην. The λιμήν here, understandably but carelessly taken as connected with, if not actually named as, Cheimerion, must in fact be the comparatively well-known Glykys Limen at the mouth of the Acheron: a proper harbour. Instead of making the natural but non-compulsory assumption that the opening words ἔστι δὲ λιμήν must refer to the Corinthian base and to Cheimerion itself, we may reasonably prefer to interpret the passage as intended to give the reader, no doubt ignorant of this non-Greek coastline, a clear if general idea of where the ἄκρα τὸ Χειμέριον is. Thucydides begins by naming one area which is or might be known: Ephyre and its harbour, the Acherousian lake and the river Acheron. This sets one limit: the other is set by the river Thyamis. An adequate translation would be of the form: 'Now there is (1) a harbour and a city above it, Ephyre ...: and there is also (2) the river Thyamis, which forms the boundary between Thesprotia and Kestrine: between these two limits, there juts out the promontory of Cheimerion.' If we do not interpret along these lines (which in any case seem to me a more natural rendering of the Greek), we can hardly see the point of Thucydides mentioning the Thyamis at all.

(c) What remains a much more open question is whether Cheimerion actually did, or was thought by Thucydides to, entitle a particular promontory within these limits, or stood rather as a general name for the

whole mountainous block. I should not regard the latter as impossible;
but the word used is ἄκρα, and the former gives us a perfectly good
candidate where Hammond places it (i.e. Cape Varlam: see map).
Hammond's candidates for the anchorage, Arila Bay or the Paramythia
bay, are also clearly correct: they are indeed the only possible
anchorage in the area within striking distance of the Corcyreans.
Neither bay is much more than a shallow curve or bight in the
the coastline, and neither affords good shelter. It is likely that
the Corinthians would have wished to beach as many of their 150 ships
as they could - if possible, all of them. That would be very difficult if only one bay was used; the Paramythia is the larger of the
two, but offers not much more than 1000 yards of suitable shore-
line, something between six and seven yards per ship - extremely awkward, to say the least. Almost certainly they used both bays together with the small indentation between the two. Their camp may
have been at Vemocastro, which is certainly the most easily-defended
site, and was probably at least one of the places where they established a garrison after Leukimme in 435 (I.30.3); but on this occasion they had their barbarian allies, and may not have thought they
needed such a strong position. A better alternative is somewhere
between the two bays, where its position would be more central:
possibly the slightly elevated ground (over 300 ft.) just north of
the Paramythia bay.

2. *Leukimme*

Of the two eastern capes of Corcyra, only the southern (Asprokavo)
is prominently white, being over 300 ft. high with outstanding white
cliffs: the northern is a low sandy spit. It is incredible that the
name Λευκίμμη could have been bestowed on the latter rather than the
former. Bloomfield (*ad. loc*) unsurprisingly writes (in 1829) 'now
the name, Cape Bianco, is given only to the southern one': but there
is no evidence that such a name was ever given to the northern one in
antiquity. Gomme (p.183) argues for the northern, on the grounds that
there is deep anchorage to the west of it (15-17 fathoms): but this
depth is irrelevant to Greek ships of that period.
Hammond produces three arguments for Leukimme being the northern
cape. The first is 'the persistence of the ancient name' (Lefkimo):
but this argument is weak to the point of non-existence, in view of
the large number of known topographical changes in this sort of nomen-
clature. The second is that 'it alone affords the beaching facilities required for a naval base'; but (a) this is not true, beaching
being entirely possible at a number of points; and (b) it is not clear
that it was used as a 'naval base' in any important sense. The
Corcyreans preferred the more sheltered Sybota Islands in 433; and
Thucydides' description of what happened after the battle in 435 does
not necessarily imply a permanent base rather than a summer encamp-
ment: ἀντεστρατοπεδεύοντο δὲ καὶ οἱ Κερκυραῖοι ἐπι τῇ
Λευκιμμῃ ναυσί τε καὶ πεζῷ ... ἀντικαθεζόμενοι χειμῶνος ἤδη
ἀνεχώρησαν ἐπ' οἴκου ἑκάτεροι (30.4). (Hammond remarks on this
passage: 'In both cases the meaning of ἀντι appears to be 'opposite'
in the geographical sense', and adds 'In the bay west of Cape Lefkimo
there is excellent anchorage, according to the *Mediterranean Pilot*.'
But there is no serious sense in which a camp at the northern cape,
particularly if the ships anchored to the west of it, is geographically

ἀντι the Corinthian forces at Actium and Cheimerion: the point holds
much better for the southern cape.)   The third argument is that
'This accords with Strabo vii,7,5, who describing the coast from north
to south, mentions Buthrotum and then the Sybota islands κατὰ τὸ
ἑῷον ἄκρον τῆς Κορκυραίας τὴν Λευκίμμαν κείμεναι. ['lying
opposite the eastern cape of Corcyra, Leukimme']; sailing south one
sights Cape Lefkimo and not Cape Bianco.'   This also is an *argumentum
adversus sese*.   For (1) the Sybota islands are very much more κατὰ
the southern than the northern cape; and (2) *from those islands*, at
least, 'one sights' the southern much more clearly than the northern.
Indeed the flat and marshy northern promontory is in general much
less visible.

In any case, more general features of the situation speak strongly
for the Corcyreans trying to hold a line, as it were, from Asprokavo
to Sybota: and their base must have been at, or very near, one end of
the line.   The Corinthians were not only trying to defeat them in a
sea-battle but were (or were thought to be) dangerous in two quite
different ways.   First, they could make a descent on the Corinthian
mainland; and secondly, they could sail past Corcyra and conduct
operations to the east and north of it, most obviously at Epidamnos.
These dangers made something like the Asprokavo-Sybota position necessary for the Corcyreans: in no other way could they be so certain
of bringing the Corinthians to battle.   A base at the Sybota islands,
at least, was absolutely required: it is in fact virtually the only
possible location, since the Thesprotian mainland was occupied by
pro-Corinthian troops; and even a line from Sybota to the northern
promontory of Corcyra would give more latitude for a possible Corinthian descent on the territory to the south (nearer to Asprokavo).
The Asprokavo-Sybota line also made the presence of the Athenian ships
more effective.   For if the Corinthians had been able to land on
Corcyra (between the southern and northern capes) before meeting the
Corcyrean line of battle, the Athenians could not have participated
in an attack on them without deliberate aggression; but so long as
the Corinthians were forced to attack the Corcyreans in order to land,
the Athenians could adopt a defensive posture.

It is perhaps possible to identify the Corcyrean camp with more
precision.   Thucydides talks always of τὸ στρατόπεδον in the
singular, and the implication is that there was s single locale for
both the fleet and the land forces: they must at least have been close
to each other if the soldiers were to give immediate support to the
fleet.   Look-out men would no doubt have been posted on the heights
of the cape itself, but the camp could not have been there: nor is
there anywhere suitable, from the viewpoint of weather conditions
and easy beaching, round the coastline facing south and south-east.
The bight (rather than bay) by the modern Kavos, however, offers
plenty of space, easy beaching on a sandy bottom, and as much weather
protection as is available on the Corcyrean coastline at the eastern
end of Corycra: most importantly, it is sufficiently near the narrows -
in effect, directly on them - to perform the essential strategic
function described above.   It will be clear from later remarks that
this fits in with other features of the battle.

3. Mainland Sybota

The Corinthians brought the salvaged ships to the mainland Sybota
(50.3). This was the nearest point to Corcyra on the mainland,
and had clearly been agreed in advance as a temporary base (hence the
barbarian supporting army had already gone there: προσεβεβοηθήκει,
pluperf.). The τὸν ἐν τοῖς Συβότοις λιμένα of 52.1 must surely
refer to the same place. It seems equally clear that the place must
be near the Sybota islands. Συβότα or τὰ Συβότα, 'the Swine-
pastures', perhaps referred to the whole non-mountainous area south
and west of the modern Mourtso. The λιμήν, then, will include
the west-facing harbour of the modern Mourtso, and the bays which
afford shelter some few yards along the coast to the south (see map).

It is important to note here, as being relevant to the Corinthian
fleet's position at the third encounter, that Port Mourtso itself
would not be sufficiently large for a fleet of 150 ships. The shore-
line suitable for beaching is not more than 50 yards long; and the
bay itself, though shallow, not more than some 50 x 50 yards in size.
The Corinthians would certainly have used the bays to the south, which
add some hundreds of yards to possible beaching areas, and also enjoy
the protection of the Sybota islands which face them. Thucydides'
description of Sybota as a λιμήν does not tell against this: here,
as at Pylos, λιμήν may refer rather to a sheltered area of sea than
a particular area of land (of course the two are often coextensive).
The λιμήν at Pylos was simply that (fairly large) area of sea which
the shelter of Sphacteria made comparatively safe from the weather,
not some particular bay within that area: so here, the λιμήν which was
called τὰ Συβότα may refer generally to the sheltered water and coves
east of the Sybota islands.

4. The Corcyrean camp at Sybota

Gomme (ad loc.) is worried by the small size of the Sybota islands as
a camping-ground. But so far as the size, rockiness, etc. of the
Sybota islands are concerned, we have only to think of the far worse
position of the Athenian fleet at Pylos in 425 (described in IV.26
and elsewhere). The islands are less than five miles from the
Corcyrean mainland, so that the fleet could easily be supplied: and
though they had (if the figures are correct) more ships than the
Athenians in 425, they also had more space and more sheltered water.
Above all, the camp had only to be maintained for a short time.
Thucydides says that the troops encamped only ἐν μιᾷ τῶν νήσων,
'in one of the islands' (47.1) (which suggests no particular space
shortage). This is more likely to have been the western island:
not only because there is more flat ground for sleeping and eating, but
because it provides a better vantage-point for observing the Corinthians
and maintaining contact with the Corcyrean mainland, and (more important)
has better landing-places (see map).

More worrying, at least prima facie, is the nearness of the Sybota
islands to the mainland, and hence their vulnerability to the Corinthian allied land forces. The nearest distance between Ayios Nikolaos
and the mainland is now not more than 25 yards: and assuming (as we
must) a rise of 1-2 metres in sea-level since classical times, would
have been somewhat less (not much, since the shore-line is in general
precipitous). Some of this can be waded; and more could then have
been. The distance between that island and the other is at one point
no greater.

41

Determined men, it seems, could have ousted the Corcyreans from
their base or at least contested it; even if, as I have suggested,
it was on the western island. In fact the Corinthian allies probably
did not reach that part of the mainland until the Corcyreans had
sailed from Sybota; and they would, of course, in any case have had
to contend with the well-armed *epibatai* of the whole Corcyrean fleet
- not an easy task for barbarians who probably did not dispose of
many hoplite troops. But it would have paid the Corinthians to have
sent them on ahead with at least the threat of an attack, on the day
before the night in which they set sail. This would certainly have
confused and alarmed the Corcyreans: they would have had either to
abandon the base or guard it. Either alternative would have been at
best a nuisance, and at worst a severe handicap, for a fleet that
had to be ready to deploy against the Corinthians before they passed
through the narrows.

Did the Corinthians miss a trick here? Perhaps they did not know
that the Corcyreans were based at Sybota, or perhaps their barbarian
allies refused to undertake the task: but the most probable exaplan-
ation is that they were unwilling to part with their allies before
actually embarking. They had to guard against the possibility of
a Corcyrean attack on their camp at Cheimerion, and the allies may
have seemed a necessary part of their defence. Even so, the allied
force might have been divided, and part sent to Sybota: though we
do not know their total numbers, and they may have been insufficient.

E. The Engagements

1. *The Corinthians' night embarkation*

At what time of night did the Corinthians start, and why? The answer
to the first of these questions is given by ἅμα ἕω πλέοντες,
which must mean something like 'at dawn, as they were sailing on':
that is, the Corinthian ships were in motion and not just hanging
about. The Corcyrean fleet, for reasons given above, was ensuring
that the battle took place in the narrows between Leukimme and
Sybota. It is about seven miles from Cheimerion to the narrows:
the Corinthians must have left not earlier than about an hour or
two before dawn.

No doubt they did this, as Hammond says, to 'escape observation'.
But to what end, and why did they not start much earlier in the night?
There would have been time, if they had wished and if the Corcyrean
fleet did not intervene, for them to have moved from Cheimerion
through the narrows, round the north-east cape of Corcyra and even as
far as the town of Corcyra itself (about thirty miles from Cheimerion):
or they could have blockaded the Sybota islands, or made a landing at
more or less any suitable point on the western half of Corcyra, or
simply gained the open water north of the narrows. They did none of
these things: the fact that they started so late must mean that they
wished to be by dawn where in fact they were - in the narrows. But
that, it might seem, could have been just as well achieved by starting at dawn or a bit later, without all the trouble of a night embark-
ation.

The point must be that they wished to be in the narrows *at dawn and
neither earlier nor later*. So we need to ask (1) why there, and (2)

why then? Their other options must all have seemed less satisfactory
to them. (a) The more open water north of the narrows would break the
Corcyrean line of defence (Leukimme-Sybota), and give them some
chances - after a naval victory, though only after a naval victory
(see below) - of a successful landing on Corcyra. But it would take
the fleet away from the support of its land forces on the mainland,
and might (in the event of defeat) threaten its line of retreat,
enabling the Corcyreans in effect to cut the Corinthian fleet off.
(b) The same would apply to attempted landings on Corcyra by any
route north of the narrows: landings in any case extremely risky
if they could be interrupted by an undefeated Corcyrean fleet.
(c) Landings on the south (south-west) coast of Corcyra would not
involve passing the narrows, but would still mean that the undefeated
Corcyrean fleet was on their flank and could intervene. It is in
general clear that the Corinthians thought it necessary to defeat
the Corcyrean fleet first, before attempting any landings on
Corcyra (as with Alcidas and Brasidas in 427 see III.76ff.). Their
plan was to fight in the narrows: hence they arranged for land support at Sybota.
(2) To arrive in the narrows at night would be not only pointless
(since they did not wish to go further) but dangerous, as exposing
them to a possible night attack by the Corcyreans. The Corinthians,
justifiably in the event, must have believed their fleet superior,
and not wished to expose it to the unnecessary chances of an engagement during darkness. The point of arriving at dawn rather than later
seems to lie in their hope of catching the Corcyreans unprepared and
still at anchor in the Sybota islands. But just what would be gained
by this? Hammond suggests, not without reason, that there would be
a considerable advantage to the Corinthians if they could gain a
position between the Corcyrean fleet and Leukimme: the Corcyreans
would then have a hostile mainland at their backs, and (if the
Corinthians won) might thus be totally destroyed. On the other hand,
the same point holds in reverse: if the Corcyreans won, the Corinthians
might be forced back against the hostile Leukimme and adjacent area
of Corcyra island. Perhaps the Corinthians, trusting in their superiority, backed the former rather than the latter possibility.. But
a clear and non-controversial advantage would be gained if the
Corinthians could occupy a position which at once allowed them an
easy retreat, in the case of defeat, towards their own coastline
rather than towards Leukimme, and also put the Corcyreans in a very
difficult tactical situation: that is, a position very close to the
Sybota islands, south and west of them. This would virtually blockade the Corcyreans in their anchorage, where they could be destroyed
piecemeal or forced back on the hostile mainland. Such a possibility
depended, of course, on the Corcyreans remaining at anchor and letting
this happen: they had more sense, but it was worth trying.
All this assumes, of course, that each fleet had reasonably good
information about what the other was doing, but for most purposes
that can be taken as more or less certain. Vemokastro and the Sybota
islands are intervisible, and only about seven miles apart; and the
Corinthians, at least, would have been able to receive information
from scouts on the friendly mainland. The only doubtful point is
whether the Corcyreans knew that the Corinthians were going to embark

at night, and on that particular night: and, if so, how they knew.
It is possible that the Corcyreans kept their fleet at sea during
however many nights the Corinthians were at Cheimerion (we do not know
how many, though they spent some time in making preparations:
παρεσκεύαστο, 48.1): that would have been tiring, but they could
have rested in the day-time with the security of good look-out men
at Leukimme and Sybota. Possibly they had boats posted between
Cheimerion and Sybota: such boats might have had enough time, between the beginning of the (necessarily lengthy) Corinthian embarka-
tion and the Corinthians' arrival in the narrows, to warn the
Corcyreans; but this seems doubtful, since the Corcyreans would
also have needed some time to embark, even though they had less far
to go. Possibly, despite the hostility of the mainland, they had
spies there or even in the Corinthian camp, who could have covered
the distance by land soon enough. But it is perhaps equally likely
that, if there was a moon and good visibility (about which we cannot be certain), they may have been able to see - perhaps even hear -
the Corinthians preparing to embark, or at least embarking, even at
night: in time for them to deploy in the narrows before the
Corinthians got there.

The Corinthians took food for three days. It is difficult to draw
any very specific conclusions from this, because the Corinthians
themselves may not have taken up any specific tactical options.
They may have thought more generally about the possibilities of
a landing on Corcyra, a blockade of the Sybota anchorage, a running
sea-fight lasting several days, and so on: and made the best general
provision against any of these that they could by taking three days'
food. Nor is it wholly clear whether they could have been fed from
their anchorage in mainland Sybota. The place was ἔρημος ('uninhabited', 50.3); and though the barbarian army was en route (and
must have arrived before the battle) it does not follow that these
allies would be either willing or able to provide food for the
crews of 150 ships (about 30,000 men) - not, at least, for long.

2. The Composition of the battle-lines

It is not certain whether these positions were agreed or actually
adopted before or after the fleets saw each other. But some discussion must have taken place, and contingency plans at least laid;
and ὡς κατεῖδον ἀλλήλους ('when they saw each other', 48.3) might
be thought to imply that there was time (because both sides allowed
themselves and each other time) to deploy as they thought best. So
it is worth while trying to make sense of the arrangements.
    The Athenians had orders to engage the Corinthians only if they
were going to land on Corcyra or Coryrean-owned territory (45.3).
These orders were both vague and hard to carry out; but it is at least
understandable that they took a position on the extreme right of the
Corcyrean line, as near as possible to Corcyra, for they had some
hope of positioning themselves between the Corinthians and the land.
The division of the Corcyreans into three squadrons is also intelligible as an attempt to introduce some order and effective decen-
tralisation of command: though in fact the battle seems to have been
devoid of any kind of coherent manoeuvres - at least to start with,

the ships just grappled each other and slugged it out (as 49.1-3 makes clear). Partly for this reason, it seems unlikely that the twenty victorious Corcyreans on the Corcyrean left were a separate squadron, under a single command throughout: they were probably just twenty ships that had defeated the adversaries opposite them and then pursued them on their own initiative. A separate squadron of twenty would in any case seem rather odd: the other two squadrons, if equally divided, would amount to forty-five each (110 less twenty divided by two), and the anomalously small squadron of twenty would have had to face a total of thirty-nine (twelve Megarian and twenty-seven Ambracian) on the Corinthian right. To make sense of this we should have to postulate a specially-designed squadron of twenty selected ships with a specific job to do: and there is no evidence for this. We do best to assume that the three squadrons were more or less equally divided.

On the Corinthian side, there was some reason for the Corinthians to station themselves on the left. Their best ships were there, and they would be more able to give a good account of themselves against the redoubtable Athenians: moreover, in the event of a decisive victory and the possibility of a landing, they would be nearer Corcyrean territory. It may even be that the Corinthians wished to put the Athenians diplomatically on the spot, as it were, by forcing them to fight against the Corinthians themselves rather than against their allies. The Megarian and Ambracian contingents were larger than any other allied contingents, and might be thought to make a more coherent right-wing squadron than a mixture from a greater number of allies. What Thucydides calls τὸ μέσον ('the centre') consisted only of the other allies, numbering just twenty-one ships (ten from Elis, ten from Leucas, and one from Anaktorion).

There is a problem here, inasmuch as the different parts of the Corinthian line seem *prima facie* to be unequally weighted: ninety Corinthians on the left, twenty-one allies in the middle, and thirty-nine allies on the right. Most scholars assume that the descriptions are not strictly topographical, and that in effect the ninety Corinthians must have held most of the centre as well as the left wing. But Thucydides does not say so; indeed he repeats that the Corinthians were on the left (ἐπὶ τῷ εὐωνύμῳ, 49.6) and it may well be that the left side of the Corinthian line was, at least, much more heavily weighted with ships than the rest of it was. That would certainly help to account for the Corcyrean defeat in this section: together with the fact which Thucydides reports that the twenty victorious ships on the Corcyrean left were not available to reinforce the Corcyrean right (*ibid.*). The Corinthians perhaps aimed at some sort of breakthrough on their left wing. If they had placed their sixty allies against an equal number of Corcyreans (on the Corinthian right and in the centre), they would have been able to deploy their own ninety ships against the remaining fifty Corcyreans and ten Athenians. That is quite a sensible tactical plan, and accords with what actually happened; though of course we cannot hope for anything like certainty here. In particular we cannot know how the Corcyreans might have reacted: if this was the Corinthians' deployment, if the Corcyreans perceived it in time, and if they adjusted their own deployment in view of it, they might have reinforced their right wing. One might guess that they did

not have much time to do this successfully, and were further thwarted
by the absence of their victorious twenty ships on their left, thus
allowing the Corinthian tactics to succeed.

3. The Attack on Cheimerion

49.5 and 52.2 must refer to Cheimerion rather than Sybota: not so
much because Thucydides 'has not yet mentioned the latter' (hardly
a decisive point), still less because 'the σκηναί and χρήματα
would be there and not at the advanced base' (Gomme, p.195) (even less
decisive), but because the Corinthian allies on land would certainly
be at Sybota in time for the battle (the whole point of having them
there), and would have prevented the Corcyreans from plundering the
camp. The σκηναί and χρήματα show that the Corinthians intended
at least to return to Cheimerion; in any case they might be thought
to need a base for supplies nearer than Actium. But it is not clear
what sort of supplies these would be, nor how far (if at all) the
Corcyrean descent affected the Corinthian position as described in
52. Χρήματα is not the normal Thucydides word for 'equipment':
the usual term is σκεύη (as in VII.4.5; see also VI.97.5 where
the distinction is made in σκεύεσι καὶ χρήμασιν); and since the
Corcyreans plundered it rather than setting fire to it, χρήματα
here probably means just 'valuables' or 'money'. There is no positive evidence that the Corinthians brought any σκεύη to Cheimerion
at all, and some suggestion from Thucydides' silence that they did
not: though they no doubt brought simple 'spares', either carried with
them on board, left at Cheimerion or left at Sybota - supplies of
arrows and other weapons, perhaps oars and rigging.

Since they anticipated the possibility of a campaign lasting
for some days, this may seem improvident; and we should have to believe,
despite Thucydides' silence, that there was σκεύη at Cheimerion and
that the Corcyreans burned it. That might, of course, account in one
way for the Corinthians' difficulty which they express in 52.2 - that
ἐπισκευὴν οὐκ οὖσαν τῶν νεῶν ἐν χωρίῳ ἐρήμῳ. But this must
mean 'there were no facilities for repairing their ships in this
uninhabited locality'; and (1) it is not clear that the kind of
facilities they needed were such as they could have carried with
them to Cheimerion: any serious repairs to damaged ships might involve
too heavy and complex equipment to be easily portable; (2) ἐν χωρίῳ
ἐρήμῳ only makes sense in this light; they require something like a
port or dockyard, or at least skilled workmen, to do the job. The
Corinthians do not say 'We can't repair our ships because our equipment was destroyed', but 'We can't repair our ships because there are
no facilities in this uninhabited place.' The Corinthians, then,
brought with them all the things they could reasonably bring and (I
should guess) kept them either on board or at Sybota; but these did
not include what was necessary for major repairs. What they left at
Cheimerion was precisely what they did *not* immediately need for the
sea-fight: their tents and valuables.

There were twelve Megarian and twenty-seven Ambracian ships on the
Corinthian right, and one suspects that they were not very efficient.
That may apply particularly to the Ambracians, who lived remote
from the main centres of Greek power and naval affairs: moreover on
the previous expedition (in 435) they had sent eight ships only,

46

and hence most of their fleet would be totally unpractised. The Megarians, who also sent eight on the first expedition, might have been rather better. It is a bit surprising that the Corinthians did not, in the course of the battle, bear in mind the possibility of these allies suffering defeat.

We are not told when these victorious Corcyreans returned, but it must be at some time after the defeat of the Corcyrean right in 49.6-6, and before the second action in 50.4, for which the Corcyreans used every available ship. The distance to Cheimerion and back is about ten miles from the scene of the first action, and some time must be allowed for burning and plundering: perhaps three or four hours altogether. Unless these victorious Corcyreans were unusually cowardly or egocentric, the chances are that they would have joined in the fight on the Corcyrean right if they had observed what was happening and had had time to get there: they could have taken the Corinthians in the rear and done much to affect the course of the battle. They might well have intervened not only before the τροπή in 50.1, but also while the Corinthians were mopping up - killing the survivors and forcing the Corcyreans ashore. The fighting was ended ἐπειδὴ κατεδίωξαν τοὺς Κερκυραίους ... ἐς τὴν γῆν ('when they had pursued the Corcyreans ... to the shore', 50.3), and we may thus reasonably assume that this did not last longer than three or four hours: perhaps not as long. The victorious twenty ships had no time to intervene. The towing of the wrecks would have taken many hours, and it is clear from the Corinthians' revewal of the battle (they formed up again, sang the paean, and so forth) that they were not blockading the Corcyrean camp with their ships. Most if not all of the Corinthian fleet was either occupied with towing or had retired towards Sybota. While this was going on, the victorious Corcyreans could have returned to Leukimme with comparative safety. They perhaps took a detour westwards in order to avoid tangling with the Corinthians (see map).

4. Details of the Corinthian Victory

(a) What the Corinthians do in 50.3 'seems hardly consistent' (Gomme, p.186) with what they do in 50.1-2. But the first few words of each give the key. τῆς δὲ τροπῆς γενομένης (50.1) is meant with a precise use of τροπή, the 'turning' of the enemy: 'once the enemy had begun to flee'. There would have been a fair amount of time between this and the stage referred to in 50.3. It is only after they had pursued the Corcyreans as far as the land (ἐπειδὴ ... ἐς τὴν γῆν) that they turn their attention to the wrecks. ἐτράποντο is deliberately used in both 50.1 and 3, to mark the two different Corinthian interests.

(b) We meet an apparent contradiction between διεκπλέοντες ('break-ing the line', 50.1) and διέκπλοι δ᾽ οὐκ ἦσαν (49.3). It is easy to say that Thucydides employs διεκπλέοντες 'not, of course, in the tactical sense in which διέκπλοι was used' (Gomme, p.185); but this tells us nothing about what it is supposed to mean. There seem to be two possibilities:
(i) If the object of διεκπλέοντες is (as in 'the tactical sense') the enemy's line of battle, then we may argue that a victorious fleet may make one διέκπλους at any rate, even if it does not

employ the sophisticated tactics of the 'tactical sense':
namely, when as a whole it breaks through that line, having
already won the battle by sinking or damaging many enemy ships.
(ii) We may take the object to be, not the battle line, but the sunk
or damaged Corcyrean ships (specifically, τὰ σκάφη, 50.1)
through and past which the victorious Corinthians sailed in
their pursuit.

These two alternatives are conceptually, if not substantially,
distinct. It is hard to choose between them, and perhaps Thucydides
did not himself distinguish in this way. What he means, however,
is clear. The Corinthians spent some time in close and fairly
static combat with the Corcyreans, damaging and sinking ships until
the Corcyreans had had enought and begun to flee. Through this area
of static combat - that is, both through what had been the enemy
battle-line and through the ruck of damaged ships - the Corinthians
sailed, and eventually out of it (διά + ἐκ), pursuing them ἐς τήν
γῆν. As they sailed in this manner they killed the enemy troops,
who were in the water or on the wreckage.

(c) Why did the Corinthians act in this way? Unless we ascribe
it merely to revenge (as Hammond does), or to insensate blood-lust,
we must presume that they considered the death of enemy troops more
important, at that stage, than either (a) taking prisoners, or (b)
salvaging the sunken ships. (a) is readily intelligible: taking
prisoners would have cost more time (under these circumstances)
than killing them, and they would be a nuisance to look after (as
Thucydides says in 52.2). (b), however, is less obvious. Perhaps
the Corinthians felt that their superiority in ship-numbers was
already sufficient; but it is more likely that they did not feel
secure in trying to salvage any ships until their enemy was at a
safe distance, i.e. until they had chased them ἐς τήν γῆν.

The failure of the Corinthians to distinguish between their own
and Corcyrean survivors is on any account striking; but the reasons
for it are not immediately clear. Thucydides' argument seems to be:
they killed their friends in ignorance because they had not grasped
that their right wing had been beaten, and they did not grasp this
because (γάρ, 50.2) there was a large number of ships over a wide
area of sea, so that it was not wasy to see who was winning or being
beaten. The implication seems to be that they simply assumed the
survivors to be Corcyrean, because they assumed that their own
fleet was victorious on the right wing as it had been on the left.
It still seems curious (1) that the Corinthians could not have identified the *ships* that had been crippled of waterlogged as their own,
or the victorious ships as Corcyrean, both during and after the
victory; and (2) that they could not have identified the *survivors*.
There would be some survivors on crippled ships, some clinging to
pieces of wreckage, some swimming. Did the Corinthians say to themselves in all or any of these cases 'Well, our ships have won, so
these people must be Corcyrean'? Could not some of these survivors
have established their identity before being killed - if only by shouting 'Hoi, I'm an Ambracian!'?

(1) is more understandable if, as seems to be the case (see on 50.5
- 51.5 below), ships were not easily identified as belonging to this
or that state, except at very close range. Thucydides more or less says

48

this, and we have to accept it. They could not, then, have carried easily recognisable ensigns or markings which could be recognised at some distance. The hoisting of some kind of signal, a common practice, occurred on this occasion (τὰ σημεῖα ... ἤρθη, 49.1). But these σημεῖα, like modern signals, may only have been raised and then lowered again: and probably they were raised only in the flagships. No doubt also any distinctive markings were obliterated on some ships, those which had been severely damaged and the survivors on or around which were killed by the Corinthians: intact ships might have been recognised at close quarters and left alone.

(2) may be largely explained by the chaos and heat of battle. There may have been nothing particularly distinctive about the dress of appearance of the survivors, and any attempt they made to identify themselves vocally would have been drowned by the general cries and cheering. Many of them, in fact, may have been in no fit state to identify themselves at all: wounded, half-drowned, or unconscious. It is even possible that the survivors, being from the right of the line and hence mostly Ambracian, used a dialect which was unlike Corinthian and may even have been more like Corcyrean. The Corinthians, in any case, were in no mood of calm reflection.

5. Ship numbers and Corcyrean losses

Most editors have expressed discontent with the ship-numbers as given in the Mss. Naturally these are always suspect; but there is in fact no reason for particular suspicion here. The major worry is again expressed by Gomme (p.191), who doubts the figure of seventy as the Corcyrean losses, on the grounds that 'this would be an overwhelming advantage' to the Corinthians in a second battle. But to this there are two replies:
(i) The Corinthians had, at most, 120 ships. They begin with 150 (46.1) of which thirty had been out of action (διαφθείραντες 54.2). διαφθείραντες may of course mean 'having destroyed', with the implication of total destruction; but it is more likely to mean 'having disabled' - as it must, for instance, in II.90.5, where the Peloponnesians διέφθειραν Athenian ships which were afterwards taken in tow and then recovered by the Athenians. The word is also used of the Leucadian ship which was actually sunk (II.92.3), and is likely to be a term of pretty general application. Something like 'put out of action' seems best. Ships can be put out of action by sinking, or breaking their oars, or all sorts of other methods. Thucydides prefers, however, to use this word of the Corcyreans where he uses κατα-δύσαντες of the Corinthians; the implication must be that some or most of the Corinthian ships were not put out of action by actually being sunk, but by some lesser feat. Nevertheless, διαφθείραντες implies more than just damage; and it is likely that a good many additional Corinthian ships were in fact damaged, though not put out of action.

The Corcyreans' numbers are more uncertain. For this battle they manned 110 ships (47.1): after about seventy had been sunk (καταδύσαντες 54.2) they reformed not only with the surviving ships but, apparently, with whatever (other) ships they had left (ταῖς πλωίμοις καὶ ὅσαι ἦσαν λοιπαί, 50.4). The only in-dication we have as to the numbers of these ships comes from

49

25.4, where we are told τριήρεις γὰρ εἴκοσι καὶ ἐκατὸν
ὑπῆρχον αὐτοῖς ὅτε ἤρχοντο πολεμεῖν. This might seem
to suggest a maximum of ten, as Gomme assumes (a total fleet
of 120, of which 110 had been committed). It is not clear to
what precise point of time ἤρχοντο πολεμεῖν applies,
and (partly because of this) we cannot even guess at possible
losses, or additional launchings, between that date and the
battle of Sybota. We can, however, reasonably assume that they
had available a fair number of ships *which were not triremes*
(remembering that the figure of 120 is for triremes alone): and
this, in a battle which was more like a πεζομαχία ('land-
battle', 49.2) and in which οὐ ῥᾳδίως ἀπελύοντο ('they
could not easily get clear', 49.3), may well have augmented the
Corcyreans' strength considerably. We must, in any case, add
the thirty unscathed Athenian ships- and this gives us a total
of eighty (110 less seventy, plus at least ten additional ships,
plus thirty Athenians). A preponderance of 120 over eighty,
particularly when many of the 120 had probably been damaged and
the eighty probably augmented by older craft, is not overwhelming.
(ii) In any case there were other factors, which Thucydides states
quite clearly in 52.2: (a) the undamaged (and redoubtable) thirty
ships from Athens; (b) the need to guard prisoners. Further, the
Corinthians were just as anxious as the Athenians to avoid direct
conflict between the two of them for wider political reasons. In
the first encounter, the Corinthians could easily have involved
the Athenians had they wished to do so, by an immediate attack
on the ten ships- indeed,they must (like the Athenians) have exercised a good deal of care in trying to avoid this. They would
have remained anxious to avoid it however overwhelming their
numerical advantage. All this makes it entirely intelligible
that the conjoined Corcyrean and Athenian fleet should have taken
the initiative by sailing over to Sybota and challenging the
Corinthians to fight (52.1). Both parties, in fact, recognised
that if either side had an advantage, it was the Corcyreans and
Athenians.

How crippling a blow was this to the Corcyrean navy? In particular,
were the Corcyrean losses sufficient in themselves to account for the
inadequacy of the Corcyrean navy in later years? The answer to this
last question must, I think, be negative: but some discussion is required.

As we have just seen, the Corcyreans had some fifty triremes in
effective operation after the battle (having suffered losses of seventy
out of a fleet of 120). In 431 they assist the Athenians with fifty
triremes; and though this fleet probably did not go further than the
southern Peloponnese, and may have returned to Corcyra before the
Athenian expedition was complete, it is still very unlikely that the
Corcyreans would have assisted Athens with their whole naval strength:
particularly since the possibility of Peloponnesian fleets in the
north-west was a real one.

It is highly probable that the Corcyreans would have rehabilitated
any of their own (no doubt also any Corinthian) hulls that they managed to acquire, assuming that they were not damaged beyond repair;
but it is very hard to say just how many of these there were, even if

we assume that most of the waterlogged hulls were not so damaged (a fair assumption, since both sides were anxious to recover them). There were seventy Corcyrean ones, and an indefinite number of Corinthian: as argued above, not many of the latter - something like eighty hulls in all. The Corcyreans gained some of these (54.1), though the Corinthians got most of them (50.3). But what did the Corinthians do with theirs after they had decided to retreat? It is not to be believed that they towed them all the way home: the most sensible thing was to destroy them totally, but Thucydides does not tell us that they did this, and it is not immediately obvious how they could have done it easily (perhaps by fire, if they were not too waterlogged). We cannot, at least, rule out the possibility that the Corcyreans managed to get some of them back and reconstitute them. If (just for the sake of example) they acquired and reconstituted half of the total number - that is, forty - that would have brought their fleet up to a total of ninety. The work could well have been done between Sybota and the Athenian expedition of 431.

All that is of course highly speculative and uncertain. Nor do we know how many new ships, if any, the Corcyreans built, or when. Fortunately we know that in 427 they are able to man sixty ships (III.77.1). These, together with twelve Athenians, were to confront only fifty-three Peloponnesian ships. It is possible that the Corcyreans had more ships available but either felt no need to man them (having already a numerical advantage) or - more probably - were uncertain about their crews: in III.80 their difficulty is that they cannot get enough men, perhaps particularly enough hoplites, to man more than thirty ships. In the battle against the Peloponnesians they lost thirteen ships (irrecoverably, since the ships were captured and retained by the Peloponnesians, rather than damaged or sunk); but that still leaves Corcyra with a minimum of forty-seven. We may legitimately suspect that there were more.

It is sufficiently clear, despite these numerical uncertainties, that the fifteen Corcyrean ships which helped Demosthenes at Leucas in 426 (III.94) and the fifteen which Eurymedon obtained from Corcyra for the Athenian force in Sicily (VII.31) cannot have represented more than a fraction of Corcyra's naval strength. Whatever the reasons for her unimpressive naval performance after Sybota, or at any rate after 431 - they are, I think, primarily political, and discussed in Part II - it was not that Sybota had dealt her a shattering blow. If compelled to guess, I should be inclined to say that she may have had anything up to ninety or a hundred ships soon after Sybota, or at least by 431: and that most of these ships were retained even after the *stasis* in 427. They may well have been in bad shape (leaky, rotten, not properly equipped, etc.); but if so, that was because other (political) reasons inhibited the Corcyreans from actually manning and using them.

6. *Arrival of Athenian reinforcements (50.5-51)*

Just before the Athenians were sighted, the Corcyrean fleet would at this point have been ranged along their own coastline roughly along a north-south line. It is therefore certain, as Hammond says, that the reinforcing Athenians sailed west of Paxos, and were initially hidden from the Corcyreans by Cape Asprokavo (Leukimme), becoming visible to them shortly after they were visible to the more easterly Corinthians. The fact that the Athenians sailed to the Corcyrean camp διὰ τῶν νεκρῶν καὶ ναυαγίων ('through the corpses and wreckage') tells us something about the position of the first encounter: that is dealt with below. Otherwise there is nothing controversial under this particular heading.

One interesting point, however, emerges from the text. Given that Cape Asprokavo is Leukimme (see above), there would certainly have been look-out men on the heights there, even if (as suggested) the camp itself was nearer to the modern Kavos. These men would have seen the Athenian fleet well before the Corcyrean sailors saw it: not only because of their unimpeded view, but more importantly because of their advantage in elevation. Indeed they would have seen it before the Corinthians did. They would have reported it to the camp; and the implication is that there was no effective signal system between the camp and the Corcyrean fleet. The point is reinforced by the sentence beginning τοῖς δὲ Κερκυράιοις στρατοπεδευομένοις. Gomme (p.187) makes an unnecessary fuss on stylistic grounds about this; in fact Thucydides is obliged to repeat τοῖς Κερκυράιοις from 51.2, since there has been an intervening reference to οἱ Κορίνθιοι; and he adds στρατοπεδευομένοις to show that they were by now back in camp - it does not refer only to the land army, as Gomme supposes, but to the whole Corcyrean force. ὤφθησαν must refer to the sighting by the fleet, not the army (for, as shown just above, the army or their scouts would have seen them from the heights a long time before they arrived, and οὐ πολλῷ ὕστερον ('not long afterwards') would be inappropriate).

There is also confirmation of the somewhat surprising point for which our chief evidence is in 50.1-2 - that recognition of ships as belonging to this or that state was not easy. In that passage, the Corinthians appear to do it chiefly by induction: the confirmation is not as good as we should like, because it is not wholly clear just how much visibility there was at particular points of the narrative. However, it was only when the paean had been sounded and the Corinthians backed water because they had caught their first glimpse of the ships (50.5); a little time elapses while the Corcyreans wonder at this phenomenon, and then come to see the ships themselves (the ships having made enough progress to be past Leukimme and therefore visible), at which point ὤφθησαν ('they were seen'). Before that point, surely, the observers on the Leukimme heights should have been ideally placed to identify them; but they did not, since the Corcyreans were still worried about them when they reached their camp (51.5). The observers, then, could not be certain of identification even at fairly close range (a mile or two south of Leukimme). Perhaps identification was only by ensigns or other small-scale devices, which (for lack of telescopes) could not be discerned except at very close quarters. We should like to know how the Corcyreans eventually ἔγνωσαν (recognised) them in the dark: perhaps only when they were within hailing distance.

This is perhaps the most appropriate point at which to raise the questions of why the Athenians only sent ten ships in the first place, and why they sent the twenty afterwards. Thucydides gives us no answer to the first question; but the context in which he says that they sent them (I.45.1-3, immediately following the Athenian thoughts re-

ported in 44.1-2, and joined to them at the beginning of 45 by
τοιαύτη μὲν γνώμῃ ('with this sort of idea in their heads'),
makes the general intention fairly plain. The intention was not to
prevent a sea-fight - something which the Athenians welcomed as
increasing their naval monopoly (44.2): - but to stop the Corinthians
taking over Corcyra and the Corcyrean navy. Athens was anxious not
to break the truce (45.3), and hence did not want positively to in-
itiate a sea-fight; but she was prepared to fight in order to prevent a Corinthian take-over. She may have hoped that it would be
sufficient merely to place her ships between the two contestants.

Clearly ten ships were not enough to do this; but the gesture
was diplomatic. It was directed at the Corinthians, who must have
known about it: 'If you continue your war against Corcyra, you will
run up against us Athenians.' The hope was that the Corinthians would
hold back their armada, and either give up their plans or at least
enter into negotiations with Athens. When this hope proved vain,
the Athenians sent an additional twenty ships - just in time - for
the reasons Thucydides give (50.5): δείσαντες, ὅπερ ἐγένετο, μὴ
νικηθῶσιν οἱ Κερκυραῖοι καὶ αἱ σφέτεραι δέκα νῆες ὀλίγαι
ἀμύνειν ὦσιν, 'they feared (as actually happened) that the Corcyreans would be beaten and their own ten ships would be too few to
keep the Corinthians off.' ἀμύνειν, I suspect, refers not to the
sea-fight (which would be somewhat tautologous, after the earlier
νικηθῶσιν) but to the protection of Corcyra itself: as we have said,
it was a Corinthian take-over which the Athenians were out to avoid,
not a bloody battle.

The Athenians' actions may have been affected by internal politics:
Plutarch (*Pericles* 29) has an unconvincing story about Pericles trying
to humiliate Cimon's family by giving his son Lacedaimonius a contempti-
bly small squadron (the ten ships). If there is anything in the choice
of commander at all, it is more likely to represent Pericles' attempt
to pacify the Peloponnesians by choosing someone with a pro-Spartan
background. But there is no need to look for further political motivation here: what the Athenians did makes perfectly good strategic
and diplomatic sense in itself.

7. *Diplomatic interchange*

ἄνευ κηρυκείου (53.1) ('without a herald'): as Gomme (p.190) says,
because that would be 'a confession that the peace between Athens and
Corinth had already been broken'. The Corinthian delegation shows
some ingenuity (and courage) in making a test case of themselves, as
it were. Either it is war, in which case treat us as enemies (kill
us or take us prisoner: but doing that would put the Athenians very
clearly in the wrong); or it is peace, in which case don't stop us
from sailing where we want, either (a) against Corcyra or (b) elsewhere. The Athenians are obliged to accept the second general alternative, but only as regards (b), not (a). That is in accord with
the Athenians' orders, and also suits the Corinthians, who want to
go home.

It is of some interest in relation to Corcyrean feeling generally
that the Corcyreans within earshot press the Athenians to opt not only
for the first alternative, but for actually butchering the delegation
(not just taking them prisoner). This may of course have been simply a
natural reaction after a bloody battle, not a well-considered diplo-

matic judgement: and perhaps, though we cannot say, the Corcyreans within earshot were unrepresentative. But they would have been mostly men of the hoplite class, the *epibatai* (the slave-rowers either not giving opinions, or not being attended to): and the willingness of these men, some of whom would naturally count as *oligoi* or potential *oligoi*, perhaps also as δυνάμει πρῶτοι τῆς πόλεως (55.1), to butcher helpless Corinthians at such a juncture suggests a strong general anti-Corinthian feeling. Later, as described elsewhere, feelings changed in favour of Corinth and against Athens.

8. The Corinthian Retreat (52-3)

This passage is of considerable interest from a tactical point of view. For the implication is that the Corinthians did not feel safe in retreating (a) along a coastline still dominated (we presume) by their own allies, (b) with something like 120 ships against thirty Athenians and perhaps fifty Corcyreans, (c) with far more hoplites and other *epibatai* per ship than were on the Athenian ships, and with a great preponderance of *epibatai* over the Athenians and Corcyreans in general. Even granted their other difficulties - the need to guard the prisoners, and the bad state of repair of some (perhaps many) of their ships - this is striking. Nor, in fact, do those difficulties seem to make much difference. The prisoners (securely tied up) would not require very many guards, and they would not occupy more than a few ships: if the worst came to the worst, not much would be lost by killing 800 slaves, leaving only 250 high-ranking Corcyreans to attend to (or less: not all of them were high-ranking: 55.1). If their own ships were damaged, so (presumably) were some at least of the remaining Corcyreans. These difficulties are much more intelligible as reasons for a decision not to continue the fight: for the battle would be in open water, against thirty un-scathed Athenians. But it is harder to understand them as reasons for fearing that the Athenians could prevent their retreat. Could they not, at least, have limped back as far as Cheimerion (only six or seven miles) and indeed as far as Actium (not much over forty), keeping close to the coastline and accompanied by their supporting land forces?

Evidently not: or not without severe risk. The passage contrasts with II.83, in which the Corinthians with a flotilla of only forty-seven ships against Phormio's twenty, and that organised for troop-movement rather than a sea-fight (στρατιωτικώτερον παρεσκευασμένοι, 83.3), did not (at least to begin with) think that Phormio would dare to engage them. Such confidence seems surprising four years after the Corinthians' apparent terror of the Athenians at Sybota, even granted that the ratio of strength was 2:1 in the 429 battle, as against only 3:2 at Sybota. Of course we may accuse the Corinthians in 429 of irrational over-confidence; but that still leaves the problem of what, in fact, the Athenians could have done to prevent the Corin-thian retreat from Sybota.

The difficulty lies, perhaps in our tendency to suppose that the Athenian superiority lay solely or chiefly in their ability to manoeuvre in open water: in particular, to win by means of the διέκπλους ('breaking the line'). That point is, indeed, often stres-sed by Thucydides, and is especially relevant to Phormio's battles, in which his major concern is to get enough εὐρυχωρία ('space') to manoeuvre in (see II.83.2, 89.8). But this would certainly not have been practicable against the retreating Corinthians, who would have hugged the shore. Nor could the Athenians have relied on grapple-and-board tactics, being inferior both in numbers of ships and in hoplite strength. Further, it might seem as if the Corinthians could always have put into shore at once, whenever the Athenians attacked, and thus availed themselves of the strength of their supporting land army. It is thus not immediately obvious just what the Athenians could have done, and done with decisively effective nautical skill, in order to prevent the Corinthian retreat: yet there must have been something.

Part of the answer is that the Corinthians' route did not, in fact, very often allow them to put into shore if the Athenians attacked. Much of it lay past sheer or rock-bound coast-line (particularly from Cape Varlam to Cape Trophale), where their allies on land would be unable to help, and where their ships would simply be dashed against the rocks. It would be possible for them to try a series of moves from one bay to another: for instance, first to Cheimerion, then (moving perhaps by night) to Glycys Limen, and then down the somewhat easier coast as far as Actium. But this might certainly entail severe losses, their fleet being in part already crippled and no doubt slow-moving. It would mean a series of running fights, as the Athenians moved in to attack them on their flank and the Corinthians turned, of necessity, through ninety degrees to face them.

But that in itself is hardly sufficient. It is more helpful to consider the kind of skill shown by the Athenians in the sea-fight at Pylos in 425 B.C. (IV.14). There the waters are comparatively enclosed, and the shore-line was dominated by Spartan hoplites: yet the Athenians managed to inflict a decisive defeat on a greater number of Peloponnesian ships. Details of this battle suggest that there were a number of nautical skills, in particular the speed, effective organisation of command, and general seamanship of the Athenians, which enabled them to win even under these conditions, and without the help of any such open-water manoeuvres as the διέκπλους. Here lies the real analogy with the professionalism of the Spartan army: the Athenians were trained to think and move fast and efficiently, without muddle.

9. Wrecks and Corpses (50.3 and 54.1)

Hammond talks of 'the drifting wreckage some three or four miles northward from the scene' of the first engagement (in the narrows), which he claims to be 'in accord with local conditions' (current-flows and winds): he is obliged to do this by a mistranslation of the text (see below) and by the assumption that the Corcyreans can only be occupying a position somewhat to the north of the Sybota islands when they pick up the wrecks and corpses. This latter is certainly unnecessary: whatever position the Corcyrean fleet adopted in 52.1 (certainly somewhere near Sybota, as Thucydides says), the picking up of the wrecks and corpses need not refer only to what they could find at that particular point and time. The Corcyreans reaslied, by the time of 54.1, that the Corinthians were unlikely to attack: certainly they would have felt safe in sparing a few ships to scour the whole area for the wrecks and corpses.

55

The mistranslation of 54.1 is shared by Hammond with almost all other scholars. He translates '... the Corcyreans took up the wrecks and the dead, carried out to them by the current and wind, which arising in the night had scattered them widely'. The implication is that *all* the wrecks and the dead - that is, all those not already collected by the Corinthians the day before - were carried by the current and wind in a certain direction, namely to where the Corcyreans were. That cannot be right, if only because παντᾳχῇ does not mean, as translated here, 'widely' but 'in every direction' - perhaps a slightly loose usage, since they were not driven literally in *every* direction or to every single point of the compass, but certainly implying in more directions than one. The more natural sense of ναυάγια ... τὰ κατὰ σφᾶς ἐξενεχθέντα is, in any case, 'those of the wrecks that had been carried out to them': that is, not 'the wrecks (all of which had been) carried out to them', but 'the wrecks - that is, the ones which had been carried out to them'.

In 50.3 the Corinthians get possession of and bring to Sybota most of the wrecks and their own dead. The term ἐκράτησαν ('gained mastery of') may mislead here, for it does not seem likely that the Corcyreans would at this stage have been able to dispute possession of these: they had already been routed and driven to the land (ἐς τὴν γῆν). Possibly there was some fighting round wrecks and corpses that had been washed up on or very near the shore to which the Corcyreans had been driven; but that cannot have been true of all the wrecks, since the Corcyreans salvage some of them in 54.1, the passage we have just considered. These at least must have been floating free: some explanation is needed of why the Corinthians did not manage to get hold of all of them and bring them back to Sybota. The likeliest is that they were short of time: towing wrecks is a slow process, and Sybota was about five miles away. They wanted to engage the Corcyreans again, and it was late when they did so, as 50.5 - 51.5 makes clear. We can translate ἐκράτησαν in some way as 'managed to get hold of', but we should resist the implication that their possession was disputed: they were trying to beat the clock, not the Corcyreans.

10. Positions of the fleets

The position of the first action (48-49) must be somewhat to the south of the Sybota islands, since the Corinthians meet the Corcyreans when the latter are ἐπὶ σφᾶς πλεούσας ('sailing towards them', 48.2): that is, having gone some distance from their anchorage at Sybota. The Corcyreans' tactical objective was to prevent the Corinthians forcing their way through the narrows on a line roughly from Leukimme to Sybota: on their part, the Corinthians needed to defeat the Corcyrean fleet before they could think of making a landing. They met, then, roughly as shown on the map.

The length of their battle-line is more doubtful. Hammond, who assumes that 'both sides formed a single line for boarding tactics', makes the Corinthian line three miles long, which allows forty yards per ship, twenty-four yards of clear water between one ship and the next if sailing ahead, and four yards between them broadside on. That seems far too tight for safety, particularly in a motley fleet contributed by many different states. But it does not follow that the line was much longer, for it is not clear that they formed a single line.

56

On the contrary: Thucydides means what he says when he talks of the
Conrinthians (alone) forming the left wing, the Megarians and
Ambracians the right wing, and the other allies the centre. That
means a distribution in spatial terms of ninety on the left, thirty-
nine on the right, and twenty-one in the centre: and however this
worked out, the left was probably not formed into a single line.
Here the Corinthians would have stacked their ships some numbers
deep, the ships in the rear being ready to assist the ones in front
as required when battle was joined. We cannot hope to be much more
precise: perhaps they were two or three deep. If so, if they allowed
rather more space for themselves than Hammond gives them (say, sixty
yards a ship), and if the rest of their fleet was in a single line -
and all these are uncertain - the total line would have been something
between 5,000 and 6,000 yards. But that is extremely speculative.
Equally speculative is the length of the Corcyrean line, since that
depends both on some of the unknown factors just mentioned, and also
on whether the Corcyreans adjusted their line on meeting the
Corinthians: though no doubt their line was roughly similar in
length, to avoid encirclement.

After the τροπή (rout), the Corcyrean right is driven back to
the land (ἐς τὴν γῆν). To judge from 49.6 and 7, this seems to
have been a fairly slow or at least not a sudden process; it no doubt
gave time for the Corcyrean centre, and those ships of the Corcyrean
left that were not going to Cheimerion, to move towards their right
wing and reinforce it, and/or eventually to retreat to the land along
with the ships on the right wing. If the στρατόπεδον was at or
near the modern Kavos, they would not have had far to retreat.

The Corinthians begin the second encounter by collecting their
ships together again (αὖθις ἀθροισθέντες, 50.3) and sailing
against the enemy: that is, after collecting the wrecks and corpses
and taking them back to Sybota, they reform their fleet - presumably
in line of battle again - at or near Sybota and sail more or less due
west at the Corcyreans. This gives the Corcyreans time to meet them
without being pinned to their coastline: they were frightened of the
Corinthians making a landing, and no doubt moved as soon as possible,
using all the ships they could - the additional ones must have been
at their camp already, since there would be no time to get them
from Corcyra city. Their fear of a Corinthian landing would induce
them to meet the Corinthians in the open sea, rather than wait very
close to their own shore: for in the latter position the Corinthians
might out-manoeuvre them by sailing straight to a landing elsewhere.
The fleets met somewhere between Kavos and Sybota, probably somewhat nearer to Corcyra (since the Corinthians started to move first).

The action was abortive, and the third position also did not result in any fighting. This position is much more uncertain because
of the comparatively complicated topography. In 52.1-2 the Athenians
and Corcyreans sail to or towards (ἐπί) the harbour of mainland
Sybota - that is, Port Mourtso and the nearby bays which were
necessary to accommodate the Corinthian fleet. The Corinthians must
have seen them coming, and thus had time to form a line of battle out
of their ships in the open water (παραταξάμενοι μετεώρους 52.2):
for fear, presumably, of being blockaded in their anchorage by the
enemy. They would hardly have formed line right in front of their
anchorages between the Sybota islands and the mainland, even if

μετεώρους allows of such an interpretation (at some points the islands are only a few yards from the mainland): where, then, did they go?

Hammond is right in implying that they would not want to go far from their land force; but not necessarily right in placing both fleets north-west of Mourtso without argument. He is led to this, I suspect, by the view that Mourtso alone was the Corinthian anchorage, since the natural exit from Mourtso is to the north-west. But if they used all the nearby bays, as they had to, the position is more obscure. Almost certainly they saw the Athenians and Corcyreans coming in time to deploy their own ships where they wanted: to the north-west of the islands, to the south-west of them, or perhaps further out to sea due west of them. The Athenians and Corcyreans would then have gone to wherever the Corinthian fleet had placed itself. On balance, a deployment to the south-west seems most probable: the Corinthians were thinking primarily about how to get back home, which could be more easily attempted from that position; at the same time it would be fairly close to the support of their land allies.

F. Prisoners and the Corcyrean Navy

We have here to consider the evidence of the Corcyrean prisoners, since this bears importantly on the constitution of the Corcyrean navy and the possibilities of support from Athens in pursuance of certain strategic aims (see Appendix).

In I.54.2 Thucydides describes the Corinthians as ἄνδρας ἔχοντες αἰχμαλώτους οὐκ ἐλάσσους χιλίων, 'having not less than 1000 men as prisoners'; and in 55.1 τῶν Κερκυραίων ὀκτακοσίους μὲν οἳ ἦσαν δοῦλοι ἀπέδοντο, πεντήκοντα δὲ καὶ διακοσίους δήσαντες ἐφύλασσον κτλ ('they sold 800 of the Corcyreans who were slaves, and kept 250 bound in prison', etc.). The most natural interpretation of this is that the total number of prisoners was 1050: that is, 800 slaves and 250 free (and mostly high-ranking) Corcyreans. It might just be argued that the figures in either category, or both, were higher, and that what Thucydides means is that they sold 800 out of the total of those who were slaves, and 250 out of the rest. But (a) that is a priori unlikely for the second category at least. For if there were free Corcyrean prisoners over and above the 250, what did the Corinthians do with them? Cut their throats? Enslave them? If so, the chances are that Thucydides would have said so. For the first category, the slaves, it is of course possible that the Corinthians kept some as their own slaves, and sold off the 800; but (b) the slightly awkward οἳ ἦσαν δοῦλοι seems deliberately chosen to make the point that he did not mean '800 slaves' or '800 out of the slave-category', but precisely '800 of the Corcyrean prisoners, 800 who were in fact slaves'. The division of the total number into two exhaustive categories is reinforced (c) by the sentence ἐτύγχανον ... πόλεως. For, in view of ἐτύγχανον, that must mean 'It was the case that most of them [i.e. of the total numbers of free men, 250] were powerful and leading men in the state', not 'These [i.e. 250 selected by the Corinthians from a larger category of free men] were mostly the powerful and leading men in the state'.

58

These figures are remarkable, because they suggest *prima facie* that the Corcyrean navy was composed of both slaves and leading citizens (πρῶτοι), which is virtually unique for any society in the ancient history of Greece and Rome, and quite unlike the composition of other navies in classical Greece. Fighting was invariably a high-status job, indeed the specific mark of a citizen: and slaves were almost always excluded. When in times of crisis slaves had to be used, they were freed before they fought. Hence both the presence of slaves, and the absence of ordinary lower-class citizens, is highly anomalous: and we should not be inclined to accept it without some further discussion.

One thing, however, has to be accepted. Even if these figures do not represent a random sample of manpower from the Corcyrean fleet, we can hardly deny (unless we accuse Thucydides of gross and quite untypical falsehood) that *slaves were present in substantial numbers*. That fact, however contrary to normal practice, has to be accounted for somehow. The natural way of accounting for it is to suppose that the slaves were used as rowers. It is barely possible to think that they were used as attendants to the fighting-men or *epibatai*, on the analogy of the Spartan helots: but (a) that still goes against the normal practice of using slaves in battle (the helots were a special case), and hence does not redress the anomaly; and (b) the absence of citizen rowers from the prisoners leaves a gap - if the slaves did not row, who did? We are, then, bound to suppose that some slaves, at least, were rowing the ships.

The only escape from this anomaly would be the assumption that the Corcyreans had freed the slaves beforehand for the special purpose of meeting this crisis. It would still be surprising that no citizens (apart from the πρῶτοι, who would not have been rowers) were taken prisoner; but various reasons may be found to account for this (see below). The decisive objections to the assumption are surely (1) that the slaves would have been highly inefficient as rowers if they had only been given this task for the first time, and (2) we know that Corcyra had a large and efficient navy before the crisis, which must have had well-trained rowers: slaves would not have been brought in, or not in any large numbers, to row ships for which there was already an adequate complement of men. We must then suppose that slaves normally rowed the ships in this navy.

Various arguments may still be used to bring these figures more into line with normal practice, by suggesting reasons why the citizen rowers (assuming these to exist in significant numbers) were not taken prisoner, whereas the slaves and πρῶτοι were. There are no insuperable difficulties about the πρῶτοι: we may say, if we wish, that they would have been heavily armed, and hence both more worthwhile and more easily identifiable targets for capture: also that their armour may have given them less chance of swimming to safety. The slaves present greater problems. One might maintain (1) that slaves, unlike free citizens, might be sold for a good ransom-price, as being the property of wealthy men, so that the Corinthians chose to capture them rather than the citizens (though it is quite possible that the Corinthians could have sold the citizens as slaves). Or (2) perhaps the slaves were worse swimmers than the citizens, and hence less able to escape capture; or (3) better swimmers, and hence more liable to capture (since they would not drown); or (4) perhaps the slaves were more willing to be captured than the citizens. All these argu-

59

ments seem to me (to speak frankly) only likely to commend themselves
to those who are anxious to avoid the facts as Thucydides gives them.
As well as their inherent implausibility, most of them run up against
the fact that the Corinthians were evidently not in a position to be
particularly deliberate or selective. They had preferred in general
to kill rather than capture (50.1): there was a great deal of chaos,
in which they even killed some of their own men by mistake (*ibid.*).
The idea of the Corinthian commanders having the time (or inclina-
tion) to make judicious enquiries about the social status of 1050
Corcyreans in various stages of shipwreck and drowning seems absurd.

If the figures of 800 and 250 represent a fair sample, and if
the former were all rowers and the latter all non-rowers, then there
were about three times more rowers than non-rowers in the Corcyrean
fleet. In terms of a single trireme, the rowing crew of which was
about 170, that would mean rather more than fifty non-rowers:
apart from a few nautical officers, they would consist almost exclu-
sively of hoplites, javelin-men and archers. That is, of course,
a very high figure compared with the standard ten to twelve *epibatai*
on Athenian ships: but it fits a battle in which the Corcyreans had
decided on old-style tactics. The truth is probably slightly to one
side of this: it is very unlikely that slaves would have been armed,
so that all the 800 would have been rowers but some of the 250 may
well have been rowers also. The proportion may have been more like 5
to 1: that is, 170 rowers to 40 fighting men, by no means an implaus-
ibly large number of the latter. In fact we may reasonably argue
the other way round: the plausibility of the proportion suggests
that the sample was a fair one.

The Corcyreans manned 110 ships, which would give us something
like 18,700 slaves to row them. That is a strikingly large figure,
but one which seems to be forced upon us. We may round it off to
18,000; but there cannot have been many non-slave rowers, for
rowing is not a natural job for πρῶτοι τῆς πόλεως (who formed
the majority of our sample 250). Moreover, the slaves cannot have
been totally untrained. Even at Sybota, on the Corcyrean left wing
twenty ships, at least, were completely victorious; and on the right
it was by no means a walk-over for the Corinthians (Thucydides gives
as a reason for the Corcyrean defeat there that τοῖς Κερκυραίοις
τῶν εἴκοσι νεῶν ἀπὸ ἐλάσσονος πλήθους ... οὐ παρουσῶν.
Had the slaves' lack of training been a major factor in the battle,
Thucydides would surely have mentioned it.) On *a priori* grounds,
indeed, it is quite possible that slave labour made at least as efficient
a rowing force as citizen or mercenary rowers; and the Corcyrean navy's
performance at Leukimme in 435, when eighty-five Corcyrean ships sank
fifteen of a Corinthian-led fleet of seventy-five and won a decisive
victory, was presumably based on slave-rowers. Much of course would
depend on the way the slaves were treated; but in view of the pride
taken by the Corcyreans in their navy, and their realisation of its
practical importance, they are likely to have been treated as least
well enough for efficiency.

Two other pieces of evidence may be fitted in here, albeit our conclusions can only be rough. (1) Both sides are described as having
many hoplites on the decks, and also many archers and javelin-men
(49.1), though there would naturally be a preponderance of hoplites,
since they would be of most use for the grapple-and-board tactics
used in the battle: they 'relied for victory mostly on their hoplites

on the decks'. We may perhaps assume a ratio of something like
5:3 - that is, twenty-five hoplites to fifteen others (other plausible
ratios, as perhaps 3:1 or 4:1, make no difference to our general conclusions in this and the following section). (2) Only the majority
(55.1) of the free men captured were *protoi*: if we take them to have
numbered 150, as against 100 who were not *protoi*, the 5:3 ratio above
is preserved. We assume, that is, that the Corinthians captured a
random sample of *epibatai*: the 150 *protoi* are hoplites, the 100 others
are archers and javelin-men.

G. Hoplite Numbers

Perhaps the most intractable problem of the whole campaign concerns
the hoplite numbers on both sides. On the Corcyrean side, if we stick
to the ratio of hoplites to other *epibatai* suggested above (roughly
5:3), and assume something like forty *epibatai* per ship, we reach a
figure of 110 x 25 hoplites: 2,750. That still leaves uncertain the
number of hoplites in the army at Leukimme (reinforced by 1,000
Zacynthians); but that is connected with the Corinthian numbers,
since those numbers must have been sufficient to give the Corinthians
a good chance of conquering Corcyra. Even granted that they might
have obtained some help from their barbarian allies on the mainland,
few of these would have been armed as hoplites.

Unfortunately Thucydides gives no figures of Corinthian hoplites
for the Sybota campaign; and the figures for the Epidamnus campaign
of 425 are of no help. First, either the mention of 3,000 hoplites
(27.2), or the mention of 2,000 (29.1), or perhaps both, must be
corrupt (like many numbers in Thucydides): for the 3,000 are specifically Corinthian, not allied (αὐτῶν Κορινθίων, 27.2), and the
2,000 seem to represent the total force. Had the figures been the
other way round, some sense could be made of it: we would assume
2,000 Corinthians plus 1,000 allies. But they are not, and a short-
fall of 1,000 Corinthians plus any allied contributions at least
needs explanation; Thucydides gives none. Secondly, as Gomme (p.164)
sensibly points out, different expeditions had different purposes
and hence different hoplite-strengths: the Epidamnus expedition did
not aim at a complete conquest of Corcyra, whereas the Sybota expedition did.

We may get some help from the battle itself. Corinthians won not
by naval tactics but by hard infantry fighting (49.2), and their
epibatai can hardly have been fewer than the Corcyreans'. If the
same ratio holds, that argues 150 x 25 hoplites in the Corinthian
fleet: 3,750. Would that have been sufficient for conquest, assuming a decisive naval victory? Much depends here on the Corcyrean
losses, which may also be roughly calculated. Seventy Corcyrean
ships were sunk: 250 *epibatai* were taken prisoner, of which (on our
ratio) 150 were hoplites. On those seventy ships, the total of
hoplites would have been 70 x 25: 1,750; of other *epibatai*, 70 x 15:
1,050. It is fairly clear that at one stage of the battle (in 50.
1-3) the Corinthians are in complete control; and it is at this stage
that they kill (rather than take prisoner) those in and around the
wrecks. We may thus assume that a high proportion of the *epibatai*

61

in the seventy sunken ships were killed; of the hoplites, perhaps
as many as 1,000, with 150 taken prisoner and 600 survivors. On
the remaining forty ships (of the total of 110) would have been
40 x 25 hoplites, 1,000, most of whom presumably got safely to
land. After their naval victory, then, it seems that - again very
roughly - the Corinthians had to face a total of 1,600 Corcyrean
hoplites from the fleet. The Corinthians themselves would have had
some losses: let us stipulate, 250 hoplites out of their original
3,750.

That leaves 3,500 Corinthian hoplites against 1,600 Corcyreans
on the Corcyrean ships; but we must of course add the numbers in the
Corcyrean army. Even if (unlikely) there had only been 1,000
Corcyrean hoplites at Leukimme, these when reinforced by the 1,000
Zacynthians would still swell the total numbers to 3,600. This
number seems to be more than the Corinthians would have felt com-
petent to face in their conquest of the island, particularly since the
town of Corcyra itself was defended by walls. But two factors might
modify this judgement: (1) the Corinthians may not have known about
the Zacynthian reinforcement, while knowing about Corcyrean hoplite
weakness in general; and (2) Corinth may well have put a good deal
of trust, not unreasonably, in the quality of her troops as against
the unpractised and no doubt by comparison unskilled Corcyreans.
It is also possible, indeed likely, that there was a higher proportion of hoplites in the Corinthian fleet (since they intended
conquest of the island, not just a sea-fight): an extra 1,500 hoplites (ten more per ship) is a plausible figure, and the total
(5,250) not too large for an expedition whose ship-numbers were double
that of the Epidamnos expedition. On that reckoning, 5,000 Corinthian
hoplites would have confronted 1,600 Corcyreans from the fleet, 1,000
Zacynthians, and whatever hoplite strength the Corcyreans had at
Leukimme - perhaps as much as 2,000. Such a confrontation might well
have seemed satisfactory to the Corinthians, insofar as they could
predict the numbers at all.

Much of this is of course dangerously speculative, but the specu-
lation is not idle. It appears from almost any reasonable account of
the numbers of hoplites involved that the Corcyrean hoplite strength
cannot have been very great. Corcyra in such a crisis would certainly have mustered almost every hoplite she had: but the total could
not have been much above 5,000 - roughly, 2,750 in the fleet and
2,250 on land. If we suppose that it had been significantly greater
- say, 8,000 - then Corinth would have to have brought something
like 10,000 hoplites to have a fair chance of conquest. But, quite
apart from whether Corinth could produce that number of hoplites
even with allied help, the figure involves about 66 hoplites per ship
in their fleet of 150. That is, perhaps, not logistically impossible;
but it is highly unlikely, and would not have been passed over in
silence by Thucydides. The conclusion that Corcyrean hoplite
strength was remarkably weak must stand.

H. Results

In a strictly military sense, Sybota was not a decisive victory for

Corcyra, indeed not a victory at all. The Corinthian fleet (admittedly in part newly-built and much more powerful than usual) routed the Corcyreans at their full strength, and supported by ten Athenians. That it gave way to the additional reinforcement of twenty Athenians may have boosted or confirmed Athenian morale and prestige, but did nothing to show the Corcyreans that they could defend themselves by their own resources. Unless Athens and Corcyra were more closely allied, as in a coherent and effective north-west strategy, Corcyra could not rely on sufficient Athenian aid being avilable when danger threated. Corinth could have tried again.

Why did she not? The Athenians did not keep a permanent fleet in the area, nor even at Naupactos until the winter of 430/29: and granted that they made fairly lengthy summer expeditions in 431 and 430 round the Peloponnese, the Corinthians could have either anticipated them or waited till they had returned. Nor, indeed, does it appear at first sight that they were alarmed by the possibility of Athenian intervention: the Corinthians themselves operated with forty ships in Acarnania and Cephallenia during what must have been a fairly long campaign in the winter of 431; and the Spartan Alliance as a whole spent some time at Zacynthos in the summer of 430, with 100 ships. These numbers are less than would be required for the conquest of Corcyra; but many more must have been available, in view of the minimal Corinthian losses in 433 (only the disablement of about thirty ships from Corinth and her allies together).

Many reasons may have operated, either singly or collectively. One is that after the outbreak of war Corinth was not in a position to act independently, or at least that her plans must have been strongly influenced by her membership of the Spartan Alliance; and perhaps Sparta either did not think the conquest of Corcyra of major importance or regarded it as too great a military risk. She had in some sense supported Corcyra earlier (in 435, when Spartan envoys accompanied the Corcyrean envoys to Corinth: I.28.1); and though she intervened in 427, that intervention depended on a planned uprising in Corcyra, and even then the Spartan commander, under virtually ideal circumstances, refused to attack the city. Expeditions which went only as far as Acarnania, Zacynthos or Cephallenia, in any case, did not commit the Peloponnesians from operating too far from the safety of their home bases (chiefly Cyllene); by the time that Athens had sent a fleet round the Peloponnese, they could get news of it and withdraw in time. But the distance to Corcyra does not admit of this security; and indeed when the Spartans tried it, they were nearly caught (III.80). Further, it became apparent (at least after Corcyrean aid to Athens in 431) that Corcyra was not supporting Athens in any very active way; and this may have made it at least seem of only peripheral importance for the war - an appearance which was certainly a reality after the devastating *stasis* of 427.

As we shall see in Part II, Corinth at least preferred to put her money on the Corcyrean prisoners. Her skilful use of these, together with the less obvious fact that a good many potential *oligoi* had been killed at Sybota, were perhaps the most important results of the battle. For, in combination, they ensured (a) that an uprising took place, but (b) that the *oligoi* were too weak to take control or play any further part in Corcyrean affairs. This was as disastrous for Athens as for Corcyra, since Corcyrean military support depended

on the *oligoi*: and from the Peloponnesian viewpoint should have hence
seemed not unsatisfactory. Athens could still use Corcyra as a base,
of some value in the Sicilian expedition; but otherwise Corcyra had
in effect been put out of the war, and could give Athens no effective
help.

All this, however, would be true only in default of adequate Athenian
diplomacy. For the most obvious and immediate result of Sybota was to
demonstrate beyond doubt to the Corcyreans that they could defend themselves against Corinth if, but only if, the Athenians supported them.
The shape of the battle was ideal for making that particular point:
if the Corcyreans had only been defeated by themselves, they might have
believed that Athenian assistance would not have saved them; and if
they had only been victorious in Athenian company, they might have
believed that they could have won by themselves. In the event,
they were defeated when fighting virtually by themselves (with only
ten mostly passive Athenian ships), and then triumphant - at least
triumphant enough to make the Corinthians turn tail - when the twenty
additional Athenians arrived. No demonstration could have been clear-
er. Moreover, the small Corinthian losses did not permit the
Corcyreans to believe that the Corinthian navy would take years to
recover; they knew well enough that Corinth and her allies had the resources to mount another attack, and after the outbreak of war in 431
those resources would have the backing of the whole Spartan Alliance.
Everything, in other words, pointed to the need for a full and immediate alliance between Athens and Corcyra - an alliance that could
have been as beneficial to Athens as it must have seemed necessary to
Corcyra (see Appendix). But no such full alliance was then made:
Athens missed her chance.

PART II

THE STASIS AND AFTER (427-410 B.C.)

There are three relevant passages of continuous narrative:
III.69-81, with 85 (I have omitted the famous reflections
on *stasis* in general, 82-84, which have no specific relevance to our concerns); IV.46-48; and Diodorus Siculus
XIII.48.

69 Αἱ δὲ τεσσαράκοντα νῆες τῶν Πελοποννησίων αἱ
Λεσβίοις βοηθοὶ ἐλθοῦσαι, ὡς τότε φεύγουσαι διὰ
τοῦ πελάγους ἔκ τε τῶν Ἀθηναίων ἐπιδιωχθεῖσαι
καὶ πρὸς τῇ Κρήτῃ χειμασθεῖσαι καὶ ἀπ' αὐτῆς
σποράδες πρὸς τὴν Πελοπόννησον κατηνέχθησαν,
καταλαμβάνουσιν ἐν τῇ Κυλλήνῃ τρεῖς καὶ δέκα
τριήρεις Λευκαδίων καὶ Ἀμπρακιωτῶν καὶ Βρασίδαν
τὸν Τέλλιδος ξύμβουλον Ἀλκίδᾳ ἐπεληλυθότα.

2 ἐβούλοντο γὰρ οἱ Λακεδαιμόνιοι, ὡς τῆς Λέσβου
ἡμαρτήκεσαν, πλέον τὸ ναυτικὸν ποιήσαντες ἐς
τὴν Κέρκυραν πλεῦσαι στασιάζουσαν, δώδεκα μὲν
ναυσὶ μόναις παρόντων Ἀθηναίων περὶ Ναύπακτον,
πρὶν δὲ πλέον τι ἐπιβοηθῆσαι ἐκ τῶν Ἀθηνῶν
ναυτικόν, ὅπως προφθάσωσι, καὶ παρεσκευάζοντο
ὅ τε Βρασίδας καὶ ὁ Ἀλκίδας πρὸς ταῦτα.

70 Οἱ γὰρ Κερκυραῖοι ἐστασίαζον, ἐπειδὴ οἱ αἰχμάλωτοι
ἦλθον αὐτοῖς οἱ ἐκ τῶν περὶ Ἐπίδαμνον ναυμαχιῶν
ὑπὸ Κορινθίων ἀφεθέντες, τῷ μὲν λόγῳ ὀκτακοσίων
ταλάντων τοῖς προξένοις διηγγυημένοι, ἔργῳ δὲ
πεπεισμένοι Κορινθίοις Κέρκυραν προσποιῆσαι.
καὶ ἔπρασσον οὗτοι, ἕκαστον τῶν πολιτῶν μετιόντες,
ὅπως ἀποστήσωσιν Ἀθηναίων τὴν πόλιν.   καὶ

2 ἀφικομένης Ἀττικῆς τε νεὼς καὶ Κορινθίας πρέσβεις
ἀγουσῶν καὶ ἐς λόγους καταστάντων ἐψηφίσαντο
Κερκυραῖοι Ἀθηναίοις μὲν ξύμμαχοι εἶναι κατὰ τὰ
ξυγκείμενα, Πελοποννησίοις δὲ φίλοι ὥσπερ καὶ

3 πρότερον.   καὶ (ἦν γὰρ Πειθίας ἐθελοπρόξενός τε
τῶν Ἀθηναίων καὶ τοῦ δήμου προειστήκει) ὑπάγουσιν
αὐτὸν οὗτοι οἱ ἄνδρες ἐς δίκην, λέγοντες Ἀθηναίοις

4 τὴν Κέρκυραν καταδουλοῦν.   ὁ δὲ ἀποφυγὼν ἀνθυπάγει
αὐτῶν τοὺς πλουσιωτάτους πέντε ἄνδρας, φάσκων
τέμνειν χάρακας ἔκ τοῦ τε Διὸς τοῦ τεμένους καὶ
τοῦ Ἀλκίνου· ζημία δὲ καθ' ἑκάστην χάρακα ἐπέκειτο

5 στατήρ.   ὀφλόντων δὲ αὐτῶν καὶ πρὸς τὰ ἱερὰ ἱκετῶν
καθεζομένων διὰ πλῆθος τῆς ζημίας, ὅπως ταξάμενοι
ἀποδῶσιν, ὁ Πειθίας (ἐτύγχανε γὰρ καὶ βουλῆς ὤν)

69.   The forty Peloponnesian ships which had gone to help the Lesbians
fled, on that occasion, across the open sea, closely pursued by the
Athenians: they ran into bad weather off Crete, and came back from
there to the Peloponnese in small groups.   At Cyllene they met up
with fifteen triremes from Leucas and Ambracia, and also Brasidas the
son of Tellis, who had come as adviser to Alcidas.   For the Spartans,
when they had failed at Lesbos, wanted to reinforce their fleet and
sail to Corcyra, which was at that time in a state of *stasis*: there
were only twelve Athenian ships at Naupactos, and they wanted to get
there before any reinforcements arrived from Athens.   Brasidas and
Alcidas made their preparations with this in view.

70.   For the Corcyreans were in a state of *stasis*, because of the
prisoners who had returned home.   The Corinthians had released them
after their capture at the sea-battles which had been fought because
of the Epidamnos affair: the story was that they had been set free on
the security of 800 talents paid by their official representatives
at Corinth, but in fact they had been persuaded by the Corinthians
to win Corcyra over.   These men set about the task of detaching the
city from Athens, approaching the citizens individually.   When an
Attic ship and a Corinthian one arrived, bringing ambassadors, the
matter was debated: and the Corcyreans voted to be allies of the
Athenians (in accordance with what had already been agreed), but to be
friendly towards the Peloponnesians as in time past.

   Their next move was to bring to trial Peithias, the voluntary
representative of the Athenians and a leader of the *demos*, claiming
that he was enslaving Corcyra to Athens.   He was acquitted, and in
his turn charged the five richest of them with cutting vine-props
from the sacred precinct of Zeus and Alcinous, for which the fine
was a stater for each stake.   They were found guilty; and because
the fine was so heavy, they sat as suppliants in the temples, trying
to get the payments reassessed.   But Peithias, who was also at the
time a member of the council,

6 πείθει ὥστε τῷ νόμῳ χρήσασθαι. οἱ δ' ἐπειδὴ
   τῷ τε νόμῳ ἐξείργοντο καὶ ἅμα ἐπυνθάνοντο τὸν
   Πειθίαν, ἕως ἔτι βουλῆς ἐστί, μέλλειν τὸ πλῆθος
   ἀναπείσειν τοὺς αὐτοὺς Ἀθηναίοις φίλους τε καὶ
   ἐχθροὺς νομίζειν, ξυνίσταντό τε καὶ λαβόντες
   ἐγχειρίδια ἐξαπιναίως ἐς τὴν βουλὴν ἐσελθόντες
   τόν τε Πειθίαν κτείνουσι καὶ ἄλλους τῶν τε βουλευτῶν
   καὶ ἰδιωτῶν ἐς ἑξήκοντα· οἱ δέ τινες τῆς αὐτῆς
   γνώμης τῷ Πειθίᾳ ὀλίγοι ἐς τὴν Ἀττικὴν τριήρη
71 κατέφυγον ἔτι παροῦσαν. δράσαντες δὲ τοῦτο καὶ
   ξυγκαλέσαντες Κερκυραίους εἶπον ὅτι ταῦτα καὶ
   βέλτιστα εἴη καὶ ἥκιστ' ἂν δουλωθεῖεν ὑπ' Ἀθηναίων,
   τό τε λοιπὸν μηδετέρους δέχεσθαι ἀλλ' ἢ μιᾷ νηὶ
   ἡσυχάζοντας, τὸ δὲ πλέον πολέμιον ἡγεῖσθαι. ὡς
   δὲ εἶπον, καὶ ἐπικυρῶσαι ἠνάγκασαν τὴν γνώμην.
2 πέμπουσι δὲ καὶ ἐς τὰς Ἀθήνας εὐθὺς πρέσβεις περὶ
   τε τῶν πεπραγμένων διδάξοντας ὡς ξυνέφερε καὶ τοὺς
   ἐκεῖ καταπεφευγότας πείσοντας μηδὲν ἀνεπιτήδειον
72 πράσσειν, ὅπως μή τις ἐπιστροφὴ γένηται. ἐλθόντων
   δὲ οἱ Ἀθηναῖοι τούς τε πρέσβεις ὡς νεωτερίζοντας
   ξυλλαβόντες, καὶ ὅσους ἔπεισαν, κατέθεντο ἐς
   Αἴγιναν.
2   Ἐν δὲ τούτῳ τῶν Κερκυραίων οἱ ἔχοντες τὰ
   πράγματα ἐλθούσης τριήρους Κορινθίας καὶ
   Λακεδαιμονίων πρέσβεων ἐπιτίθενται τῷ δήμῳ, καὶ
3 μαχόμενοι ἐνίκησαν. ἀφικομένης δὲ νυκτὸς ὁ μὲν
   δῆμος ἐς τὴν ἀκρόπολιν καὶ τὰ μετέωρα τῆς πόλεως
   καταφεύγει καὶ αὐτοῦ ξυλλεγεὶς ἱδρύθη, καὶ τὸν
   Ὑλλαϊκὸν λιμένα εἶχον· οἱ δὲ τήν τε ἀγορὰν κατέ-
   λαβον, οὗπερ οἱ πολλοὶ ᾤκουν αὐτῶν, καὶ τὸν λιμένα
73 τὸν πρὸς αὐτῇ καὶ πρὸς τὴν ἤπειρον. τῇ δ' ὑστεραίᾳ
   ἠκροβολίσαντό τε ὀλίγα καὶ ἐς τοὺς ἀγροὺς περιέ-
   πεμπον ἀμφότεροι, τοὺς δούλους παρακαλοῦντές τε
   καὶ ἐλευθερίαν ὑπισχνούμενοι· καὶ τῷ μὲν δήμῳ τῶν
   οἰκετῶν τὸ πλῆθος παρεγένετο ξύμμαχον, τοῖς δ'
   ἑτέροις ἐκ τῆς ἠπείρου ἐπίκουροι ὀκτακόσιοι.

persuaded the council to enforce the law. The men were thus constrained by the law; and they also learned that Peithias intended,
while he was still a member of the council, to persuade the people to
make a full offensive and defensive alliance with the Athenians. So
they joined with others of their party, took daggers, and suddenly
burst in upon the council: they then killed Peithias and other members of the council, as well as some private citizens, to the number
of about sixty. Some few of those who were of Peithias' opinion
escaped to the Attic trireme, which was still there.

71. Having done this, they called the Corcyreans together and told
them that it was all for the best, and would most effectively prevent
their being enslaved by the Athenians; also that for the future they
should receive neither side unless they came in peace with only a
single ship - any more than that, and they should consider them hostile. They said all this, and forced the assembly to ratify it.
They also sent representatives to Athens at once to give a version
of events favourable to themselves, and to persuade the refugees there
to do nothing inconvenient, in order to avoid any counter-revolution.

72. When they came, the Athenians arrested the representatives,
and those whom they had persuaded, on a charge of being revolutionaries,
and put them in custody on Aegina.

Meanwhile, when a Corinthian trireme with Lacedaimonian representatives came, those in power in Corcyra attacked the *demos* and were
victorious in the fighting. At nightfall the *demos* fled to the
acropolis and the high parts of the city, concentrated their forces
there, and set up their base; they also held the Hyllaic harbour.
The other party occupied the *agora* (market-place), where most of them
lived, together with the harbour next to it which faces the mainland.

73. On the next day there was some skirmishing at long range, and
both sides sent messages round the country seeking the support of the
slaves and promising them their freedom. The majority of the household servants joined the *demos*: the other party had the support of
800 mercenaries from the mainland.

69

74 διαλιπούσης δ' ἡμέρας μάχη αὖθις γίγνεται καὶ
νικᾷ ὁ δῆμος χωρίων τε ἰσχύι καὶ πλήθει προύχων·
αἵ τε γυναῖκες αὐτοῖς τολμηρῶς ξυνεπελάβοντο
βάλλουσαι ἀπὸ τῶν οἰκιῶν τῷ κεράμῳ καὶ παρὰ

2 φύσιν ὑπομένουσαι τὸν θόρυβον. γενομένης δὲ τῆς
τροπῆς περὶ δείλην ὀψίαν, δείσαντες οἱ ὀλίγοι μὴ
αὐτοβοεὶ ὁ δῆμος τοῦ τε νεωρίου κρατήσειεν ἐπελθὼν
καὶ σφᾶς διαφθείρειεν, ἐμπιπρᾶσι τὰς οἰκίας τὰς ἐν
κύκλῳ τῆς ἀγορᾶς καὶ τὰς ξυνοικίας, ὅπως μὴ ᾖ
ἔφοδος, φειδόμενοι οὔτε οἰκείας οὔτε ἀλλοτρίας,
ὥστε καὶ χρήματα πολλὰ ἐμπόρων κατεκαύθη καὶ ἡ πόλις
ἐκινδύνευσε πᾶσα διαφθαρῆναι, εἰ ἄνεμος ἐπεγένετο
τῇ φλογὶ ἐπίφορος ἐς αὐτήν.

3   Καὶ οἱ μὲν παυσάμενοι τῆς μάχης ὡς ἑκάτεροι
ἡσυχάσαντες τὴν νύκτα ἐν φυλακῇ ἦσαν· καὶ ἡ Κορινθία
ναῦς τοῦ δήμου κεκρατηκότος ὑπεξανήγετο, καὶ τῶν
ἐπικούρων οἱ πολλοὶ ἐς τὴν ἤπειρον λαθόντες διεκομίσ-

75 θησαν. τῇ δὲ ἐπιγιγνομένῃ ἡμέρᾳ Νικόστρατος ὁ
Διειτρέφους Ἀθηναίων στρατηγὸς παραγίγνεται
βοηθῶν ἐκ Ναυπάκτου δώδεκα ναυσὶ καὶ Μεσσηνίων
πεντακοσίοις ὁπλίταις· ξύμβασίν τε ἔπρασσε καὶ
πείθει ὥστε ξυγχωρῆσαι ἀλλήλοις δέκα μὲν ἄνδρας
τοὺς αἰτιωτάτους κρῖναι, οἳ οὐκέτι ἔμειναν, τοὺς
δ' ἄλλους οἰκεῖν σπονδὰς πρὸς ἀλλήλους ποιησαμένους
καὶ πρὸς Ἀθηναίους, ὥστε τοὺς αὐτοὺς ἐχθροὺς

2 καὶ φίλους νομίζειν. καὶ ὁ μὲν ταῦτα πράξας
ἔμελλεν ἀποπλεύσεσθαι· οἱ δὲ τοῦ δήμου προστάται
πείθουσιν αὐτὸν πέντε μὲν ναῦς τῶν αὐτοῦ σφίσι
καταλιπεῖν, ὅπως ἧσσόν τι ἐν κινήσει ὦσιν οἱ ἐναντίοι,
ἴσας δὲ αὐτοὶ πληρώσαντες ἐκ σφῶν αὐτῶν ξυμπέμψειν.

3 καὶ ὁ μὲν ξυνεχώρησεν, οἱ δὲ τοὺς ἐχθροὺς κατέλεγον
ἐς τὰς ναῦς. δείσαντες δὲ ἐκεῖνοι μὴ ἐς τὰς
Ἀθήνας ἀποπεμφθῶσι καθίζουσιν ἐς τὸ τῶν Διοσκόρων

4 ἱερόν. Νικόστρατος δὲ αὐτοὺς ἀνίστη τε καὶ παρε-
μυθεῖτο. ὡς δ' οὐκ ἔπειθεν, ὁ δῆμος ὁπλισθεὶς
ἐπὶ τῇ προφάσει ταύτῃ, ὡς οὐδὲν αὐτῶν ὑγιὲς
διανοουμένων τῇ τοῦ μὴ ξυμπλεῖν ἀπιστίᾳ, τά τε

74. After a day's interval the fighting started again, and the *demos* was victorious, having the advantage both of a stronger position and of greater numbers; their women assisted them bravely, hurling tiles from the houses and standing up to the noise of the battle in a way unusual for their sex. Towards sunset the *oligoi* were routed. They were frightened that the *demos* might without difficulty advance, capture the arsenal, and destroy them; so they set fire to the houses and the apartment blocks that surrounded the *agora*, so that there should be no passage through them. They spared neither their own nor other people's property, with the result that a good deal of valuable merchandise was burned, and the city itself ran the risk of being totally destroyed, if a wind had risen and blown the flames towards it.

Both sides in their respective positions now stopped fighting and remained quiet for the night, though they kept guard. The Corinthian ship slipped out of the harbour when the *demos* had won, and most of the mercenaries got away secretly to the mainland. 75. On the next day Nicostratos, son of Dieitrephes, the Athenian commander, arrived from Naupactos with twelve ships and 500 Messenian hoplites. He tried to make an agreement, and persuaded them to come to terms with each other: ten men (who were no longer present) should be put on trial as those most responsible, and all the rest should make a settlement with each other - and with the Athenians, in terms of a full offensive and defensive alliance - and live at peace. Having done this, he was about to sail away; but the leaders of the *demos* persuaded him to leave behind five of his ships with them, so that their enemies should be less likely to make any move: they themselves would man an equal number of ships from their own men and send them with him. He agreed: and they nominated their personal enemies for service on board. The men nominated were afraid that they might be sent off to Athens, and seated themselves in the temple of the Dioscuri. Nicostratos removed them from their position and tried to reassure them; but when he failed to convince them, the men of the *demos* armed themselves on the pretext that their intentions could not be trusted if they felt doubtful about sailing with Nicostratos. They then

71

ὅπλα αὐτῶν ἐκ τῶν οἰκιῶν ἔλαβε καὶ αὐτῶν τινὰς
οἷς ἐπέτυχον, εἰ μὴ Νικόστρατος ἐκώλυσε, διέφθει-
5 ραν ἄν. ὁρῶντες δὲ οἱ ἄλλοι τὰ γιγνόμενα καθίζουσιν ἐς τὸ Ἡραιον ἱκέται καὶ γίγνονται οὐκ
ἐλάσσους τετρακοσίων. ὁ δὲ δῆμος δείσας μή τι
νεωτερίσωσιν ἀνίστησί τε αὐτοὺς πείσας καὶ δια-
κομίζει ἐς τὴν πρὸ τοῦ Ἡραίου νῆσον, καὶ τὰ
ἐπιτήδεια ἐκεῖσε αὐτοῖς διεπέμπετο.

76 Τῆς δὲ στάσεως ἐν τούτῳ οὔσης τετάρτῃ ἢ πέμπτῃ
ἡμέρᾳ μετὰ τὴν τῶν ἀνδρῶν ἐς τὴν νῆσον διακομιδὴν
αἱ ἐκ τῆς Κυλλήνης Πελοποννησίων νῆες, μετὰ τὸν
ἐκ τῆς Ἰωνίας πλοῦν ἔφορμοι οὖσαι, παραγίγνονται
τρεῖς καὶ πεντήκοντα· ἦρχε δὲ αὐτῶν Ἀλκίδας,
ὅσπερ καὶ πρότερον, καὶ Βρασίδας αὐτῷ ξύμβουλος
ἐπέπλει. ὁρμισάμενοι δὲ ἐς Σύβοτα λιμένα τῆς
77 ἠπείρου ἅμα ἕῳ ἐπέπλεον τῇ Κερκύρᾳ. οἱ δὲ πολλῷ
θορύβῳ καὶ πεφοβημένοι τά τ' ἐν τῇ πόλει καὶ τὸν
ἐπίπλουν παρεσκευάζοντό τε ἅμα ἑξήκοντα ναῦς καὶ
τὰς αἰεὶ πληρουμένας ἐξέπεμπον πρὸς τοὺς ἐναντίους,
παραινούντων Ἀθηναίων σφᾶς τε ἐᾶσαι πρῶτον
ἐκπλεῦσαι καὶ ὕστερον πάσαις ἅμα ἐκείνους ἐπι-
2 γενέσθαι. ὡς δὲ αὐτοῖς πρὸς τοῖς πολεμίοις ἦσαν
σποράδες αἱ νῆες, δύο μὲν εὐθὺς ηὐτομόλησαν, ἐν
ἑτέραις δὲ ἀλλήλοις οἱ ἐμπλέοντες ἐμάχοντο, ἦν
3 δὲ οὐδεὶς κόσμος τῶν ποιουμένων. ἰδόντες δὲ οἱ
Πελοποννήσιοι τὴν ταραχὴν εἴκοσι μὲν ναυσὶ πρὸς
τοὺς Κερκυραίους ἐτάξαντο, ταῖς δὲ λοιπαῖς πρὸς
τὰς δώδεκα ναῦς τῶν Ἀθηναίων, ὧν ἦσαν αἱ δύο
78 Σαλαμινία καὶ Πάραλος. καὶ οἱ μὲν Κερκυραῖοι
κακῶς τε καὶ κατ' ὀλίγας προσπίπτοντες ἐταλαιπώ-
ρουν τὸ καθ' αὑτούς· οἱ δ' Ἀθηναῖοι φοβούμενοι τὸ
πλῆθος καὶ τὴν περικύκλωσιν ἀθρόαις μὲν οὐ
προσέπιπτον οὐδὲ κατὰ μέσον ταῖς ἐφ' ἑαυτοὺς τεταγμέναις, προσβαλόντες δὲ κατὰ κέρας καταδύουσι
μίαν ναῦν. καὶ μετὰ ταῦτα κύκλον ταξαμένων
2 αὐτῶν περιέπλεον καὶ ἐπειρῶντο θορυβεῖν. γνόντες
δὲ οἱ πρὸς τοῖς Κερκυραίοις καὶ δείσαντες μὴ ὅπερ

took the men's arms out of their houses, and would actually have
killed some of them whom they happened to meet, if Nicostratos had
not prevented it. The other *oligoi*, seeing what was going on,
seated themselves as suppliants in the temple of Hera: there were
not less than 400 of them. The *demos*, afraid that they would be
violent, persuaded them to rise and removed them to the island in
front of the temple of Hera, and provisions were sent across to
them there.

76. At this point in the *stasis*, on the fourth or fifth day after
the men had been taken across to the island, the Peloponnesian ships
from Cyllene arrived, having been at anchor and on the watch there
after their voyage back from Ionia. There were fifty-three of them:
Alcidas was their admiral, as he had been before, and Brasidas sailed with him as adviser. They came to anchor at the harbour of Sybota
on the mainland, and sailed out against Corcyra at dawn. 77. The
Corcyreans were in a good deal of turmoil; they were frightened
about things in the city and about the Peloponnesian attack. So they
prepared sixty ships and sent them straight out against the enemy as
soon as each was manned; though the Athenians advised them to let
the Athenian ships go out first, and afterwards to join them with
all their own ships in one body. Thus the Corcyrean ships came out
against the enemy in small groups; two of them immediately deserted,
and in others the crews fought amongst each other, and there was no
discipline in what they did at all.

The Peloponnesians saw the confusion, and set twenty of their ships
against the Corcyreans, and the rest against the twelve Athenian
ships (two of which were the Salaminia and the Paralos). 78. The
Corcyreans made their attacks inefficiently and in small numbers,
so that in their part of the battle things went badly for them.
The Athenians were afraid of the numbers of the enemy, and of being
encircled; so they did not fall upon the Peloponnesians where their
ships were packed together and ranged against them, nor in the middle
of the Peloponnesian line, but attacked it on the wing, and sank one
ship. After that the Peloponnesians formed a circle, and the
Athenians sailed round it and endeavoured to throw it into confusion.
Those of the Peloponnesians who were opposing the Corcyreans saw
this, and were frightened that

ἐν Ναυπάκτῳ γένοιτο, ἐπιβοηθοῦσι, καὶ γενόμεναι
ἀθρόαι αἱ νῆες ἅμα τὸν ἐπίπλουν τοῖς Ἀθηναίοις
3 ἐποιοῦντο. οἱ δ᾽ ὑπεχώρουν ἤδη πρύμναν κρουόμενοι καὶ ἅμα τὰς τῶν Κερκυραίων ἐβούλοντο προ-
καταφυγεῖν ὅτι μάλιστα, ἑαυτῶν σχολῇ τε ὑποχω-
ρούντων καὶ πρὸς σφᾶς τεταγμένων τῶν ἐναντίων.
4 Ἡ μὲν οὖν ναυμαχία τοιαύτη γενομένη ἐτελεύτα
79 ἐς ἡλίου δύσιν, καὶ οἱ Κερκυραῖοι δείσαντες μὴ
σφίσιν ἐπιπλεύσαντες ἐπὶ τὴν πόλιν ὡς κρατοῦντες
οἱ πολέμιοι ἢ τοὺς ἐκ τῆς νήσου ἀναλάβωσιν ἢ καὶ
ἄλλο τι νεωτερίσωσι, τούς τε ἐκ τῆς νήσου πάλιν
ἐς τὸ Ἥραιον διεκόμισαν καὶ τὴν πόλιν ἐφύλασσον.
2 οἱ δ᾽ ἐπὶ μὲν τὴν πόλιν οὐκ ἐτόλμησαν πλεῦσαι
κρατοῦντες τῇ ναυμαχίᾳ, τρεῖς δὲ καὶ δέκα ναῦς
ἔχοντες τῶν Κερκυραίων ἀπέπλευσαν ἐς τὴν ἤπειρον,
3 ὅθενπερ ἀνηγάγοντο. τῇ δ᾽ ὑστεραίᾳ ἐπὶ μὲν τὴν
πόλιν οὐδὲν μᾶλλον ἐπέπλεον, καίπερ ἐν πολλῇ
ταραχῇ καὶ φόβῳ ὄντας καὶ Βρασίδου παραινοῦντος,
ὡς λέγεται, Ἀλκίδᾳ, ἰσοψήφου δὲ οὐκ ὄντος·
ἐπὶ δὲ τὴν Λευκίμμην τὸ ἀκρωτήριον ἀποβάντες
80 ἐπόρθουν τοὺς ἀγρούς. ὁ δὲ δῆμος τῶν Κερκυραίων
ἐν τούτῳ περιδεὴς γενόμενος μὴ ἐπιπλεύσωσιν αἱ
νῆες, τοῖς τε ἱκέταις ἦσαν ἐς λόγους καὶ τοῖς
ἄλλοις, ὅπως σωθήσεται ἡ πόλις, καί τινας αὐτῶν
ἔπεισαν ἐς τὰς ναῦς ἐσβῆναι· ἐπλήρωσαν γὰρ ὅμως
2 τριάκοντα προσδεχόμενοι τὸν ἐπίπλουν. οἱ δὲ
Πελοποννήσιοι μέχρι μέσου ἡμέρας δῃώσαντες τὴν
γῆν ἀπέπλευσαν, καὶ ὑπὸ νύκτα αὐτοῖς ἐφρυκτωρή-
θησαν ἑξήκοντα νῆες Ἀθηναίων προσπλέουσαι ἀπὸ
Λευκάδος· ἃς οἱ Ἀθηναῖοι πυνθανόμενοι τὴν στάσιν
καὶ τὰς μετ᾽ Ἀλκίδου ναῦς ἐπὶ Κέρκυραν μελλούσας
πλεῖν ἀπέστειλαν καὶ Εὐρυμέδοντα τὸν Θουκλέους
81 στρατηγόν. οἱ μὲν οὖν Πελοποννήσιοι τῆς νυκτὸς
εὐθὺς κατὰ τάχος ἐκομίζοντο ἐπ᾽ οἴκου παρὰ τὴν
γῆν· καὶ ὑπερενεγκόντες τὸν Λευκαδίων ἰσθμὸν τὰς
ναῦς, ὅπως μὴ περιπλέοντες ὀφθῶσιν, ἀποκομίζονται.
2 Κερκυραῖοι δὲ αἰσθόμενοι τάς τε Ἀττικὰς ναῦς

the same thing would happen as had happened at Naupactos: so they came to the rescue, and all the ships together then bore down on the Athenians. The latter began to give way and back water: they wanted to give the Corcyrean ships the best opportunity to retreat, so they themselves retreated slowly, with the whole fleet of the enemy arrayed against them.

Such was the sea-fight, and it ended at sunset. 79. The Corcyreans were afraid that the victorious enemy would sail to attack their city, or pick up the men on the island, or make some other bold move; so they brought the men back again from the island to the temple of Hera and put the city under guard. However, the Peloponnesians did not dare to sail against the city when they had triumphed in the sea-fight, but sailed off to the mainland, from where they had put out to sea, with thirteen Corcyrean ships which they had captured. On the next day they still did not sail against the city, even though the Corcyreans were in turmoil and extremely alarmed. Brasidas is said to have advised Alcidas to do so (though his vote did not weigh as heavily as Alcidas'): but they made a landing on the headland of Leukimme and ravaged the fields. 80. The Corcyrean *demos* were, meanwhile, very frightened that the Peloponnesian fleet might attack, and entered into discussion with the suppliants and the others for the safety of the city: and they persuaded some of them to serve on the ships. They managed, in fact, to man thirty ships at that time when they expected the Peloponnesian attack. The Peloponnesians ravaged the land till about midday and sailed away; and about nightfall they were informed by fire-beacons from Leucas that sixty Athenian ships were sailing towards them. These ships the Athenians had sent off when they learned about the *stasis*, and about the ships with Alcidas which were going to sail to Corcyra: the commander was Eurymedon son of Thucles. 81. The Peloponnesians immediately sailed home with all speed along the coastline: they dragged the ships over the Leucadian isthmus, to avoid being seen sailing round Leucas, and so got away.

The Corcyreans saw that the Attic ships

75

προσπλεούσας τάς τε τῶν πολεμίων οἰχομένας, λαβόντες
τούς τε Μεσσηνίους ἐς τὴν πόλιν ἤγαγον πρότερον
ἔξω ὄντας, καὶ τὰς ναῦς περιπλεῦσαι κελεύσαντες
ἃς ἐπλήρωσαν ἐς τὸν Ὑλλαϊκὸν λιμένα, ἐν ὅσῳ
περιεκομίζοντο, τῶν ἐχθρῶν εἴ τινα λάβοιεν,
ἀπέκτεινον· καὶ ἐκ τῶν νεῶν ὅσους ἔπεισαν ἐσβῆναι
ἐκβιβάζοντες ἀπεχρῶντο, ἐς τὸ Ἡραιόν τε ἐλθόντες
τῶν ἱκετῶν ὡς πεντήκοντα ἄνδρας δίκην ὑποσχεῖν
3 ἔπεισαν καὶ κατέγνωσαν πάντων θάνατον. οἱ δὲ
πολλοὶ τῶν ἱκετῶν, ὅσοι οὐκ ἐπείσθησαν, ὡς ἑώρων
τὰ γιγνόμενα, διέφθειρον αὐτοῦ ἐν τῷ ἱερῷ ἀλλήλους,
καὶ ἐκ τῶν δένδρων τινὲς ἀπήγχοντο, οἱ δ' ὡς ἕκασ-
4 τοι ἐδύναντο ἀνηλοῦντο. ἡμέρας τε ἑπτά, ἃς
ἀφικόμενος ὁ Εὐρυμέδων ταῖς ἑξήκοντα ναυσὶ παρέ-
μεινε, Κερκυραῖοι σφῶν αὐτῶν τοὺς ἐχθροὺς
δοκοῦντας εἶναι ἐφόνευον, τὴν μὲν αἰτίαν ἐπι-
φέροντες τοῖς τὸν δῆμον καταλύουσιν, ἀπέθανον δέ
τινες καὶ ἰδίας ἔχθρας ἕνεκα, καὶ ἄλλοι χρημάτων
5 σφίσιν ὀφειλομένων ὑπὸ τῶν λαβόντων.

85   Οἱ μὲν οὖν κατὰ τὴν πόλιν Κερκυραῖοι τοιαύταις
ὀργαῖς ταῖς πρώταις ἐς ἀλλήλους ἐχρήσαντο, καὶ ὁ
Εὐρυμέδων καὶ οἱ Ἀθηναῖοι ἀπέπλευσαν ταῖς ναυσίν·
2 ὕστερον δὲ οἱ φεύγοντες τῶν Κερκυραίων (διεσώθησαν
γὰρ αὐτῶν ἐς πεντακοσίους) τείχη τε λαβόντες,
ἃ ἦν ἐν τῇ ἠπείρῳ, ἐκράτουν τῆς πέραν οἰκείας
γῆς καὶ ἐξ αὐτῆς ὁρμώμενοι ἐλήζοντο τοὺς ἐν τῇ
νήσῳ καὶ πολλὰ ἔβλαπτον, καὶ λιμὸς ἰσχυρὸς
3 ἐγένετο ἐν τῇ πόλει. ἐπρεσβεύοντο δὲ καὶ ἐς τὴν
Λακεδαίμονα καὶ Κόρινθον περὶ καθόδου· καὶ ὡς
οὐδὲν αὐτοῖς ἐπράσσετο, ὕστερον χρόνῳ πλοῖα καὶ
ἐπικούρους παρασκευασάμενοι διέβησαν ἐς τὴν
νῆσον ἑξακόσιοι μάλιστα οἱ πάντες, καὶ τὰ πλοῖα
ἐμπρήσαντες, ὅπως ἀπόγνοια ᾖ τοῦ ἄλλο τι ἢ κρατεῖν
τῆς γῆς, ἀναβάντες ἐς τὸ ὄρος τὴν Ἰστώνην, τεῖχος
ἐνοικοδομησάμενοι ἔφθειρον τοὺς ἐν τῇ πόλει καὶ
τῆς γῆς ἐκράτουν.

were sailing towards them, and that the enemy's ships had gone: so they took the Messenians inside the city (hitherto they had been outside), and ordered the ships which they had manned to sail round to the Hyllaic harbour. Then, while the ships were on their way round, they killed all their personal enemies they could get hold of: after that, they made all those whom they had persuaded to serve on the ships disembark, and butchered them. Next, they went to the precinct of Hera, persuaded about fifty of the men there to undergo a trial, and condemned them all to death. Most of the suppliants, who had not been so persuaded, killed each other there in the precinct when they saw what was going on; some hanged themselves on the trees, and others committed suicide as best they could. During the seven days which Eurymedon with his sixty ships spent there after his arrival, the Corcyreans continued to massacre those whom they took to be their personal enemies: they charged them with wanting to destroy the *demos*, but some of them were killed because of purely private enmity, and others by their debtors because of the money they owed.

Anyway, these were the sort of wild passions which the Corcyreans displayed towards each other (and they were the first to do so). Eurymedon and the other Athenians sailed away in their ships. Later, those of the Corcyreans who escaped (about 500 of them managed it) captured some fortifications on the mainland and gained control of Corcyrean territory opposite Corcyra. Using that as a base, they plundered those on the island and did them a great deal of harm: and there was a serious famine in the city. They also sent embassies to Lacedaimonia and Corinth to discuss their restoration; but when they had no success, they later got some boats and some mercenaries and crossed over to the island, numbering about 600 in all. They burned their boats, so that they should have no hope except in actually conquering the land, and went up to Mount Istone: there they built a fortification, did much harm to those in the city, and exercised control of the country districts.

Εὐρυμέδων καὶ Σοφοκλῆς, ἐπειδὴ ἐκ τῆς Πύλου ἀπῆραν
ἐς τὴν Σικελίαν ναυσὶν 'Αθηναίων, ἀφικόμενοι ἐς
Κέρκυραν ἐστράτευσαν μετὰ τῶν ἐκ τῆς πόλεως ἐπὶ
τοὺς ἐν τῷ ὄρει τῆς 'Ιστώνης Κερκυραίων καθιδρυμένους, οἳ τότε μετὰ τὴν στάσιν διαβάντες ἐκράτουν
2 τε τῆς γῆς καὶ πολλὰ ἔβλαπτον. προσβαλόντες δὲ
τὸ μὲν τείχισμα εἷλον, οἱ δὲ ἄνδρες καταπεφευγότες
ἀθρόοι πρὸς μετέωρόν τι ξυνέβησαν ὥστε τοὺς μὲν
ἐπικούρους παραδοῦναι, περὶ δὲ σφῶν τὰ ὅπλα παρα-
3 δόντων τὸν 'Αθηναίων δῆμον διαγνῶναι. καὶ αὐτοὺς
ἐς τὴν νῆσον οἱ στρατηγοὶ τὴν Πτυχίαν ἐς φυλακὴν
διεκόμισαν ὑποσπόνδους, μέχρι οὗ 'Αθήναζε
πεμφθῶσιν, ὥστ', ἐάν τις ἁλῷ ἀποδιδράσκων, ἅπασι
4 λελύσθαι τὰς σπονδάς. οἱ δὲ τοῦ δήμου προστάται
τῶν Κερκυραίων, δεδιότες μὴ οἱ 'Αθηναῖοι τοὺς
ἐλθόντας οὐκ ἀποκτείνωσι, μηχανῶνται τοιόνδε
5 τι· τῶν ἐν τῇ νήσῳ πείθουσί τινας ὀλίγους, ὑπο-
πέμψαντες φίλους καὶ διδάξαντες ὡς κατ' εὔνοιαν
δὴ λέγειν ὅτι κράτιστον αὐτοῖς εἴη ὡς τάχιστα
ἀποδρᾶναι, πλοῖον δέ τι αὐτοὶ ἑτοιμάσειν· μέλλειν
γὰρ δὴ τοὺς στρατηγοὺς τῶν 'Αθηναίων παραδώσειν
47 αὐτοὺς τῷ δήμῳ τῶν Κερκυραίων. ὡς δὲ ἔπεισαν,
καὶ μηχανησαμένων τὸ πλοῖον ἐκπλέοντες ἐλήφθησαν,
ἐλέλυντό τε αἱ σπονδαὶ καὶ τοῖς Κερκυραίοις
2 παρεδίδοντο οἱ πάντες. ξυνελάβοντο δὲ τοῦ τοιούτου
οὐχ ἥκιστα, ὥστε ἀκριβῆ τὴν πρόφασιν γενέσθαι
καὶ τοὺς τεχνησαμένους ἀδεέστερον ἐγχειρῆσαι,
οἱ στρατηγοὶ τῶν 'Αθηναίων κατάδηλοι ὄντες τοὺς
ἄνδρας μὴ ἂν βούλεσθαι ὑπ' ἄλλων κομισθέντας,
διότι αὐτοὶ ἐς Σικελίαν ἔπλεον, τὴν τιμὴν τοῖς
3 ἄγουσι προσποιῆσαι. παραλαβόντες δὲ αὐτοὺς οἱ
Κερκυραῖοι ἐς οἴκημα μέγα κατεῖρξαν, καὶ ὕστερον
ἐξάγοντες κατὰ εἴκοσιν ἄνδρας διῆγον διὰ δυοῖν
στοίχοιν ὁπλιτῶν ἑκατέρωθεν παρατεταγμένων,
δεδεμένους τε πρὸς ἀλλήλους καὶ παιομένους καὶ

46.   After Eurymedon and Sophocles had set sail from Pylos for
Sicily with the Athenian ships, they reached Corcyra and made an
expedition with those from the city against the men who had established themselves on Mount Istone (these men had crossed over to the island after the *stasis* - they controlled the country districts and
did a great deal of harm). They attacked the fortification and took
it: the defenders escaped in a body and went up together to high
ground. There they surrendered on the terms that they should hand
over their mercenary troops, and their own arms, and give themselves
up to the judgement of the Athenian *demos*. The Athenian commanders
took them under truce to the island of Ptychia, and put them under
guard to wait there until they should be sent to Athens: the understanding was that if any of them tried to escape and was captured,
the truce was no longer valid for them all. The leaders of the
Corcyrean *demos* were afraid that when the prisoners got to Athens
the Athenians might not condemn them to death: so they devised the
following strategem. They secretly sent in to the island people who
were friends of the prisoners, instructing them to say (as if for
the prisoners' own good) that it would be best for them to run off
as soon as they could, and that they would prepare a boat for them;
since the Athenian commanders were intending to hand them over to the
Corcyrean *demos*.   47.   This persuaded some of the prisoners; and
when they had been persuaded, it was so arranged that they were caught
as they were actually escaping on the boat. So the truce was broken
and they were all handed over to the Corcyreans. The Athenian
commanders helped considerably in making the story plausible, and
allowing those who engineered the plot to do so more boldly; for
they made it clear that, since they themselves were on the way to
Sicily, they did not want the prisoners to be brought back to Athens
by others who would thereby get all the glory.

When the Corcyreans had got them, they shut them up in a large
building and then led them out, twenty at a time. They tied them
together and made them pass between two rows of hoplites drawn up on
each side: as they went, they were beaten and

κεντουμένους ὑπὸ τῶν παρατεταγμένων, εἴ πού τίς
τινα ἴδοι ἐχθρὸν ἑαυτοῦ· μαστιγοφόροι τε
παριόντες ἐπετάχυνον τῆς ὁδοῦ τοὺς σχολαίτερον
48 προϊόντας. καὶ ἐς μὲν ἄνδρας ἑξήκοντα ἔλαθον
τοὺς ἐν τῷ οἰκήματι τούτῳ τῷ τρόπῳ ἐξαγαγόντες
καὶ διαφθείραντες (ᾤοντο γὰρ αὐτοὺς μεταστήσοντάς
ποι ἄλλοσε ἄγειν)· ὡς δὲ ᾔσθοντο καί τις αὐτοῖς
ἐδήλωσε, τούς τε Ἀθηναίους ἐπεκαλοῦντο καὶ ἐκέλευον
σφᾶς, εἰ βούλονται, αὐτοὺς διαφθείρειν, ἔκ τε τοῦ
οἰκήματος οὐκέτι ἤθελον ἐξιέναι, οὐδ᾽ ἐσιέναι
2 ἔφασαν κατὰ δύναμιν περιόψεσθαι οὐδένα. οἱ δὲ
Κερκυραῖοι κατὰ μὲν τὰς θύρας οὐδ᾽ αὐτοὶ διενο-
οῦντο βιάζεσθαι, ἀναβάντες δὲ ἐπὶ τὸ τέγος τοῦ
οἰκήματος καὶ διελόντες τὴν ὀροφὴν ἔβαλλον τῷ
κεράμῳ καὶ ἐτόξευον κάτω. οἱ δὲ ἐφυλάσσοντό τε
3 ὡς ἐδύναντο καὶ ἅμα οἱ πολλοὶ σφᾶς αὐτοὺς διέφθειρον,
οἰστούς τε οὓς ἀφίεσαν ἐκεῖνοι ἐς τὰς σφαγὰς
καθιέντες καὶ ἐκ κλινῶν τινῶν αἳ ἔτυχον αὐτοῖς
ἐνοῦσαι τοῖς σπάρτοις καὶ ἐκ τῶν ἱματίων παραιρή-
ματα ποιοῦντες ἀπαγχόμενοι, παντὶ <τε> τρόπῳ τὸ
πολὺ τῆς νυκτός (ἐπεγένετο γὰρ νὺξ τῷ παθήματι)
ἀναλοῦντες σφᾶς αὐτοὺς καὶ βαλλόμενοι ὑπὸ τῶν
4 ἄνω διεφθάρησαν. καὶ αὐτοὺς οἱ Κερκυραῖοι, ἐπειδὴ
ἐγένετο, φορμηδὸν ἐπὶ ἁμάξας ἐπιβαλόντες ἀπήγαγον
ἔξω τῆς πόλεως. τὰς δὲ γυναῖκας, ὅσαι ἐν τῷ
5 τειχίσματι ἑάλωσαν, ἠνδραποδίσαντο. τοιούτῳ
μὲν τρόπῳ οἱ ἐκ τοῦ ὄρους Κερκυραῖοι ὑπὸ τοῦ
δήμου διεφθάρησαν, καὶ ἡ στάσις πολλὴ γενομένη
ἐτελεύτησεν ἐς τοῦτο ὅσα γε κατὰ τὸν πόλεμον
τόνδε· οὐ γὰρ ἔτι ἦν ὑπόλοιπον τῶν ἑτέρων ὅτι
καὶ ἀξιόλογον.

stabbed by those between whom they passed, whenever anyone saw some prisoner whom he regarded as a personal enemy. Men with whips went with them and hurried them up, if any of them went forward too slowly. 48. In this way about sixty of them were brought out and killed before those in the building realised it (they thought they were just taking them to another place). When somebody told them and they did realise, they kept on appealing to the Athenians and told them to kill them themselves, if they wished: they said that they were not going to leave the building, and would not allow anyone else to come in, so far as they had strength to stop them. The Corcyreans had no intention of forcing their way in through the doors; they went up onto the top of the building, tore away the roof, and then threw tiles at them as well as shooting down upon them. The men inside took cover as best they could; but most of them killed themselves, driving into their throats the arrows that had been shot at them, or strangling themselves with ropes taken from some beds which happened to be in the building, or with strips of their own clothing. They committed suicide in every way they could, and were being shot at by those above them; and this went on for a large part of the night (for the sun had set on this horrific scene). So they perished. When it was day, the Corcyreans piled them up onto wagons and took them outside the city. They made slaves of the women whom they had captured at the fortification. In this way the Corcyreans from the mountain were destroyed by the *demos*; and so the *stasis*, which had reached enormous proportions, came to an end, at least so far as this particular war was concerned: for one of the two parties had virtually ceased to exist.

Συνέβη δὲ περὶ τοῦτον τὸν χρόνον ἐν τῇ Κορκύρᾳ
γενέσθαι μεγάλην στάσιν καὶ σφαγήν, ἣν δι' ἑτέρας
μὲν αἰτίας λέγεται γενέσθαι, μάλιστα δὲ διὰ τὴν
2 ὑπάρχουσαν αὐτοῖς πρὸς ἀλλήλους ἔχθραν. ἐν οὐδεμιᾷ
γάρ ποτε πόλει τοιοῦτοι πολιτῶν φόνοι συνετελέσ-
θησαν οὐδὲ μείζων ἔρις καὶ φιλονεικία πρὸς ὄλεθρον
ἀνήκουσα. δοκοῦσι γὰρ οἱ μὲν ἀναιρεθέντες ὑπ'
ἀλλήλων πρὸ ταύτης τῆς στάσεως γεγονέναι περὶ
χιλίους καὶ πεντακοσίους, καὶ πάντες οὗτοι πρω-
3 τεύοντες τῶν πολιτῶν. τούτων δ' ἐπιγεγενημένων
τῶν ἀτυχημάτων ἑτέραν αὐτοῖς συμφορὰν ἐπέστησεν ἡ
τύχη, τὴν πρὸς ἀλλήλους πάλιν αὐξήσασα διαφοράν.
οἱ μὲν γὰρ προέχοντες τοῖς ἀξιώμασι τῶν Κορκυραίων
ὀρεγόμενοι τῆς ὀλιγαρχίας ἐφρόνουν τὰ Λακεδαιμονίων,
ὁ δὲ δημοτικὸς ὄχλος ἔσπευδε τοῖς Ἀθηναίοις
4 συμμαχεῖν. καὶ γὰρ διαφερούσας τὰς σπουδὰς
εἶχον οἱ περὶ τῆς ἡγεμονίας διαγωνιζόμενοι δῆμοι·
Λακεδαιμόνιοι γὰρ τοὺς πρωτεύοντας ἐν ταῖς συμ-
μαχίσι πόλεσιν ἐποίουν ἐπὶ τῆς διοικήσεως τῶν
κοινῶν, Ἀθηναῖοι δὲ δημοκρατίας ἐν ταῖς πόλεσι
5 καθίστανον. οἱ δ' οὖν Κορκυραῖοι θεωροῦντες
τοὺς δυνατωτάτους τῶν πολιτῶν ὄντας πρὸς τῷ τὴν
πόλιν ἐγχειρίζειν Λακεδαιμονίοις, μετεπέμψαντο
παρ' Ἀθηναίων δύναμιν τὴν παραφυλάξουσαν τὴν
6 πόλιν. Κόνων δ' ὁ στρατηγὸς τῶν Ἀθηναίων πλεύσας
εἰς Κόρκυραν, ἑξακοσίους μὲν τῶν ἐκ Ναυπάκτου
Μεσσηνίων κατέλιπεν ἐν τῇ πόλει, αὐτὸς δὲ μετὰ
τῶν νεῶν παρέπλευσε καὶ καθωρμίσθη πρὸς τῷ τῆς
7 Ἥρας τεμένει; οἱ δὲ ἑξακόσιοι μετὰ τῶν δημοτικῶν
ὁρμήσαντες ἐπὶ τοὺς τὰ Λακεδαιμονίων φρονοῦντας
ἐξαίφνης ἀγορᾶς πληθούσης οὓς μὲν συνελάμβανον,
οὓς δ' ἐφόνευον, πλείους δὲ τῶν χιλίων ἐφυγάδευσαν·
ἐποιήσαντο δὲ τοὺς μὲν δούλους ἐλευθέρους, τοὺς
δὲ ξένους πολίτας, εὐλαβούμενοι τό τε πλῆθος καὶ
8 τὴν δύναμιν τῶν φυγάδων. οἱ μὲν οὖν ἐκπεσόντες

About this time a serious civil war and a massacre occurred in
Corcyra, which is said to have been due to various causes, but
particularly to the Corcyreans' mutual hatred. For in no other city
have so many citizens ever been slaughtered, nor has there been so
much quarrelling and contentiousness, culminating in bloodshed.
For it appears that there were about 1,500 Corcyreans killed by
other Corcyreans before this civil war, and all these were leading
citizens. After these misfortunes had come upon them, fate
brought them another disaster by again increasing their differences with each other. For the most notable citizens of the
Corcyreans wanted an oligarchy and favoured the Lacedaimonian cause,
whereas the mass of the people were keen on an alliance with Athens.
Indeed in general different groups involved in struggles for power
had different kinds of politcal enthusiasm; for the Lacedaimonians,
when cities were allied to them, used to put the control of the
state in the hands of the leading citizens, whereas the Athenians
set up democracies in their cities.

Anyway, the Corcyreans saw that their most powerful citizens
were on the point of handing the city over to the Lacedaimonians,
and sent for some force from the Athenians to protect the city.
Conon, an Athenian general, sailed to Corcyra and left 600 of the
Messenians from Naupactos in the city; he himself with his ships
sailed on and anchored by the sacred precinct of Hera. The 600,
together with the party of the *demos*, made a sudden attack against
those who favoured the Lacedaimonians, when the market-place was
full; they arrested some, killed others, and exiled more than 1,000.
They freed the slaves, and made the resident aliens into citizens,
as a precaution against the number and the strength of the exiles.
The exiles, then,

ἐκ τῆς πατρίδος εἰς τὴν καταντίον ἤπειρον ἔφυγον·
μετὰ δέ τινας ἡμέρας τῶν ἐν τῇ πόλει τινὲς
φρονοῦντες τὰ τῶν φυγάδων κατελάβοντο τὴν ἀγορὰν
καὶ μεταπεμψάμενοι τοὺς φυγάδας περὶ τῶν ὅλων
διηγωνίζοντο.   τέλος δὲ νυκτὸς καταλαβούσης εἰς
ὁμολογίας ἦλθον πρὸς ἀλλήλους, καὶ τῆς φιλονεικίας
παυσάμενοι κοινῶς ᾤκουν τὴν πατρίδα.

left their country and went to the mainland opposite; but after a
few days some of those in the city who favoured the exiles' cause
seized the market-place, recalled the exiles, and tried to gain
control of affairs. Finally when night fell they came to an agreement with each other, ceased their quarrelling, and inhabited their
country in common.

We are concerned with the Corcyrean *stasis* primarily in reference to
the Athenian alliance and the possibilities of support given by
Corcyra to Athens. This involves trying to establish in detail
exactly what happened and when, but it is not much affected by any
topographical question (if indeed any are seriously in doubt): it
is sufficient to say here that I accept the orthodox view on which
the map is based.

A. Opening Moves and Objectives

The *oligoi* - I shall use this term to refer to organised anti-
democrats, without prejudice to their nature or numbers - began by
spending some time (perhaps considerable: see on the timing, section
B below) in persuading individual citizens (70.1). This process must
have attracted attention outside Corcyra, for the arrival of an
Athenian and a Corinthian trireme (both with accredited representatives on board) just before the debate cannot be coincidental; both
sides must have known that the debate (a critical one) was to take
place, and sent their representatives in time for it. Perhaps they
were even invited by the Corcyreans.

The outcome of the vote was that Κερκυραῖοι Ἀθηναίοις μὲν
ξύμμαχοι εἶναι κατὰ τὰ ξυγκείμενα, Πελοποννησίοις δὲ
φίλοι ὥσπερ καὶ πρότερον: 'the Corcyreans to be allies of the
Athenians, according to the agreement, but friendly to the Peloponnesians as before'. Not all of this is clear. I.44 shows that
Athens had only an *epimachy* (defensive alliance) with Corcyra, and
there is no evidence that this had yet become a full *symmachy* (an
offensive and defensive alliance) either *de iure* or - for Corcyra
had only once given actual support to Athens, in 431 - *de facto*.
However, συμμαχια is a very general term for 'alliance', and can
include the concept of *epimachy*: and κατὰ τὰ ξυγκείμενα makes
it clear that the vote was for a defensive alliance only, as is also
shown by Πελοποννησίοις δὲ φίλοι. We must conclude, then,
that no change to a full *symmachy* had taken place. ὥσπερ καὶ
πρότερον is more difficult. It may mean 'as they had (also) been
hitherto', referring only to the formal or official position (as
κατὰ τὰ ξυγκείμενα does). But there are two objections to
this. (1) ὥσπερ καὶ πρότερον would be pleonastic, if Thucydides
means no more by these words than he does by κατὰ τὰ ξυγκείμενα;
(2) since Corcyra had in fact been fighting the Peloponnesians, at
least in 433 at Sybota and in 431 round the Peloponnese, it is
straining even a *de iure* concept to describe the Corcyreans as φίλοι.
A better interpretation would be to take ὥσπερ καὶ πρότερον as
referring to a time when Corcyra was, at least, not actively or
militarily hostile to Corinth: that is, before 433 or 435.

The μεν and δε, and the context (the passage immediately follows
a description of the returned prisoners persuading the Corcyreans),
both strongly support this. If that is right, the outcome of the
debate was highly satisfactory to the Peloponnesians, who are not now
to be regarded as in any sense enemies but as friends. That might
not mean much, but it would at least mean that Athens could not
rely (if she ever could) on Corcyrean support against the Peloponnese.

The *oligoi*, however, are not content, and make three moves. (1)
They try to use the law to get their way, but fail (70.3.5). (2)
They assassinate Peithias and sixty others (70.6). (3) They force
a decree μηδετέρους δέχεσθαι ἀλλ' ἢ μιᾷ νηὶ ἡσυχάζοντας:
'to receive neither side unless they came in peace with a single
ship' (71.1). This decree clearly amounts to a total withdrawal
from any sort of alliance with Athens. That might be thought
sufficient for the *oligoi* and the Peloponnesians, but they go
further still: on the arrival of a Corinthian trireme with Spartan
delegates they attack the *demos*, with ultimately disastrous results
for the *oligoi*.

In making these moves the *oligoi* seem to have grossly overplayed
their hand. Their motivation for playing a hand at all is clear
enough: they wanted to take power. For there were no other advantages to them in siding with Sparta against Athens; on the contrary,
Corcyra as a whole and Corcyrean interests would be as much, perhaps
more, threatened with Athens than with Sparta as an enemy, since
Athens had as much control of the sea in that area as her opponents,
or more. To remain neutral might be better than either alternative;
but the *oligoi* must have believed that their own power would only
be secure with Spartan support. That is not, however, sufficient
to explain their mistakes. The first mistake was to misjudge the
temper of the jurymen who acquitted Peithias and condemned the five
oligoi. The second, and worse, was to suppose that they could defeat
the *demos* in open warfare. It is incredible that men whose specific
task had been to persuade individual Corcyreans and to test the
political temperature should not have been aware of the odds.

Part of the explanation may be that their hand was forced by the
Spartans. That will also explain two other odd facts: (1) that the
Spartans did not intervene earlier (if they could have done so: see
on the timing below, section B), and (2) the attention paid by the
oligoi to securing the second vote of complete neutrality, even
though the vote was forced. We are to suppose that the *oligoi* were
promised Peloponnesian support (which they needed in face of possible Athenian intervention) if and only if (a) they got the Corcyreans in general to agree to a total rejection of the Athenian
alliance, so that *de iure* Corcyra was at least neutral; and (b) they
obtained power *de facto*. The method of political trial was worth
attempting even against the odds, and in attacking the *demos* they
counted on keeping their end up long enough for Peloponnesian support
to arrive. Against that background the *oligoi* acted at least intel-
ligibly and indeed not too rashly. They did in fact keep their end
up for some days; if the Spartans had come before Nicostratos, and
established a rallying-point for the potential *oligoi* in the city,
the coup would have succeeded. Indeed the *demos* were in certain
respects so weak and so clearly terrified of the *oligoi* (see section
C. below), that a sufficient Spartan presence in the city at any
time before the massacre, even during Nicostratos' presence, would
have turned the tide in favour of the *oligoi*.

So much is perhaps reasonably certain: on other points we have to
speculate. It is striking that all the initiative seems to have been
taken by the returned prisoners: surely there were other *oligoi* in
Corcyra who could have been expected to play a leading part? Yet
it is the ex-prisoners alone who bring Peithias to trian (οὗτοι οἱ
ἄνδρες, 70.3), and five of them (αὐτῶν ... πέντε ἄνδρας,

70.4) who are accused in their turn. They are also the subject of
ἐπυνθάνοντο (70.6), as if only they realised the Peithias was
planning to get a total alliance with Athens, which can hardly be
true. It is not even clear, when they ξυνίσταντο (*ibid.*), that
the five condemned men joined with other *oligoi* (besides the ex-
prisoners): they may only have joined with the rest of their ex-
prisoner associates.

The 250 who were captured must have been more or less a random
sample of Corcyrean *epibatai*: no doubt because of their rank and
social position politically opposed to the *demos*, but not a pre-
selected group of particularly passionate anti-democrats. There
were not, I believe, all that many *oligoi* or even potential *oligoi*
throughout the *stasis*; but certainly a good many more than 250,
who must have made their appearance when the fighting started (ch.
72) if not before. We must assume, I think, not so much that the
250 had been 'brainwashed' by the Corinthians into playing such a
leading part, but rather that only they - in the early stages, at
least - were working in conjunction with the Peloponnesians: perhaps
were even bribed by promises of money or power when Corcyra was
won over to the Peloponnesian side. They may not have trusted other
oligoi or potential *oligoi* with their plans.

The timing of the initial coup, as described in 70.6, sounds
slightly *ad hoc*. The five *oligoi* τῷ τε νόμῳ ἐξείργοντο καὶ
ἅμα ἐπυνθάνοντο τὸν Πειθίαν κτλ: 'they were constrained by
the law, and at the same time learned that Peithias', etc. At
first sight the implication is that only at this point did they
appreciate Peithias' intentions, and that this additional stimulus
combined with their own unfortunate personal position made them
undertake the coup: as if the timing was more or less forced upon
them in their desperation. There may, of course, be elements of
truth in this: revolutionaries cannot always choose their time for
striking the first blow, nor do they always act rationally. But
it consorts ill with the idea of a long-term plot carefully organised in conjunction with the Peloponnesians.

Probably we should put a good deal of weight on ἕως ἔτι βουλῆς
ἐστί, 'while he was still a member of the countil'. The revolutionaries' hand may have been forced, not so much by the personal misfortunes of the five rich men, but by the need to stop Peithias.
We cannot know for certain how long was the tenure of a member of
council, or at what date it ended; but it may well have been that
Peithias was about to make his political move within a very short
space of time, and that the *oligoi* only realised this at the last
moment. Of course they were aware of the general policy and intentions of Peithias: what they learned was that he intended to imple-
ment it *while he was still a member of council*. So they had to
act fast. Probably the council was largely pro-*demos*, and constitutional methods of persuasion would have failed in any case. Force
was needed, and in a hurry.

B. The Timing

One or two scholars have had shots at this, notably Busolt and Gomme
(see Gomme, *ad loc.*): in my view, very bad shots, allowing far too

much time to elapse in the earlier stages of the *stasis*, chiefly because they fail to take the text seriously enough.

We begin with what we may call Day O (72.2), on which the *oligoi* defeat the *demos*: at night the *demos* digs in on the acropolis. Next day, Day 1 (τῇ δ᾽ ὑστεραίᾳ, 73.1), both sides offer freedom to the slaves.

After a pause of one day (Day 2) the battle starts again on Day 3 (διαλιπούσης δ᾽ ἡμερᾶς, 74.1): the *demos* wins, the mercenaries leave, and the Corinthian trireme sneaks away (74.1-3). On Day 4 Nicostratos comes (τῇ δὲ ἐπιγιγνομένῃ ἡμέρᾳ, 75.1). So far as the slaves and mercenaries are concerned, it looks as if both the household slaves (who joined the *demos*) and the mercenaries of the *oligoi* were actually present (παρεγένετο, 73) and helping their respective sides on Day 1. The country slaves had farther to go: we do not know which side (if either) they supported, or when they arrived (if they did). The mercenaries must have been prepared well in advance by the *oligoi*, if they arrived on Day 1; they were certainly in the fighting on Day 3, at the end of which they left for the mainland.

So far we have something like certainty. But we cannot be sure how much time was spent on the events of ch. 75. There is nothing there that need have taken very long, however; probably about two to three days, which brings us to Day 6. If we allow many more days we unnecessarily raise an insoluble problem about why the Spartan fleet did not arrive earlier: see below). Four or five days (τετάρτη ἢ πέμπτῃ ἡμέρᾳ, 76) after that, let us say Day 10, Alcidas' fleet anchors at Sybota. On Day 11, at dawn (ἅμα ἕῳ, *ibid.*) the Peloponnesians sail to Corcyra, and the sea-fight goes on till sunset (ἐς ἡλίου δύσιν, 78.4). On the next day, Day 12 (τῇ δ᾽ ὑστεραίᾳ, 79.3), they ravage Corcyra till noon, and then at night sail away. They use the Leucadian isthmus, τὸν Λευκαδίων ἰσθμὸν (81.1), so Eurymedon's fleet must have been close; no doubt he arrives either the next day or the day after (Day 13 or 14). He stays for seven days (ἡμέρας τε ἑπτά, 81.4).

We must distinguish in ch.81 between two stages of the massacre. The *demos'* actions in 81.2-3 - bringing the Messenians in, ordering the fleet to sail, killing the enemies on the spot, killing the men as they landed from the ships, and procuring the death of the suppliants - are introduced by οἱ Κερκυραῖοι δὲ αἰσθόμενοι τάς τε Ἀττικὰς ναῦς προσπλεούσας, 'the Corcyreans seeing the Athenian ships sailing towards them' (81.2): all this happens before Eurymedon arrives. Then, for the seven days that he stayed, they continued to slaughter (ἐφόνευον, 80.4) on a wider basis: they charged their victims with trying to overthrow the democracy, but some of them were killed because of personal hatred, and others by their debtors. All this takes us to Day 20 or 21.

The wording of 85.1-2 (ὕστερον δὲ ... πεντακοσίους) suggests that the 500 escapees had fled during and not after the reign of terror, unsurprisingly. We cannot time their subsequent actions precisely. It was late summer in 425 (after the Pylos campaign) when the Athenians returned to expel them from Mt. Istone, and the horrific events which finally destroyed the *oligoi* were completed in time for the Athenians to sail on to Sicily towards the end of the season.

To go backwards from Day 0 is more difficult. There is, however, good
reason to believe that the actual coup of 70.6 (the murder of
Peithias and sixty others), and the events which followed it, occurred in rapid succession. (1) the *oligoi* would naturally call the
Corcyreans together (71.1) as soon as possible after the coup, in
order to give their explanations and avert any backlash. (2) The
proposal was made at the same time as the explanation (it is part
of the same sentence, *ibid.*), and the same applies to (3) their forcing the proposal through the assembly (*ibid.*) (4) Sending the
ambassadors to Athens occurred immediately afterwards (εὐθὺς, 71.2),
either on the same day or the day after. The ἐν τούτῳ ('meanwhile'), of 72.2 refers to what happened outside Corcyra (the trireme
went to Athens, and the Athenians put the delegates in prison). We
can hardly allow more than one or two days for these events: I am
inclined to put (1)-(3) at Day -2, and (4), which may have required
some debate, at Day -1.

The possibilities are (1) that they did in fact return in or short-
Going a step further back, we cannot hope to time Peithias' trial
and acquittal, and the counter-accusation, which precede the coup:
no doubt we should allow some weeks for these events (the Athenian
trireme in 70.6 could have stayed for a long time). Nor can we be
certain about the return of the prisoners in ch.70, though some
scholars are in no doubt. Gomme, in a note on ὑπὸ Κορινθίων
ἀφεθέντες (70.1) says (p.359): 'Clearly not long before the sedi-
tion broke out in Kerkyra in the spring of 427', but gives no argument (that I can see). He adds that 'Some have thought that this
argues too long a time taken in the persuasion of the prisoners,
whom the Corinthians had cherished from the beginning (i.55.1); but
perhaps the majority of them were moderately honest and patriotic
men'. It seems clear, however, that the prisoners would have needed
the high-minded idealism of a Regulus (*mutatis mutandis*) to stay
in prison; the Corinthians would in any case have had no hold on them
once they had returned to Corcyra. Indeed their enthusiasm in the
event for the task of political persuasion shows clearly enough
that they themselves were already willing to engage in anti-Athenian,
and/or anti-democratic, *stasis*. These were men who, shortly before,
had fought for their country at Sybota in the company of Athenian
allies: neither their patriotism nor their honesty seems particularly
durable. The time taken in the persuasion of the prisoners need not
have been very long.

The possibilities are (1) that they did in fact return in or shortly before 427; (2) that they returned a good deal earlier. If (1),
the Corinthians must have kept them in Corinth, judging that they had
no chance of success till then. If (2), something similar would apply:
they must have lain low, or risked only the most gentle persuasion,
before 427. We may reasonably guess, in either case, that Corcyra
remained pro-Athenian until some date after 431 (when she sent fifty
ships to help Athens). She is not known to have sent any in 430,
though Athens then conducted another naval expedition against the
Peloponnese; and the desperation of Phormio's position in 429, when
his twenty ships had to face first forty-seven and then seventy-seven
Peloponnesians, evoked no help from Corcyra, despite Corcyra's interest in north-west Greece and hatred of the Corinthians. Nor did
she send aid to Athens at the time of the Mytilene revolt (428).
It looks much as if, from 430 (or perhaps even a year or so before),
Corcyrean support for Athens was on the wane. Perhaps the returned

prisoners had been working in Corcyra from 430 or earlier, their coup (which plainly required a good deal of preparation) flowering early in 427.

We may now make some informed guesses at ship movements:

(i) The Spartans

Most of the information we have about the Spartans' intentions and actions comes from ch.69. The major question is the time to which στασιάζουσαν refers.

(1) We may refer it to ἐβούλοντο γάρ, and take the sense to be that Corcyra was first in a state of *stasis*: then the Spartans form their plans - thirteen ships are collected at Cyllene, Brasidas is sent there, Alcidas' ships are collected and sent there, and Brasidas and Alcidas make preparations. This has the advantage of giving a clear and full sense to γάρ: i.e. 'all these arrangements were made because the Spartans wanted ...'; and also to the opening words of 70, οἱ γάρ Κερκυραῖοι ἐστασίαζον: 'For the Corcyreans were [*sc.* while all this was going on] in a state of *stasis*'. The trouble is that the timing becomes impossibly tight. As the famous passage on *stasis* (82-83) makes clear, not just any political disagreement counts in Thucydides' eyes as *stasis*. The central criterion is surely the overthrow or disregard of the constitution, together with some use of illegitimate force by one or both of the two parties. If that were not so, all Greek cities would have to be described as permanently in *stasis*. Hence the Corcyrean *stasis* cannot be said to begin with the persuasion by the *oligoi* and the free vote in 70. 1-2, nor even with the political but quite constitutional trial and counter-trial in 70.3-5. It can begin, at the earliest, only with the use of force by the *oligoi* in 70.6: or, more probably with the actual fighting in 72.2. (Hence in 70 Thucydides writes ἐπειδή and not, for instance, ἐξ οὗ: 'they were in *stasis*, because ...' or 'after ...', not 'ever since'.) But the former can hardly be timed earlier than Day -2 or Day -3. Between then and the fleet's departure from Cyllene on Day 8, we have to fit in the time needed for the news to reach Sparta (4 or 5 days at least), for the collection of the Leucasian and Ambracian triremes, the despatch and arrival of Brasidas, the collection and journey of Alcidas with his forty ships, and the 'preparations' mentioned at the end of ch.69. That seems out of the question.

(2) At the other extreme, we may start with the idea - surely a very plausible one - that the *oligoi* were working in conjunction with the Spartans from the beginning. We may then hypothesise that both parts of the combined fleet, Alcidas' as well as Brasidas', had been at Cyllene for some time (certainly before the beginning of the coup): they were 'preparing' and waiting until the *oligoi* had achieved some initial success. στασιάζουσαν would then have to be taken proleptically or with some sort of future sense: 'having failed at Lesbos, they wanted to reinforce their fleet and sail to Corcyra when the *stasis* broke out', or '... which would then be in a state of *stasis*'. That, however, is a somewhat questionable if not impossible sense; and the ἐστασίαζον of 70.1 is strongly against that interpretation of 69. For the imperfect tense suggests the *stasis* had broken out

92

while *some* elements, at least, of those reported in 69 were going on.

The natural logic of 69-70.1, having particular regard for each use of γαρ, is surely this: (a) Alcidas' ships come to Cyllene, where there was Brasidas and his fleet; (b) they were sent there because the Spartans wanted to sail to Corcyra, which was then in *stasis*, with a bigger fleet; (c) Corcyra was in *stasis*, because ... We must suppose, then, that the thirteen triremes had been collected at Cyllene, and perhaps Brasidas sent there, before the *stasis* broke out; and that Alcidas was not despatched there with his fleet until after it had broken out. This makes perhaps the best sense of 69, at any rate (whatever the difficulties in timing, which we shall look at in a minute). The first sentence of 69 suggests that there was no delay in using Alcidas' fleet as soon as it was available: the fleet was part of a prearranged plan for an expedition to Corcyra. The plan was made as soon as they heard of the failure at Lesbos (which they would have done well before: see III.26ff. for the timing), and no doubt the Spartans despatched it as soon as it was collected. Being part of the plan, they might be said to 'catch up with' (καταλαμβάνουσι) the smaller fleet ready and waiting at Cyllene: a fleet by itself inadequate (thirteen against twelve Athenians from Naupactos). στασιάζουσαν will then refer, not to the time when the *whole* Spartan plan (including the thirteen ships at Cyllene) was made, nor to the time when the ships actually sailed to Corcyra, but to the time when the thirteen ships were reinforced by Alcidas' fleet, or when the Spartans ordered the reinforcement. The phrase πλέον τὸ ναυτικον ποιήσαντες has to be stressed.

When did Alcidas arrive at Cyllene? He sailed for Corcyra on Day 8, and we must allow a day or two for the 'preparations' made with Brasidas, whatever these were (perhaps collecting troops to fight at Corcyra if necessary?); so not after Day 6. But not much before Day 6 either; for if the Spartans put their reinforcement plan into effect at the beginning of the *stasis*, it would still take them a few days to issue orders for the ships to go to Cyllene, and for the ships to get there. That remains true wherever they were in the Peloponnese, and whether or not they had been collected together after arriving σποράδες ('in small groups', 69.1). Also the Spartans wanted the fleet to anticipate any reinforcements from Athens, so there should have been no undue delay at Cyllene after Alcidas' arrival. However, on Day 5, by our reckoning, the Corinthian trireme with Spartan delegates probably arrived at Cyllene, having left Corcyra on Day 3: it brought news of the failure of the *oligoi* in their fighting against the *demos*, and may well have caused some debate and hesitation in the minds of the Spartan commanders. We cannot hope for precision here: but Alcidas seems to have reached Cyllene sometime around Day 4-6.

One question remains: why did not the central Spartan authorities reinforce the thirteen ships earlier, thereby avoiding delay? It is possible that they did not anticipate the *stasis*; or, somewhat more plausibly, that they did not fully believe that the *oligoi* meant business, and were unwilling to commit forty ships to an indefinite wait at Cyllene until the *oligoi* proved their good faith by an actual coup. But that seems unlikely, since it is probable that the coup had been timed in conjunction with the Spartans, as the arrival of the Corinthian trireme (72.2) strongly suggests. The other possibility is that the Spartan authorities were unable, rather than unwilling,

to get Alcidas' ships to Cyllene any quicker than they did. We do
not of course know how much time, if any, elapsed between their
arrival in the Peloponnese and their being ordered to Cyllene; and
it is, admittedly, somewhat of a coincidence if they arrived only
just in time for the first days of the *stasis*. Nevertheless, the
first sentence of ch.69 (and perhaps καταλαμβάνουσιν ('met up
with') in particular) might be thought to suggest this; and of
these two alternatives, the latter seems to me on the whole preferable.

(ii) The Athenians

The timing here is in general simpler. In 70.6 Peithias' associates
escape to the Athenian trireme: this trireme must sail at once for
Athens, since it is very soon afterwards followed by the delegates
of the *oligoi* who are to persuade τοὺς καταπεφευγότας ('the
fugitives': these must be Peithias' supporters). The Athenians
know about the coup probably first from this trireme, which left
(see above) on Day -2, arriving about Day 3. Earlier than this, the
news had reached Naupactos: probably the trireme had passed the message
on to be carried by a ship or boat in the Cephallenia-Zacynthos area
(both these places being allies of Athens) - this could be timed at
perhaps Day 0, and the news reached Naupactos on Day 2. Nicostratos
starts at once, and reaches Corcyra on Day 4. Nicostratos was about
to sail away soon after that (Days 5 or 6: 75.2) but did not. In
fact he must have stayed at least until Eurymedon arrived (Day 13),
since just before that arrival the Messenian hoplites, whom surely
he would not have permanently relinquished to Corcyrean control,
are still there (81.2). Probably he left as soon as Eurymedon
came, in order to get back to his job at Naupactos as soon as possible.

Eurymedon arrived on Day 13, presumably therefore starting from
Athens about Day 8, some five days after the Athenians had heard th
news. The Athenians sent him πυνθανόμενοι τὴν στάσιν καὶ τὰς
μετ' Ἀλκίδου ναῦς ('when they learned about the *stasis* and about
the ships with Alcidas', 80.2). They knew of the initial coup about
Day 3 from the single Athenian trireme, but waited for further information - the trireme would not have brought news about Alcidas'
instructions. Alcidas, as we saw earlier, arrived at Cyllene round
about Day 4-6; hardly time for news of this to reach Athens and for
the Athenians to prepare sixty ships to sail on Day 8. But Thucydides
says nothing about Cyllene; and the Athenians could have had news
of Spartan intentions and Alcidas' instructions from other sources,
before he reached Cyllene. Such news perhaps arrived about Day 6,
leaving two days for preparing the fleet: for the Athenians would have
made no delay, once they realised that the twelve ships from Naupactos
would be insufficient to handle things in Corcyra.

There is one other piece of evidence to be fitted in, relevant to
the timing but also interesting in itself. Of the twelve Athenian
ships at the sea-fight, two were the Salaminia and the Paralos (77.3).
These must be the same twelve ships which Nicostratos first came
with (75.1), and the two special triremes were therefore at
Naupactos then. They are also very likely to be the same twelve
ships which the Spartans refer to in 69.2, despite attempts by
Steup and Gomme (see Gomme, p.365) to juggle with the numbers. That
reference is difficult to date exactly, but it is certainly some

time before the beginnings of the coup: the Spartan plans were formed
before those beginnings, and the plans took account of the twelve
ships. The Salaminia and Paralos were therefore at Naupactos at
that time. Our own time-scheme does not require orders to be sent
from Athens to Naupactos by one or both of these special triremes,
so there is no problem there.

These two ships were in the Aegean earlier in the summer
(see III.33), and were presumably sent to Naupactos from Athens after
that. They can hardly have formed part of the regular squadron at
Naupactos (if there was a regular squadron, and whatever it was: we
are very badly informed on these points), and the likely implication is that they joined it just because the Athenians knew that
some kind of trouble was brewing in Corcyra. Swift ships, with some
kind of diplomatic status, might be needed nearer the scene of action.
Neither of them, however, was the trireme that arrived at Corcyra
before the first vote; if either had been, Thucydides would almost
certainly have said so: and anyway that trireme (on Day -2, by our
timing) went straight back to Athens, not to Naupactos. It is possible that when Nicostratos left Corcyra, they returned to Athens.

DAY	CYLLENE	NAUPACTOS	ATHENS	CORCYRA
?	(Brasidas' fleet present)			First vote: Corin-thian trireme leaves: Peithias' acquittal and counter-charge: *oligoi* condemned.
-2	Corinthian trireme with Spartan dele-gates sent to Corcyra			Beginning of coup (70.6): Athenian trireme leaves with Peithias' friends.
-2/-1				Assembly and second vote: *oligoi* send ships to Athens.
0				Corinthian trireme arrives from Cyllene: *oligoi* attack *demos*.
1				Freedom offered to slaves, mercenaries hired.
2		News reaches Nicostratos: he sets out for Corcyra		

DAY	CYLLENE	NAUPACTOS	ATHENS	CORCYRA
3			Trireme with Peithias' friends arrives	*Demos* victorious: mercenaries and Corinthian trireme leave.
4				Nicostratos arrives.
5	Corinthian trireme arrives.			Events of 75
6	Alcidas' fleet arrives.			Events of 75.
7				
8	Alcidas starts for Corcyra.		Eurymedon starts for Corcyra.	
9				
10				Alcidas reaches Sybota.
11				Sea-fight.
12				Alcides ravages Corcyra: leaves at night. Massacre starts.
13				Eurymedon arrives: Nicostratos leaves.
14-20				Massacres continue
20				Eurymedon leaves

C. Numbers of *Oligoi* and Weakness of the *Demos*

How many *oligoi* were there? This question is both vague and difficult, but it is important for our understanding of what opposition the *demos* had to face, and to the extent to which the destruction of the *oligoi* crippled Corcyra. Thucydides gives us enough evidence to reach some conclusions, albeit imprecise: but the reasoning is complicated.

The best place to start is 75.2-5. In 3 and 4 one group of *oligoi*, and only one, is mentioned: those whom the *demos* nominated for their five ships. These are the τοὺς ἐχθροὺς ('enemies') and the ἐκεῖνοι of 3, and must also be the same as the αὐτοὺς and the αὐτῶν (three times) in 4. They appear first in the temple of the Dioscuri and then outside it (αὐτῶν τινὰς οἷς ἐπέτυχον, 'some of them whom they happened to come across'), because in between Nicostratos has raised and removed them from their place of supplication (ἀνίστη: a common use). Then in 5 there are οἱ ἄλλοι, 'the others': that is, if Thucydides means what he says, *all* the others, not just some of the others (ἄλλοι). These, at least 400, go to the precinct of Hera. They are moved from the precinct to the island (75.5) and back again (79.1). In 80.1 the *demos* enter into negotiations with them and τοῖς ἄλλοις: again, this must mean '*the* others', and most naturally refers to the former group of *oligoi* nominated for the five ships, the only 'others' hitherto mentioned.

That, at least, is what Thucydides actually says. Editors have characteristically not taken it seriously, and assumed references to much larger numbers of *oligoi* or supporters for the *oligoi*, thereby getting into unnecessary tangles. Gomme's note, for instance, reads (p.364): 'οἱ ἄλλοι: "the rest of the oligarchs", that is, those who had not taken refuge at the temple of the Dioskoroi, as well as those who had not been called for service in the five ships'. [I do not understand 'as well as': these two groups are identical.] 'But the figure of 400 which is now given seems to describe *all* the oligarchs who are nervous of democratic promises, which means most oligarchs (82.7)'. [82.7 in fact tells us nothing about this particular situation, and nothing about numbers of *oligoi*.] '... There were, naturally, yet other "oligarchs" who were not revolutionaries (τοῖς ἄλλοις of 80.1).' [The concept of 'revolutionaries' is not in question: fighting had already begun (72-74). And τοῖς ἄλλοις does not naturally mean 'yet others' of the *oligoi*, but 'the others'.]

Prima facie, then, the *oligoi* at this stage consist of two groups. One numbered 400. The other were nominees for five ships: how many of them were there? The natural implication of what Thucydides says - τοὺς ἐχθροὺς κατέλεγον ἐς τὰς ναῦς (75.3) - is that the *demos* nominated their enemies for *all* the posts on board. But that can hardly apply to posts as rowers: Corcyrean rowers were, characteristically at least, slaves; and anyway the number - 170 x 5, plus *epibatai* - seems far too large. Nor would the *oligoi* be trained as rowers; and Nicostratos would not have been willing to accept untrained rowers. We can more reasonably assume that their posts were as *epibatai*; and the chances are, though we cannot be certain, that their numbers were on the Sybota model (perhaps forty *epibatai* per ship)

and not on the Athenian (usually about ten or twelve). An additional
reason for larger numbers of hoplite *epibatai* would be the *demos'*
desire to get rid of as many *oligoi* as possible in this way. Plausible
figures, then, are in the region of 5 x 40, i.e. something like 200
men. That gives us a total of 600 *oligoi*.

We go back now to 72-74. In 72 the *oligoi* are on top; in 73 they
acquire 800 mercenaries, and the *demos* is joined by the majority of
the household slaves; in 74 the *demos* is victorious. If we assume,
somewhat arbitrarily, that 100 *oligoi* were killed in the fighting
(which seems to have been fairly severe), we have the following
picture. To begin with, when the *demos* is disorganised and unsup-
ported, 700 well-armed and well-prepared *oligoi* are in control. But
within two days (see below on the timing), despite the 800 mercenaries,
the *demos* prevails partly because of its superior numbers (πλήθει
προύχων, 74.1); as against a minimum of 1500 well-armed men, we
must assume a very large number in the *demos*, perhaps as many as
5,000, with additional support from the majority of the slaves (73.1).
This host, after the mercenaries go off to the mainland (74.3), has only
600 *oligoi*, at most, to deal with. Then Nicostratos arrives, and
the events described above take place.

It is likely that at some stage a good many more *oligoi* must come
into the picture, and certain that there is one stage for the active
intrusion of more *oligoi*: that is, the sea-fight (77). There must have
been many men of the hoplite class, potential members of the *oligoi*
party, who might have joined it before had not Nicostratos' intervention made that difficult or impossible. Amongst these will be
epibatai on the sixty ships manned against the Peloponnesians. Two
of these ships immediately deserted, and on others the crews were
fighting amongst themselves. The Peloponnesians were described as
having (ἔχοντες, 79.2) thirteen Corcyrean ships when they sailed
back to Sybota, but nothing is said about any Corcyrean ships being
sunk or damaged: it seems clear that these ships, and perhaps others,
had at least some pro-Peloponnesian crew members, and were captured
without wholehearted resistance. On this occasion, though the Corcyreans were in a hurry, there is no reason not to assume a full
complement of *epibatai* on the ships: perhaps about forty, as usual.
That might suggest, very roughly, something like 300 *oligoi* who in
effect deserted.

This figure, though of some interest, does not help us because, of
course, they were no longer present: we are still left with only 600
oligoi in 80.1 - 'the suppliants' (τοῖς ἱκέταις) and 'the rest'
(τοῖς ἄλλοις). The *demos* persuades some of them (τινας) to go on
board the ships of the second fleet, of which thirty were manned.
The figures here are also of some significance. Suppose, generously,
that the *demos* persuaded 200 of this group of 600 to go on board:
that would amount to only six or seven *epibatai* per ship. It is
clear that they were desperately needed, otherwise the *demos* would not
have taken the risk of their deserting (as had happened in the earlier
battle); and this reinforces the hypothesis that the men of the *demos*
were, in general, not equipped as hoplites, though some of them
served as *epibatai* on the thirty ships, to keep an eye on the *oligoi*.

We now turn to the events of 81. The striking point here is that
the *demos* still feels itself weak in face of the *oligoi*, and hence
adopts a skilful 'divide and rule' set of tactics. First the leaders

of the *demos* bring in the 500 Messenian hoplites, whom they must have regarded as a necessary protection: then they get the fleet temporarily out of the way by ordering it to sail to the Hyllaic harbour. White it is doing so, they kill (a) any enemies they can find on the spot; then (b) the *oligoi* on the fleet, as they land; and (c) the suppliants in the precinct of Hera. The original 600 *oligoi* are those in (b) and (c). Those in (a) are just 'enemies' (τῶν ἐχθρῶν , 81.2); so too are those whom they kill (d) during the subsequent seven days; some are just 'thought' to be enemies (τοὺς ἐχθροὺς δοκοῦντας εἶναι) and others the victims of purely private hatred (ἰδίας ἔχθρας ἔνεκα, 81.4).

There is no evidence at this stage of any large or well-organised party or band of *oligoi*: and a strong negative argument from Thucydides' silence. No doubt there were plenty of middle- and upper-class (if these terms are appropriate) men of hoplite rank and above-average wealth, who had not - or not yet - organised themselves for military resistance, or had no strong reason to oppose the régime. The extreme care and subtlety which the *demos* showed in the first stages of the purge suggests, not a large number of *oligoi* so organised, but (1) the potentiality of this in the large number of sympathisers - the *demos* thought it necessary to act fast in order to prevent their organisation; and (2) the *demos'* own military weakness, partly no doubt due to lack of hoplite equipment and training. It was safe to kill (a) those on the spot, since those on the fleet and in the precinct of Hera would be ignorant or unable to intervene; so too with (b), at the *demos*-controlled Hyllaic harbour; and those in (c) were now totally isolated and (as they recognised by their suicide) stood no chance at all. The whole 600, parcelled up in this way, were thus effectively liquidated, together with a large number of ἔχθροι.

The 500 who eventually escaped were not, as far as we know, survivors of any organised party or band of *oligoi*. It is striking that Thucydides never describes them as such throughout III.85 and the longer passage which relates their final liquidation (IV.46-48). They are called simply οἱ φεύγοντες τῶν Κερκυραίων ('those of the Corcyreans who were fleeing', 85.2), τοὺς ἐν τῷ ὄρει ... καθιδρυμένους ('those established on the mountain', IV.46.1), or τῶν ἐν τῇ νήσῳ ('those on the island', 46.5). The same element of private vendetta occurs: the prisoners were κεντουμένους ὑπό τῶν παρατεταγμένων, εἴ πού τίς τινα ἴδοι ἐχθρὸν ἑαυτοῦ ('stabbed by those between whom they passed, whevever anyone saw a personal enemy' 47.3).

Some light is also thrown on the weakness of the *demos* and the nature of the Corcyrean state generally by 85.1-2. Only about 500 men were involved: no doubt mostly of the hoplite class, but it is doubtful whether they even managed to escape with their arms and armour, let alone many negotiable valuables (indeed they only scraped up about 100 allies, as compared with the 800 mercenaries whom the *oligoi* hired from the mainland in 73). Nevertheless they seize forts on the mainland and control the Corcyrean territory there, the *demos* apparently powerless to prevent them. Not only that: their plundering raids did a great deal of damage and produced a major famine, which continued at least until 425 (IV.2.3). This reinforces the impression that the *demos* by itself was virtually impotent from a military point of view. But it is also true that the rebels were well placed on Mt. Istone, the only major (and highly defensible) mountain on the

99

island, the modern Pandocrator: and it gives directly onto the
northern strait. The 500 with their 100 allies could have crossed
to it without risking interception, and used it to continue their
depredations in that area. They thus had a strong and (for the
demos) excessively troublesome position. Thucydides goes so far
as to say ἐκράτουν τῆς γῆς: this must mean, as Gomme says (p.386),
that they were 'masters of the open country' (i.e. the country as
opposed to the towns, not of Corcyra as a whole). But that is
remarkable for only 600 men, even if we take it to mean only the
open country in their area, the northern part of the island (it is
hard to believe that they controlled the south-east, some thirty
miles distant and only to be reached by passing very close to
the city). The *demos* can hardly have had many effective troops
under its command.

How much help did the *demos* need from the Athenians? After the
Pylos campaign in 425, the Athenian generals Eurymedon and Sophocles
arrived at Corcyra with an unspecified number of ships (Thucydides
just says ναυσίν, IV.46.1) on their way to Sicily. Hermocrates, in
his speech at the Gela conference (IV.60), speaks of the ὀλίγαις
ναυσί ('few ships') of the Athenians; but he is out to belittle
the Athenians, and ὀλίγαις is anyway not precise. In IV.65 the
Athenians punish the three generals severely on the grounds that
they could have taken control of the island: not a plausible indict-
ment if the ships had been less than, say, twenty in number. *Prima
facie* the generals had at least the ships they had set out to Sicily
with originally, i.e. forty (IV.2.2): I see no reason to suppose
otherwise. In any case, the chief point is that the Corcyrean
demos needed to wait for Athenian support (however small: and it was
probably more than minimal) in order to overcome 600 men.
  Does that mean - to put the question briefly if imprecisely - that
the *demos* had massacred vast numbers of potential *oligoi*, or that there
had never been many potential *oligoi* in the first place? The latter
is perhaps nearer to the truth than the former. There is reason to
believe that Corcyra's hoplite strength was never very great; and no
small number of these men would have been killed at Sybota, since the
Corinthians at one stage of the battle chose to kill rather than
take prisoners. It is perhaps over-bold even to suggest tentative
figures, but if we assume the ratio of killed to captured was something like 4:1 (a fairly conservative assumption) we obtain the
following:

(1) 1,000 hoplite *epibatai* killed at Sybota (250 captured);
(2) 700 *oligoi* massacred or otherwise killed before Eurymedon's arrival;
(3) 300 *oligoi* on ships deserting to or captured by Peloponnesians.

Total: 2,000. that is about the highest number we can be certain of,
if by 'potential *oligoi*' we refer (however vaguely) to men of hoplite
rank and wealth. There may, of course, have been more: for we have
omitted the two classes of (4) the 500 escapees, and (5) those massacred after Eurymedon's arrival. But it is not clear that either of
these classes included many potential *oligoi*, as opposed to ἐχθροί
(or, in the case of the escapees, potential ἐχθροί). No doubt
they contained some, but my guess is that most potential *oligoi* were
massacred before Eurymedon came: thereafter it became more of a general blood-bath than anything seriously to be described as purely

political faction. A combined total of 3,000 might be regarded as an absolute maximum. But at this point the discussion becomes impossibly speculative. (See also on the second *stasis*, section G below).

D. The Sea-fight

The Peloponnesian fleet went first to Sybota on the mainland, spent the night there, and only advanced further at daybreak (76). We do not know their movements between Cyllene and Sybota; but it is clear that they did not try to catch the Corcyreans completely unprepared, since they would certainly have been observed (from Leukimme) making for Sybota. They could have done so with profit, if they had been prepared either to spend the night further south, out of observation (perhaps at Glycys Limen: see on the Sybota campaign above), and descend as quickly as possible on Corcyra at first light: or else to sail through the night so as to arrive off the island at that time. That they did not perhaps argues their fear of meeting Athenian or Corcyrean ships en route, or at least characteristic caution in naval matters.

The Corcyreans were, in any case, not well prepared. It seems virtually certain that they occupied no base at Leukimme, as they had in the Sybota campaign: no mention of this or indeed of any point on the coast enters into Thucydides' description, and the probability is that they simply sent out their hastily-manned sixty ships from the city to meet the advancing Peloponnesians on the morning of the battle. The battle may thus have occurred anywhere between Sybota and Corcyra city; probably nearer the latter than the former. For it seems as if the Corcyreans, though they must have been aware on the previous day of the fleet at Sybota, did not man their ships in sufficient time to meet the Peloponnesians at dawn nearer to Sybota. They were either unable or unwilling to do this: perhaps they hoped that the Peloponnesians would not advance further. It would have been to the Corcyreans' advantage to get as close as possible, since (as in 433) to allow the Peloponnesians to get through the narrows before fighting gave the Peloponnesians much greater chances of monoeuvre and attack - both at sea, and in any attempts they might make at a landing on Corcyra itself (see map).

The Athenians' advice was presumably given chiefly because they thought (justifiably, in the event) that the Corcyrean fleet was too disorganised to be of much use: it would simply be a sitting target for the Peloponnesians, and perhaps interfere with Athenian manoeuvres; and its destruction by the Peloponnesians would improve Peloponnesian morale. The advice was good; but why did the Corcyreans not take it and let the Athenians sail out first? There is a problem here, since the Corcyreans would not normally be unwilling to rely on the Athenians bearing the brunt of the battle, and running the greatest risks. It is possible that they simply disagreed about tactics; but I suspect that the *demos* did not like the idea of parting with the Athenian ships even for a short period - they relied on them, overtly or tacitly, to keep the *oligoi* (including potential and suspected *oligoi*) under control.

The Corcyreans attacked κακῶς τε καὶ κατ' ὀλίγας, 'inefficiently and in small detachments'. They did not use the διέκπλους;

101

and, by bringing only small detachments at a time against the
Peloponnesians, invited the probability of being outnumbered. The
internal strife amongst the ships' crews on the Corcyrean side would
in any case be disastrous. We are to imagine, perhaps, that (apart
from the straightforward deserters) many Corcyrean ships were in
effect immobile, an easy prey for being disabled and captured. Since
thirteen were captured and none sunk, there cannot have been much
of a battle: certainly the ram could not have been much used. The
Corcyrean disorder is all the more striking in that they had three
times the enemy's numbers: sixty against twenty.

The Athenians φοβούμενοι τὸ πλῆθος καὶ τὴν περικύκλωσιν
ἀθρόαις μὲν οὐ προσέπιπτον οὐδὲ κατὰ μέσον ταῖς ἐφ' ἑαυτοὺς
τεταγμέναις, προσβαλόντες δὲ κατὰ κέρας καταδύουσι μίαν ναῦν
(see translation below). Gomme says (ad loc.): '... although κατὰ
κέρας ... is opposed to κατὰ μέσον rather than to ἀθρόαις, edd.
are probably right in taking ἀ.with ταῖς ... τεταγμέναις, rather
than as "with all their ships at once" ...' This misses the point
and does nothing to elucidate ἀθρόαις: though that word does indeed
go with ταῖς ... τεταγμέναις. ἀθρόαις is contrasted with
μίαν ναῦν as κατὰ μέσον is contrasted with κατὰ κέρας; to these
correspond their fears about τὸ πλῆθος and περικύκλωσιν
respectively. They wish (1) to avoid attacking large numbers of
Peloponnesian ships, and therefore sink (and perhaps engage) only
one; (2) to avoid attacking the Peloponnesian line in the middle for
fear of being encircled, and therefore attack on the wing. We translate: '... fearing the numbers of the enemy and the possibility of
being encircled, did not attack the ships ranged against them where
they were all crowded together, nor in the centre, but attacked on the
wing and sank one ship'. The Athenians kept their distance from the
main body, and then made a sudden advance on one wing (sinking one
ship) - an attack from which they could extricate themselves easily,
relying on superior speed and the absence of Peloponnesian ships on
one quarter. (Probably the Athenians were stationed on the right
wing: that had been their position in the Sybota campaign, and it also
makes better tactical sense. One important consideration for the
Corcyreans was to prevent a landing on Corcyra; and the more redoubtable
Athenian ships would be better placed to do that if on the right wing,
nearest to the Corcyrean coast.)

The Peloponnesians form into a circle; the Athenians sail round and
round trying to create confusion in the circle. The thirty-two ships
forming the circle are now assisted by the twenty which had been dealing with the Corcyreans: this of course prevented the Athenians from
continuing to sail around the perimeter, since their ships would have
been broadside to any kind of attack by the twenty. So the Athenians
form line and back water slowly, to give the Corcyreans time for an
ordered retreat: that is, a retreat in which they too continued to
face the enemy. This went on until sunset.

The timing is remarkable, since the Peloponnesians started out at
dawn. They might have spent perhaps two or three hours rowing to
wherever the scene of the battle was (no longer, or they would have
been at Corcyra city by that time). What happened in the battle itself does not seem enough to have occupied the remaining hours of
daylight, even granted that the Athenians' retreat was slow: it was
quite unlike the hard slogging match of the Sybota battle. We must

102

suppose that long periods of time were consumed in which neither party
chose to commit themselves to attacking. That is in general true of
the Athenians (the sudden assault on the Peloponnesian left wing was
not a major attack); and to judge from 78.1 it was true of the
Peloponnesians also, vis-à-vis the Corcyreans. For it is the
Corcyreans there who actually make the attack (προσπίπτοντες),
however badly: no mention is made of Peloponnesian attacks at all.
The implication is that the Peloponnesians simply waited - as they
might well have done, seeing the chaos of the Corcyreans and perhaps
hoping for more deserters - until the Corcyreans attacked; then the
beat them off, and captured what ships they could. The Corcyreans
themselves may well have waited also, given their chaos and disorgani-
sation, before making their attacks.

The Peloponnesians contented themselves with ravaging the eastern
part of Corcyra: should Brasidas' advice have been taken? *Prima
facie* it is difficult to see how the town could have been captured,
provded the walls were properly manned and the harbours properly
guarded or closed. But the existence of the *oligoi* - at that stage
of the proceedings still fairly numerous (see above) - increased the
chances of confusion or betrayal, and there may have been a good chance
of taking the town: or, if not that, of blockading the Athenian and
Corcyrean ships in the harbours or destroying them if they gave
battle. Unfortunately we have no evidence about the number of troops
that the Peloponnesians had with them: it cannot, however, have been
much less than about 1,000 (twenty *epibatai* per ship) and may well
have been much more, since it must have been clear to Alcidas and
Brasidas that the situation might call for operations by land. Anything between 1,000 and 2,000 would have been enough to give them a
fighting chance, so that Brasidas' advice was at least not grossly
foolhardy.

Was the real risk (and perhaps Alcidas' eventual decision) based
on the possibility that a stronger fleet might arrive from Athens,
as in fact it did? Since the Peloponnesians were only informed by
the fire-signals more or less at the last minute, it seems that they
could not rely on much advance warning of this; so that, if they had
disembarked their fleet at Corcyra (instead of being ready to sail
from Sybota, as they actually were), they would not have had time
to escape. But that is not conclusive: for the question arises whether
they would have needed to escape at all. Much would have depended on
their actual situation in Corcyra. If, for example, they had managed
to get control of the city and to put their ships in an easily-
defensible position - inside the Hyllaic harbour, which could be
closed, or even in the other harbour where land forces could defend
them -, it is hard to see what an Athenian fleet could have done
against them, since it would not have carried enough land forces to
mount its own attack by land. It could, of course, have settled down
to blockade the Peloponnesian fleet; but a permanent blockade would
have been very expensive, and would have tied up a large number of
Athenian ships and men for the doubtful advantage of preventing the
Peloponnesians from leaving Corcyra. In such a large island there
would be no possibility, as at Sphacteria, of starving them out, or
of mounting an effective land attack without a considerable number
of hoplites (which Athens could ill spare).

The civil strife in Corcyra, however, really made it impossible
for the Peloponnesians to feel secure in capturing and permanently

occupying the city and the island without risk. The *demos* was more
or less in control, and any occupying force would be in a minority:
that, together with what the Athenians might do, made the whole situation far too much a matter of chance. Nor would there have been much
gain to the Peloponnesians, other than that of denying Corcyra to
Athens - certainly an objective worth pursuing (and they were in fact
pursuing it), but not at the risk of losing substantial numbers of
Peloponnesian ships and men. For the Corcyrean navy had, by now,
been partly ruined and perhaps irremediably demoralised: the navy
was Corcyra's main potential benefit to Athens, and that benefit no
longer existed. Even if Alcidas had managed to achieve an ideal
position before the Athenians arrived, the gains to Sparta would
thus have been minimal: and the risk of being caught in a less
satisfactory position - the city uncaptured and the ships not in a
place of safety - was too great. His decision was the right one.

E. Athenian and Spartan Intervention

It is sufficiently clear that Athens should have taken Corcyra in
hand right from the start, certainly before 427. Nevertheless, the
situation was in principle retrievable even in 427, had the Athenian
generals acted sensibly. Unfortunately they displayed simple-mindedness
and criminal negligence. It is of course possible that they were acting
under strict orders from Athens, though that is not likely in the case
of Nicostratos who sailed straight from Naupactos; but the probability
is that they had a good deal of latitude. In any case their actions,
which we are to consider, speak for themselves.

Nicostratos arrived with twelve ships and 500 Messenian hoplites:
that is, if we include the usual *epibatai*, about 600 hoplites and
2,000 other crewmen. He first persuades, or at least tries to
persuade, the Corcyreans to adopt the settlement in 75.1 - political
agreement all round and a full *symmachy* with Athens. He is then *about
to sail away* (75.2), possibly imagining - if such credulity is believable - that the *demos* will stand by their agreement. The *demos* keeps
him there; perhaps unwisely in view of what he might still have done
to prevent the *stasis* (but did not: see below), but they need his
unconscious participation in getting rid of more *oligoi*. Nicostratos
agrees to take five Corcyrean ships and leave five Athenian in Corcyra
(in itself foolish, since the Corcyreans would be much less efficient
than those in his already tenuous squadron: did he think he could
rival, if necessary, Phormio's exploits with only seven Athenian
ships?), and lets the *demos* decide who is to go in them. He fails
(unsurprisingly) to reassure the nominees for the Corcyrean ships,
and fails also to prevent the *demos* stealing the arms from their
houses; having himself removed the nominees from sanctuary, thereby
making them natural targets for the *demos*, the least he can then do
is to prevent the *demos* killing them (75.4). He then fails to make
the Corcyreans deploy their ships as they ought (77.1).
    In the naval battle he performs well; and so far we might accuse
him of incompetence rather than criminal negligence. However, after
the battle he not only fails to exercise any control over the *demos*,
but allows them to use his 500 Messenians as protection during the

massacre. Some hundreds of *oligoi*, as we saw earlier, were slaughtered while Nicostratos was in Corcyra, the massacre continuing after
Eurymedon's arrival - whether or not Eurymedon ranked senior to
Nicostratos and was primarily responsible. It is thus difficult to
understand Gomme's remarks on him, particularly the reference to
his 'political intelligence and humanity' (p.366). The reverse is
true.

Could he have pleaded inability? His acquiescence in the use of
the Messenian hoplites is strongly against any such plea; and anyway
there were plenty of options open to him. He could have told the
demos that unless they abided by the settlement, Athens would leave
Corcyra open to the Peloponnesians. He could have taken hostages
from both sides. He could, in all likelihood, have controlled the
situation, confused as it was, right at the start with 600 hoplites
and 2,000 other well-organised men under his command. Indeed he had
at least two chances to do this: before and after the battle. After
the battle, the *demos* were in despair over the difficulties in producing a fleet: Nicostratos could have bargained the Athenian ships
against more or less anything. He could have refused to exchange
the five ships. He could, with his fleet, at least have prevented
the ordering of the ships round to the Hyllaic harbour and thus the
consequent slaughter. Possibilities can be multiplied: it seems
clear that the man was, in this sort of context, disastrously
incompetent.

With Eurymedon there is no question of any plea of inability: he
had sixty ships (600 hoplites and 10,000 others), and presumably the
500 Messenians until Nicostratos took them back to Naupactos.
Eurymedon simply allowed the massacre to continue. Perhaps it seemed
to him, at that stage (when the back of the resistance of the *oligoi*
had been clearly broken), simply not worth trying to restore unity
between two parties, at the cost of some Athenian lives. Nevertheless
only some 700 *oligoi* had so far died, and Eurymedon could and should
have stopped things from going further: not only for humanitarian
reasons, but because the Corcyra alliance was only worth anything
much to Athens if backed by the ship-owners and hoplites (many of
whom would be amongst the *oligoi*) as well as by the *demos*. It is
true that, at least from the viewpoint of a doctrinaire democrat,
the *demos* could be regarded as the legal or constitutional govern-
ment, and the *oligoi* as no more than a small band of terrorists;
but that viewpoint, in itself somewhat partisan, is irrelevant to
Athens' strategic needs. The final destruction of the *oligoi* two
years later (IV.46ff.) might, perhaps, be justified on the grounds
that things had gone too far for any reconciliation, and that an
omnipotent *demos* might be of more use to Athens if freed from
the rebel *oligoi* on Istone. But such a justification is barely convincing, and merely reinforces the impression of Athenian incompetence throughout the whole sad story.

In 425 the Spartans sent sixty ships to Corcyra, νομίζοντες κατα-
σχήσειν ῥᾳδίως τὰ πράγματα 'thinking that they would easily
get control of things', IV.2.3), not an unreasonable belief, in
view of the weakness of the *demos* (see above). They had already
arrived before the Athenians fortified Pylos (IV.3.1), and were not
recalled until a good mnay days later (see IV.4-8). Yet, from

Thucydides' silence, it appears that they made no impression on
Corcyra. The implication must be that, despite the *demos*' weakness,
no swift or sudden attack was likely to be successful: we remember
that the city was walled, and the Hyllaic harbour at least could
be closed. With the only *oligoi* now at some distance on Istone,
there was little chance of treachery from inside the town. If the
Spartans could have settled down to a blockade by both sea and land,
they would probably have reduced the city in a fairly short time,
particularly in view of the famine: but not short enough in relation to the time they actually had. It may also be relevant that
their commander, Thrasymelidas, seems from his behaviour at Pylos
not to have been particularly efficient (IV.13-14).

Why did they not intervene in 426? The answer must be that they
were deterred by the Athenian fleet which spent a good deal of time
at Leucas and around the Acarnanian coastline (III.94ff.). They
appreciated, perhaps, the point just made - that they required a
fairly long period of time to have much hope of success - and were
fearful of being caught between Corcyra and their home base (wherever
this was: probably Cyllene again). To the Spartans, Corcyra was a
long way off; and in view of their extremely narrow escapes (in 427
and 425), they were probably right to be cautious.

F. The Western Greeks

So far we have considered only one of the two reasons alleged for the
strategic importance of Corcyra in I.36 - the strength of the Corcyrean navy. How important was the other reason, her geographical
position? And how far were these two reasons connected? It is not
in dispute that this importance (however large or small) relates
primarily or wholly to the route between mainland Greece and the
western Greeks: Corcyra's position vis-à-vis the Adriatic route is
not in question, since that route had no obvious strategic relevance.
The Corcyreans claim firmly that τῆς τε γὰρ Ἰταλίας καὶ Σικελίας
καλῶς παράπλου κεῖται, ὥστε μήτε ἐκεῖθεν ναυτικὸν ἐᾶσαι
Πελοποννησίοις ἐπελθεῖν τό τε ἐνθένδε πρὸς τἀκεῖ παραπέμψαι,
καὶ ἐς τἆλλα ξυμφορώτατόν ἐστιν (for translation see earlier);
and we have first to determine the meaning of this claim (whether
true or false).

(a) παράπλου must mean 'sailing route along the coast', not just any
sailing route: that is, the normal route along the west coast of Greece,
across from Corcyra to the heel of Italy, and from there along the
Italian and Sicilian coastline according to the sailor's destination.
This might be thought to weaken the Corcyreans' claim, if we regard
the clause as under the influence of παράπλου: '... so that - by that
route, anyway - Corcyra can stop ships ...'. The interpretation is
possible, but perhaps slightly forced; moreover, if we adopt it, we
have to raise the question of just how much the Corcyreans' claim
amounted to. For if the Corcyreans tacitly grant that Corcyra cannot block other routes to and from Italy and Sicily we at least
need to know how easy those other routes were. We shall consider this
below.

(b) ναυτικὸν always refers to a war fleet or a naval force, not
to individual merchantmen; and anyway merchant ships could go to and
from Greece and the west without using the coastal route. The large
sailing merchant ship, the ὁλκας, could certainly do this: but it does
not follow, as some have implied, that ναυτικὸν refers only to
triremes, nor that the open waters were dangerous to triremes alone.
There is an important intermediary category, what might be called the
military or naval *convoy*: as for instance the Corinthian one which
Phormio defeated in his first battle (II.85ff.). This would include
triremes, but also other shipping, not necessarily ὁλκαδες: sometimes even λεπτὰ πλοῖα (II.83.5), 'light boats'.

(c) καὶ ἐς τἆλλα ξυμφορώτατόν ἐστιν must mean 'and it is very
useful for other relevant things also'. τἆλλα, for which '*the* other
things' is too emphatic or clumsy a translation, nevertheless seems
to me to contain the idea that not just *any* other advantages that
Corcyra might bring to Athens are in question. Particularly in a
sentence entirely devoted to Corcyra's good position on the coastal
route, it must refer to advantages relevant to the use of that route.
These would include all the benefits which Athens would enjoy from
having a friendly base on the route to the west, with facilities for
supply and repair.

We may consider various routes in round figures for simplicity.
The passage from Corcyra to the Iapygian promontory in Italy is about
fifty miles. A route from Leucas or Actium (the most northerly of
the Peloponnesian possessions) to that promontory is about 150 miles;
it would avoid the Athenian bases at Cephallenia and Zacynthos, but
would normally pass fairly close to Corcyra. From the same starting-
points due west to Croton (the nearest destination) the distance is
about 200; and from Methone or Asine to various destinations in Italy
and Sicily, about 300. (For all this see map.)
    The brevity of the fifty-mile route brings many advantages with it.
Under conditions of good visibility, land is visible at all times,
which greatly facilitates navigation: and if stormy weather threatened, there would be far greater possibilities of turning back, or racing
the last few miles across, than there were on longer routes. Most
important of all, the distance could - with some effort - be covered
in a single stint, perhaps a single day, by triremes: so that full
advantage could be taken of settled weather. Any other route involves
several days' journey, with the consequently much increased risk of
storm - much more important than the necessity, tiresome but not
disastrous, of the crew's sleeping on board and having to navigate
during the hours of darkness.
    The relevance of the other routes depends on the general strategic
position. This in turn depended, first, on the ability of Corcyra
actually to stop triremes and convoys if they were in her neighbour-
hood. If her fleet was not efficient enough to do this, the Peloponnesians would not lose much; they might not be able to use Corcyra
as a friendly base, but they could use a near-by harbour (Sybota, for
example) so as to get a short crossing. If on the other hand her
fleet was efficient, it would prevent the fifty-mile crossing, and
might even render the 150-mile crossing (to the Iapygian promontory)
very risky. Secondly, if Athens (or Athens in conjunction with Corcyra)
were able to dominate the north-west, even the 200-mile crossing from

107

Leucas to Croton would be impossible: there would be no safe starting-point anywhere in the north-west area (Leucas, Cyllene, or wherever), and the Peloponnesians would be driven to use a route of at least 300 miles, with a starting-point further south or south-east in the Peloponnese itself. (The same points apply to this route in reverse, i.e. from the west to the Peloponnese.)

It will readily be seen that almost everything turns on these factors. Had Corcyra and Athens united in the north-west strategy, it would indeed have been impossible (as the Corcyreans claim) for the Peloponnesians or their Sicilian allies to send triremes or military convoys to each other with any safety. The 300-mile route (I have taken Methone and Asine as the nearest available ports, after the Athenians held Pylos) is extremely dangerous and lengthy: and that part of it which lies near the Peloponnese was within striking distance of Athenian forces based on Zacynthos or Pylos. Further, if the recommended policy of ἐπιτείχισις in Messenia and Laconia were already in force, the risk of any ship-movements round the Peloponnese would be impossibly great for the Peloponnesians.

Did the Corcyreans foresee these factors, or take them for granted? They would have taken the first for granted, having no reason to suppose that (if the Athenians gave them assistance against Corinth) their navy would be rendered ineffective, and therefore believing in their own power to prevent any but the most prepotent fleet from using the coastal route against their will. (The devastating results of the *stasis* could not have been anticipated.) But they can hardly have foreseen the second: if they had entertained any serious conception of a genuinely functional naval alliance with Athens, used to dominate the seas of the north-west, they would no doubt have produced this as an argument to the Athenians. It is not impossible that they thought along these lines; but if so, they never acted upon them - at no time did they ever offer Athens enough assistance to suggest awareness of such a policy. They might, however, have believed that Athens herself (perhaps with some spasmodic assistance from Corcyra) would sufficiently dominate the north-west seas to make the route from Leucas or the Corinthian Gulf impossible: an assumption which would justify their claim in 36.2. Some such assumption was necessary; for as the event proved (see below), they were not in fact able to prevent Gylippus and the Corinthians from reaching Sicily from Leucas, nor prevent the arrival of Sicilian ships to join the fighting in the Aegean. (See further in Appendix.)

The events of 415 and later illustrate these *a priori* strategic considerations. Gylippus, once appointed to his task of helping the Syracusans, first fixes a rendezvous for two Corinthian (and some Spartan) ships at Asine in Messenia. But he makes no attempt to cross from there (the 300-mile route): instead, they go to the Leucas area (περὶ Λευκάδα, VI.104.1). Gylippus crosses to Tarentum (*ibid.*), and twelve Corinthian ships join him later, also from Leucas (VII.2.1, 7.1). In VII.19 merchant ships carrying hoplites leave from Taenarum in Laconia, apparently on the long direct route (ἐς τὸ πέλαγος, 'to the open sea', 19.4); and others leave from Sicyon and Corinth, the twenty Athenian ships sent to Naupactos being held in check by twenty-five Corinthians anchored opposite them (VII.34).

The earlier ships (before VII.19) will naturally be triremes: the

Spartans were anxious to send help as quickly as possible, and probably adopted Alcibiades' advice that the same men should serve both
as rowers and as hoplites (αὐτερέται, VI.91.4), this being the
quickest and most economical way of producing a maximum of fighting
troops at short notice in Sicily. There were not many of them at
any time, and an effective Athenian (or Corcyrean) presence in the
Leucas area could easily have prevented them from crossing, particularly since they probably hung around there for some time
(waiting for news: VI.104.1). The Athenians in fact sent twenty
ships round the Peloponnese to prevent crossings to Sicily; but these
went to Naupactos, where the twenty-five Corinthian triremes held
them in check. There appears to have been no adequate Athenian
force at Zacynthos or Cephallenia.

The merchantmen from the Corinthian Gulf could similarly have been
prevented, even if there had been only a few Athenian ships guarding
the exit of the Gulf of Patras. But there were not: the merchantmen
got clean away from the Peloponnese (VII.19.5). Even the ships
from Taenarum might have been threatened by a small Athenian force
at Pylos, since merchantmen are extremely slow, and their route
might have been fairly close to it. But that force did not exist
either. It is, indeed, fairly evident that Athenian command of the
sea in western Greece, never decisive, had at this time
pretty well vanished: the quality and morale of Conon's and Diphilos'
fleet at Naupactos contrasts sharply with Phormio's (VII.31,34: cf.
II.83ff., particularly 88).

But we cannot excuse the Athenians on the grounds that there were
simply not enough ships available. At the very time when the merchantmen were being sent off from the Peloponnese, and the twenty-five
Corinthian triremes were making nonsense of Naupactos as a blockade-
post, Athens despatched a fleet of thirty ships and another sixty-
five (VII.20). These were of course intended for Sicily; but the
guarding of the north-west by even a few of them would have paid
much better dividends. Finally, even the fifteen ships which Eurymedon
told the Corcyreans to man (VII.31.5) would have sufficed to do the
job, if properly placed to intercept the Peloponnesians. If the
Athenians had had even the outline of the policy recommended earlier
- a genuine naval alliance and the permanent control of the north-
west - they might, even at this late stage, have averted the
Sicilian disaster.

The movement of Peloponnesian ships to Italy and Sicily was only of real
importance because of the Sicilian Expedition: indeed, only because
the fate of that expedition was in the balance, able to be swayed by
the arrival of Gylippus' and other reinforcements (VII.1-8ff.). But
the reverse possibility of reinforcements reaching the Peloponnese
from Italy and Sicily did not depend on this: even without what many
scholars - wrongly, in my own (and Thucydides', II.65.11) judgement -
see as the fatal mistake of Athens' attempt on Scicily, naval contingents from there could have played an enormous part in the war.

This is often denied, overtly or tacitly (see Gomme, p.171); partly
perhaps because the actual contributions were meagre (even Syracuse
only sent twenty-two ships in 411: VIII.26.1), partly because the
Spartan expectation at the start of the war for 200 ships from Italy
and Sicily (see below) is thought absurd. But there seems no doubt
at least that after Athens' defeat in Sicily both sides expected that

Sicilian forces would be important. The Athenians τούς τε ἀπὸ τῆς
Σικελίας πολεμίους εὐθὺς σφίσιν ἐνόμιζον τῷ ναυτικῷ ἐπὶ
τὸν Πειραιᾶ πλευσεῖσθαι, ἄλλως τε καὶ τοσοῦτον κρατήσαντες
(VIII.1.2), '... thought that their enemies from Sicily would at once
sail against them with their fleet to the Piraeus, especially since
they had won such a great victory'; and the Spartans were particularly encouraged by the fact that their Sicilian allies would join them
in the spring 'in great force' (VIII.2.3).

Some of the Spartan preparations and hopes before the war are
described thus: καὶ Λακεδαιμονίοις μὲν πρὸς ταῖς αὐτοῦ
ὑπαρχούσαις ἐξ Ἰταλίας καὶ Σικελίας τοῖς τἀκείνων ἐλομένοις
ναῦς ἐπετάχθη ποιεῖσθαι κατὰ μέγεθος τῶν πόλεων, ὡς ἐς τὸν
πάντα ἀριθμὸν πεντακοσίων νεῶν ἐσομένων (II.7.2); 'and the
Lacedaimonians, in addition to the fleet they had at home, ordered
the cities in Italy and Sicily which took their side to build ships
(the numbers of ships depending on size of the cities), so that the
total number of ships would be 500'. Apart from very drastic emendation,
we cannot avoid a minimum figure of 500 for the Peloponnesian fleet
plus the contributions of Italy and Sicily (following Diodorus, 12.
41: 300 for the former and 200 for the latter. If the sense is that
the western Greeks alone were to produce 500, the numbers are of
course much larger). Gomme (p.7) calls 500 'an impossible number':
he implies that 150, the numbers mustered 'in a great effort' for
Sybota, was the maximum Peloponnesian strength. This is wrong on
two counts:

(1) The Corinthian war with Corcyra was not generally approved in the
Peloponnese (at least in 435, and there is no reason why opinion should
have changed); so that though some states of the Spartan Alliance
contributed to the Sybota expedtion, it would be wholly wrong to regard
their contributions as anything like a maximum effort. Sicyon and
Pellene are both on the list of naval allies (II.9), but neither
contributed at Sybota: we know that there were at least forty ships
at Nisaea (II.93.2), and no doubt more were kept by Megara at Pegai;
and in VIII.3 we hear of other naval allies whom the Spartans expected
to contribute - Boeotia (twenty-five ships), Phocis and Locris (fifteen together), Arcadians, and three states who had contributed to the
Epidamnos expedition but backed out of Sybota: Epidaurus, Hermione and
Troizen. Add to these Sparta herself, and it is entirely clear that
150 comes nowhere near the potential total. The real shortage is more
likely to have been in trained rowers than in ships: even the comparatively nautical Corinthians have to hire oarsmen for Sybota (I.31.1).
Other, perhaps political, reasons may also have reduced the number of
ships actually in operation at any one time. But for ships actually
in existence, something like 300 is a wholly plausible figure.

(2) A fortiori the pro-Spartan cities of Italy and Sicily, characteristically richer if not more powerful than those of mainland Greece,
could have contributed at least 200. Syracuse alone fought the
Athenians, in the final battle in the harbour, with seventy-six ships:
and if we consider the power of Dorian foundations in Italy and Sicily
- Gela, Taras, Camarina, Selinus, Himera and others - together with
the fact that other cities also took sides against the Athenians
(Thurii, for instance, contributed ten ships: VIII.35.1), we shall
not find 200 in the least excessive. The question of whether they

would have *wanted* to contribute early in the war is irrelevant: they
certainly *could* have done so in this quantity. The threat was there:
and since, according to Thucydides, popular opinion was heavily on
the side of Sparta (II.8.4), it could not be dismissed.

Corcyra's importance to Athens in respect of Italy and Sicily, as
in respect of the north-west strategy, was a might-have-been. We
have pursued the latter at some length because it was a visible and
realistic policy for Athens; whereas the merits of Athenian intervention in Sicily, and in particular of the Sicilian Expedition,
are more debatable. Nevertheless, although we cannot here examine
and adjudicate the objectives and handling of that venture, it is
possible to see in more general terms what Corcyra's contribution
might have been. The main point, obviously enough, is that a strong
and properly allied Corcyrean navy could have turned the geographical
advantage of Corcyra's position into something much more important.
In its general form, the idea of increasing the Athenian empire by
acquiring more allies or more tribute-paying subject states was not
necessarily misconceived; the particular strategy of starting with a
direct attack on the strongest state in Italy and Sicily may (rightly)
be seen as misguided, but a more sensible method was available, by a
piecemeal and less hasty approach. A judicious mixture of bribery,
threats and main force might have enabled Athens to acquire the support
of a good many cities in Italy and Sicily (where she already had some
allies). But this, as the history of Athens in that area shows, depended very largely on a continuous or repeated Athenian presence:
and that in turn would be a severe strain on existing Athenian resources. An efficient allied fleet at Corcyra, within easy striking
distance of Italy and Sicily, would have made all the difference to
any such enterprise; and the arrangement would also, as already noted,
have given the Athenians something to offer to Corcyra by way of
repayment - that is, a share of the spoils. It is not within the
compass of this book, and is in any case perhaps too speculative,
to suggest how the tactics of such a venture might have proceeded;
but it should at least be clear that it was a viable one. Here too
Athens, lacking both the concept of a proper alliance and the diplomacy to sustain it, missed an important chance.

Do we have any evidence of Corcyrean strength or weakness at the time
of the Sicilian expedition? The first Athenian armada is described
as having 134 triremes (or perhaps 137, since three ships had been
sent ahead: VI.42.2); 100 were from Athens, the remainder χίων καί
τῶν ἄλλων ξυμμάχων, ('from the Chians and other allies', 43).
This is tantalizing, because it is very hard to say, even in terms
of probability, whether these 'other allies' included Corcyra or
not. (1) Andrewes and Dover argue (ad loc.) that the presence of
'ships from Kerkyra or Kephallenia ... may be inferred from his
[Thucydides'] postponement of this catalogue until the fleet is leaving Kerkyra for Italy'; but it is entirely possible that he postponed
it either from dramatic reasons (describing the armada before it
launched into the open sea towards Magna Graecia and its ultimate
fate) or else simply because the total count was not complete until
then, since some elements joined it en route to Corcyra - but not
necessarily Corcyrean or Cephallenian elements. (2) Normally it is
only the Chians and the Methymnans (or the Lesbians generally)

111

who provide ships, as is made clear in VII.57 and, more relevantly,
by what the Athenian spokesman says to the Sicilians in 415 (VI.85.2).
On the other hand (3) τῶν ἄλλων ξυμμάχων does suggest that not only
the Methymnans are in question; and (4) we hear of contributions (of
men, rather than ships) from states - for instance, Cephallenia and
Zacynthos (VII.57.7) - that have not previously been mentioned
either in this initial description of the first wave or in subsequent
recruiting. Nevertheless, (5) I incline to think that Thucydides'
silence about Corcyrean contributions to the first wave is a strong
argument that there were none. If there had been, it would have been
natural to mention it either at the time when the armada was at
Corcyra, or when describing Eurymedon's recruiting in 413 (VII.31.5)
of ships and hoplites from Corcyra. In particular, no Corcyrean
hoplites are mentioned in VI.43, though other allied contributors
of hoplites are named (Argos and Mantinea): and since we know from
VII.31.5 that Corcyra was a potential contributor, it would be odd if
she contributed to the first wave but was not mentioned as doing so.
  The absence of any Corcyrean forces in itself would not be particularly strange: Athens did not put her full strength into the first
wave, and may simply not have troubled to raise forces from some of
her allies. For the second wave, however, Demosthenes and Eurymedon
seem to be scraping the bottom of the barrel: and fifteen ships must
have seemed the maximum reasonable contribution. Then, if ever,
Athens would have put pressure on a nearby ally to give as much support as she could. If (as I believe) Corcyra had not contributed to
the first wave, her fleet must have been very weak. That conclusion
is important in regard to the whole alliance, when taken in conjunction
with other factors. The conclusion would still stand even if we en-
visaged some contribution to the first wave: for the contribution
could not in any case have been very large. The Chians and Methymnans
must have accounted for the great majority of the thirty-four Athenian
ships: even if as many as ten (a generous number) came from Corcyra
alone (and not also from Cephallenia or Zacynthos or other allies),
that still puts the Corcyrean strength at only twenty-five.

G. The Second *Stasis*

The trouble here, of course, not only is that our source (Diodorus)
is characteristically unreliable, but also that he is unreliable in
ways which are hard to specify, so that we cannot say for certain
where he is to be trusted and where not. However, neither Diodorus
nor any of his sources is likely to have invented this episode, and
there are some points worth discussing.
  His dating of the *stasis* to 410 is entirely plausible, particularly
if it was at least planned (or even came into effect) early in that
year. For in April and May the decisive Athenian victory at Cyzicus
made the restoration of democracy at Athens virtually inevitable;
before that time both the existence of the oligarchy and the Athenian
naval weakness in the Aegean would have favoured an oligarchic coup.
More important than either, however, was the general conditions in
which Athens found herself at the time. In 412 and 411, chiefly as a
result of the Sicilian disaster, more and more of Athens' subject
states in the Aegean rebelled, and Athens was hard pressed to find the

ships and crews to deal with them. It looks as if the Corcyrean
oligarchs bided their time after the Sicilian disaster for a year or
two, in order to make quite sure (as they thought) of Athens' inability to support the democrats; after the suppression of the first
stasis by Athens they had reason to be cautious. For the same reason
it is more likely than Conon brought his ships from Athens rather
than from Naupactos (48.6). It is improbable that Athens had ships
to spare for a squadron at Naupactos during such a critical period;
and if she had, the *oligoi* would have thought twice before launching
their coup.

Why did Athens intervene at all? We may suggest two reasons.
First, although the probability is that there was no large Corcyrean
navy, the probability is also that some Corcyreans had recovered much
of their wealth since 427; and it was always possible that the island
could be encouraged or forced by the Spartan Alliance to produce
quite a lot of ships. Even the ones in service - we have no evidence
on this point, but fifteen seems a plausible guess, since this number
appears both in 426 and 413 - would be useful to Sparta and, in the
current crisis, dangerous to Athens. Secondly, Athens needed only a
very few ships to intervene: what she required was a small but
effective force of hoplites to put down the *oligoi*, and she had that
ready to hand in the Messenians at Naupactos. She could thus squash
a potentially dangerous rebel without much effort.

The most informative point is perhaps that the *oligoi* were strong
enough again to launch a coup at all; though this is not particularly
surprising, for seventeen years had passed since 427. In that time
Corcyrean agriculture and wealth would have revived, and much of the
latter naturally fallen into the hands of what Diodorus called the
'most powerful', τοὺς δυνατωτάτους (48.5) - indeed that was why
they were the most powerful. We can hardly suppose that the sons of
the *oligoi* massacred in 427 had by now grown up and taken over their
fathers' wealth, since no doubt the *demos* confiscated it; but there
was plenty of time for new *oligoi* to arise.

It is perhaps slightly more striking that they were strong enough
to resist a direct and open ·confrontation; Conon found it necessary
to resort to sudden mass assassination in the market-place (48.7),
and even after that (when, presumably, Conon and his Messenians had
gone) the *oligoi* attempted a second coup. Diodorus says (*ibid.*)
that they arrested some, killed others, and exiled more than 1,000;
if that is anything like the truth, there seem to have been as many
oligoi involved as in 427 - indeed rather more. As in 427, the *demos*
would have been weak and for the most part unarmed, and 600 Messenians
(even with the *demos'* support) might well have been insufficient to
win the day without resort to assassination. The numbers are at
least consistent.

The figure he gives in 48.2 (about 1,500) accords reasonably well
with the rough calculations made earlier in this book of the number
of *oligoi* killed in 427. It may be that Diodorus had his own sources
for the death-toll; but it is at least possible that he himself worked
out the figures from Thucydides. The figure seems somewhat of an
underestimate: which is rather surprising, since one would naturally
suspect exaggeration. In 427, before Eurymedon arrived, 600 *oligoi*
are killed together with an unspecified number of ἐχθροι; and the
massacre continued for seven days after Eurymedon came. That might
make a plausible total of 1,500; but if we include the 500 who escaped

to Istone and were subsequently massacred in 425, 1,500 seems too few: we allow only 300-400 to be massacred during the seven days. With this author it is hardly worth trying for statistical accuracy and consistency; but it is remarkable that he has the numbers more or less right.

There are, of course, some points which we may reasonably distrust at first sight. It is not likely that the *demos* gave freedom to the slaves, or even made the resident aliens into citizens (48.7) *after* they had beaten the *oligoi*. Conceivably something like this may have happened on a small scale; but it is quite possible that Diodorus read the freeing of the slaves in 427 into this later episode. Similarly, though naturally we cannot be certain, the ending of the *stasis* by night looks like an echo of Thucydides (III. 74.3); and the agreement to 'inhabit their fatherland in common' an echo of Nicostratos' attempts in III.75.1. There may be other echoes too. But that the *stasis* happened, and happened more or less as Diodorus describes, is quite believable.

H. Review of the Alliance

We may deal first with the question of the formal alliance. Most scholars follow Gomme (p.364), and also Andrewes and Dover (p.411), in the view that the original *epimachy* or defensive alliance was turned into a full *symmachy* either in 427 or at any rate some time before 413. But there are some doubts:

(a) To take 427 first, what Nicostratos did or set out to do is described as follows: ξύμβασιν τε ἔπρασσε καὶ πείθει ὥστε ξυγχωρῆσαι ἀλλήλοις δέκα μὲν ἄνδρας τοὺς αἰτιωτάτους κρῖναι, οἳ οὐκέτι ἔμειναν, τοὺς δ᾽ ἄλλους οἰκεῖν σπονδὰς πρὸς ἀλλήλους ποιησαμένους καὶ πρὸς Ἀθηναίους ὥστε τοὺς αὐτοὺς ἐχθροὺς καὶ φίλους νομίζειν. καὶ ὁ μὲν ταῦτα πράξας κτλ. (III.75.1-2). Thucydides mixes present and past tenses in this passage (and in the surrounding passages); but, that aside, it is not entirely clear that Nicostratos actually succeeded in his aims. Ἔπρασσε at least must mean, in the imperfect, 'he was trying to get': and πείθει ὥστε ξυγχωρῆσαι, particularly since we have the infinitive rather than the indicative (compare ξυνεχώρησεν a few lines later), may well mean 'tried to persuade them to', rather than 'succeeded in persuading them to'. Even if the latter is right, and even if πράξας refers to an accomplishment rather than just an attempt, it may still be that in one sense he persuaded them - i.e. they said they would do certain things - but that they did not in fact do them. Indeed in respect of one of the things, that the parties should live in peace with each other, Nicostratos plainly failed: fighting broke out again very shortly afterwards.

(b) Some Corcyreans, presumably those recruited by Eurymedon (VII.31. 5), were certainly present in Sicily (VII.44.6 and 57.7), but not necessarily because of the legal requirements of a full *symmachy*. The relevant passage (57.7) reads: τῶν τε περὶ Πελοπόννησον νησιωτῶν Κεφαλλῆνες μὲν καὶ Ζακύνθιοι αὐτόνομοι μέν, κατὰ δὲ τὸ νησιωτικὸν μᾶλλον κατειργόμενοι, ὅτι θαλάσσης

114

ἐκράτουν οἱ ᾿Αθηναῖοι, ξυνείποντο· Κερκυραῖοι δὲ οὐ μόνον
Δωριῆς, ἀλλὰ καὶ Κορίνθιοι σαφῶς ἐπὶ Κορινθίους τε καὶ
Συρακοσίους, τῶν μὲν ἄποικοι ὄντες, τῶν δὲ ξυγγενεῖς, ἀνάγκῃ
μὲν ἐκ τοῦ εὐπρεποῦς, βουλήσει δὲ κατὰ ἔχθος τὸ Κορινθίων
οὐχ ἧσσον εἵποντο. The ἀνάγκη does not necessarily (pace Andrewes
and Dover, p.433), refer to the obligations of an alliance. Early
in the same passage (57.4 and 5) the word is twice used, together with
ἠναγκάξοντο in 57.6, of the subject allies, and it is likely
to mean the same in all cases - that is, some kind of naked force
rather than legal obligation. Further, as the μὲν and δὲ show,
the Corcyreans are contrasted with the other islanders: and the contrast must be to the effect that, though they could plead the same
kind of ἀνάγκη as the others, in fact they came βουλήσει, 'by
thier own wish'. They are thus in effect classified amongst those
who came for private reasons, in 57.9-11, whether or not they also
had a formal alliance: like the Argives, who came οὐ τῆς ξυμμαχίας
ἕνεκα μᾶλλον ἢ τῆς Λακεδαιμονίων ἔχθρας (57.9), 'not so much
for the sake of their alliance as for their hatred of the Lacedaimonians'. We translate: 'As for the islanders round the Peloponnese,
the Cephallenians and Zacynthians on the one hand were independent,
but joined in because they were under pressure qua islanders, since
Athens had control of the sea; the Corcyreans, on the other hand
(who were not only Dorians, but also clearly of Corinthian stock,
fighting against the Corinthians and Syracusans, whilst being colonists of the one people and kinsmen of the other) could claim some
pretence of compulsion; but the truth was rather that they came of
their own volition because they hated the Corinthians'.

Of course these are only doubts: it may be that there was a full
symmachy. But if so, it must be seen as a de iure rather than a
de facto affair. For on any plausible account, Corcyrean help to
Athens was minimal: as can easily be seen if we move from formality
to fact.
    First, in 431, fifty Corcyrean ships joined the Athenian fleet of
100 ships which was conducting a periplous round the Peloponnese.
The Athenians had already begun the periplous (II.23.3) when the
Corcyreans joined them (25.1), and the next location we hear of in
their attacks is Methone (ibid.). Probably the Corcyreans came no
further than Malea, if as far, not improving on their performance
in the Persian war (see Herodotus VII.168). Subsequent references
to this expedition mention only the Athenians (there is no mention
of allies: 25.3, 25.5), and once there is a mention of 100 ships only
(30.1): finally 'the ships returned to Athens' (ἀνεχώρησαν αἱ
νῆες ἐς τὰς ᾿Αθήνας, 30.3). There is not much of an argumentum
ex silentio here; but it is at least not clear that the Corcyrean ships
or their crews did anything very useful, or even that they were
present for long after their original meeting with the Athenians in
the southern Peloponnese. This, be it noted, was the only major
support (in terms of ship-numbers at least) that the Corcyreans are
known to have given.
    It may be said, of course, that the lack of support in the period
431-427 was due to the lack of a full symmachy. But there are difficulties with that view. Why, in that case, do they send such a
comparatively large flotilla in 431? Why do they not send other
flotillas on occasions when Athens had greater need of them - for in-

115

stance, to Phormio in 429, or to assist the operations against
Oiniadai and Leucas in 428? Moreover, if the full *symmachy* was fixed
by Nicostratos in 427 - and the occasion of the *stasis* is the most
likely occasion for the change, if there ever was one - why was there
not more Corcyrean support after 427? The fifteen ships helping
Demosthenes at Leucas in 426 do not meet this difficulty: apart from
their rapid disappearance from the scene of action, the Corcyreans
sent no help at all for the important campaigns in the north-west
later in 426, nor for the Athenian initiatives round the Peloponnese
in 425-24. Fear of Peloponnesian intervention in Corcyra during
426-25 may be some excuse for this failure: and we cannot look for
Corcyrean support during the suspension of hostilities between
Athens and Sparta from 423-416. But it is not even clear that they
contributed to the Sicilian Expedition except under pressure: and
even then, probably only fifteen ships and an uncertain number of
hoplites. This gives Thucydides' statement at the beginning of the
war that τούτων ναυτικὸν παρείχοντο Χῖοι, Λέσβιοι, Κερκυραῖοι
(II.9.5) ('of these the Chians, Lesbians and Corcyreans provided a
naval force') very much a *de iure* status rather than a *de facto* status: nor
is this surprising, since the same must apply to many parallel items
in his list of allies (for instance, the Spartan naval allies).

The many occasions (not all mentioned above), both before and after
427, on which Athens could have profited greatly from Corcyrean support
and on which that support could easily have been given (particularly
over short distances in the north-west), strongly suggest that it
was not simply a matter of Athens not troubling to ask for help from
Corcyra. We should look rather for political reasons in Corcyra itself. In 431, the pro-Athenian feeling which followed Sybota is likely still to have been fairly strong; but it seems to have weakened soon
thereafter. (It may be that there was no love lost between the Athenian and Corcyran elements in the combined fleet of 431; one may en-
visage a great many possible incidents or causes of friction.)
Certainly soon after the prisoners returned to Corcyra, - if this may
be dated at about 430, as I have argued - and perhaps due to their
influence, the Corcyrean temper had returned to isolationism: they
voted (perhaps in 430?) for no more than the *epimachy* or defensive
alliance (III.70). If the prisoners had been working successfully
for some time in Corcyra, the swing to isolationism may be partly
attributed to them: but we cannot know that, and it is likely that
straightforward egocentricity was the main cause.

What exactly was the position after 427? The fifteen triremes
contributed in 426 are exceptional. So was the context, in that (1)
in the year immediately following the *stasis* the *demos* might have wished
to give direct evidence of their attachment to Athens, and (2) they
were used only at Leucas, which was very close to Corcyra and had
already been a target for Corcyrean reprisal (after Sybota). The
latter is likely to be the stronger reason: the *demos* required
Athenian aid again in 425, but made no contribution to Athens' fleet.
By that time, however, Sparta was trying to intervene, and the focus
of Athenian strategic interests had changed to the southern Peloponnese - too far, perhaps, for Corcyra to be willing to send reinforcements.

Both the *stasis* (particularly the purge of *oligoi*) and the consequent famine hit Corcyra very badly; and it is reasonable to believe
that (apart from what may have been largely a token contribution in

426) for some time after 427-25 the Corcyreans were simply unable - probably also unwilling - to give much help. Their failure during the time of the Sicilian Expedition, however, presents a problem. For it is fairly clear from the second *stasis* that the Corcyrean state, though no doubt not what it was, had regained at least a rea- sonable measure of prosperity. That is unsurprising: whatever the basis of the Corcyrean economy - agriculture or trade - there had been plenty of time between 425 and 410 for Corcyra to have regained something of her original wealth. If Diodorus is to be trusted at all, there was a flourishing group of *oligoi* in 410, which suggests a reasonably flourishing economy. Yet she apparently only contri- buted fifteen ships in 413.

Though the matter is not susceptible to direct proof, the answer is probably again political. The Corcyrean navy existed in its original strength only because of a temporary and fragile conjunction of interests between the *oligoi* and the *demos*. It was manned by slaves and (to a great extent) *oligoi*, or at least men of the hop- lite class. The *demos* allowed and encouraged it so long as it was used in the national interest; but they were extremely alarmed by any sug- gestion that it might be used in the interests of the Spartans or of the *oligoi* alone. This is dramatically represented in the 427 *stasis*, where the *demos* are torn between (a) the need to have a navy to fight off the Spartan fleet (and so they persuade the *oligoi* to man it), and (b) the fear that the *oligoi* may be victorious in the *stasis* (and so they massacre them as they step off the ships). Once the Corcyreans had joined in the war, a greater polarity of interests between *demos* and *oligoi* ensued, since there were greater temptations for both parties to use foreign power in order to secure their own position. If the *demos* allowed a navy to be built up and used, the *oligoi* might desert (as they did in the sea-fight of 427). The absence of trust is likely to be responsible for the fact - since it seems to be a fact - that the Corcyreans abdicated from their previous position as a strong naval power. No doubt they had other uses for their recovered wealth: and until the Athenian disaster in Sicily, at least, they would have counted themselves safe by virtue of Athenian naval protection.

This may also account for some of what seems to be Athens' remark- able failure to put any pressure on Corcyra: at least, after 427. If, for something like these political reasons, the Corcyrean navy was simply not viable, Athens could do little about it. But it does not account for Athens' failure between 431 and 427, particularly in view of Athens' need for help in the north-west in 429 and 428. III.70.2 shows fairly conclusively that there was no full *symmachy* before 427. Why had not Athens tried to make one, and put it to use? Partly it may be that Athens was, as it were, taken by surprise in respect of the north-west. Even after the Peloponnesian initiatives in 430 (the attempts on Zacynthos by 100 triremes and on Amphilochian Argos), Athens' only response was to send the twenty ships commanded by Phormio to Naupactos - in no sense an adequate squadron, if she really anticipated major operations in that area. In 429 Phormio kept Athens' interests alive by a combination of intelligence and good luck, without further Athenian support; and only in 428, when their attention was occupied by the Mitylene revolt, did the Athenians send a fleet of thirty ships (possibly at the request of the Acarnanians,

117

since they requested its commander), soon reduced to twelve. This
fleet failed dismally at Oiniadai and Nericos (III.7): and neither
its size nor its operations suggest a very serious Athenian interest
in the area. It is not really till Demosthenes arrives on the scene,
in 426, that the war in the north-west hots up: but by then the
stasis had taken place. At no time does the original strategic
interest in Corcyra and the Ionian islands, expressed in II.7.3, seem
to have borne fruit: Zacynthos and Cephallenia were used, if at all,
only as temporary bases for other operations (e.g. IV.8.2-3). Athens'
interest in the area may also have waned after 430, when it looked as
if the Italian and Sicilian cities would not be sending any ships
to help the Spartan Alliance.

That is, perhaps, sufficient explanation in itself: but I suspect
again that something had also gone wrong with the 431 expedition.
If so - if, for instance, the Corcyreans showed themselves (characteristically) strongly resistant to the idea of taking orders from Athens,
and proved themselves more trouble than they were worth -, then Athens
was faced with the choice either of merely hoping for Corcyrean
help whenever the Corcyreans felt like giving it, or else of mounting
a major expedition against Corcyra to enforce the terms of the alliance.
The latter was not a realistic venture, and Athens would only have
undertaken it in the case of a tribute-paying state whose defection
threatened the structure of her empire: Corcyra was sufficiently
powerful, sufficiently remote, and in that way sufficiently irrelevant, to escape Athenian reprisals when Athens was engaged elsewhere.
No doubt a good deal of diplomacy went on, about which we are not
informed. But ultimately Athens had to rely on Corcyrean goodwill,
a fairly rare commodity in Corcyra. This too was part of the price
Athens had to pay for not negotiating a proper alliance in the first
place. (This and other points of general strategic interest are
discussed in the Appendix that follows).

APPENDIX

CORCYRA AND ATHENIAN STRATEGY

1. *Corcyra and Thucydides*

I here want to consider the peculiar importance which the Corcyrean
alliance, and Corcyrean affairs in general, had or might have had
for Athens in the Peloponnesian War; and it is natural to begin
with the attention that Thucydides devotes to Corcyrean history
in the period 433-25, which contrasts fairly sharply with its comparative neglect by modern scholars. In Book I, no fewer than
thirty-two sections deal with the Epidamnos and Sybota campaigns and
negotiations (compared, for instance, with only ten on Potiadaia).
The Corcyrean *stasis* is dealt with at considerable length in III.
69.85 and IV.46-48: twenty sections, of which the famous reflections
on *stasis* in general occupy only two (III.82-83). These somewhat
striking facts may, of course, be written off in the light of some
theory - if we could be certain of any - about the composition and
drafting of Thucydides' work; perhaps the 'final draft' would have
condensed the Corcyrean material. But there is clearly some possibility that Thucydides ascribed considerable importance to Corcyra,
or at least to these lengthily-described events in Corcyrean history,
in reference to the Peloponnesian War as a whole.

If so, there could be two general reasons for this ascription.
The first, which seems to me not only more obvious but also more
probable, is to be found in the last section of Book I (146):
αἰτίαι δὲ αὗται καὶ διαφοραὶ ἐγένοντο ἀμφοτέροις πρὸ τοῦ
πολέμου, ἀρξάμεναι εὐθὺς ἀπὸ τῶν ἐν Ἐπιδάμνῳ καὶ Κερκύρᾳ.
'These were the causes of complaint and the differences between the
two sides before the war, taking their origin directly from what
had happened at Epidamnos and Corcyra'. This is more striking in
that the sections immediately preceding (139ff.), which describe
the Spartan ultimatum and Pericles' reply, do not mention the Corcyrean affair at all; the Spartans demand that Athens abandon the
siege of Potidaia, give Aegina independence, and revoke the Megarian
decree (139.1), but not that she should cancel the Corcyrean alliance.
In 146 Thucydides is looking back at all the αἰτίαι (causes) immediately prior to the war, and claiming that they took their origin 'from
what had happened at Epidamnos and Corcyra'.

Nor does his use of ἀρξάμεναι ('beginning', 'originating') make
a purely chronological point: it is not just that the Corcyrean
affair happened first. As he makes clear when discussing the
Athenian demands on Potidaia (I.56.2), the alienation of Corinth
after Sybota was directly responsible for some of the pressure on
Megara, elements of which may plausibly be dated to 432. (Megara
was virtually the only Peloponnesian state, apart from Corinth,
which had increased its ship-contribution to the Corinthian expeditions, sending eight ships to the Epidamnos expedition in 435 and
twelve to the Sybota expedtiion in 433; nearly all other Peloponnesian states dropped out of the latter.)

On this account, Thucydides felt obliged to describe 'what had
happened at Epidamnos and Corcyra' in some detail, as the most important
direct causes of the war; Potidaia is more condensed, and the other
αἰτίαι (the Megarian decree and the autonomy of Aegina) condensed

119

still more. The Corcyrean *stasis* merited a lengthy treatment,
partly as a natural follow-up to what had already been said about
Corcyra, partly because it was inextricably intertwined in military
events that had to be described anyway (the Athenian and Spartan
interventions and the sea-fight), and perhaps partly as a good
springboard for philosophical reflections on *stasis* in general
(the Melian Dialogue might be quoted as an analogous example:
V.84ff.).

The less plausible suggestion is that Thucydides believed
Corcyra to have considerable strategic importance for the war as
a whole, and hence followed her fortunes in some detail. But there
is not much positive evidence for this, and a great deal of negative
evidence against it. The positive evidence is in effect confined
to the reasons he gives for the importance of the Corcyrean alliance
to Athens: that is, the acquisition of the Corcyrean navy (or the
prevention of its falling into Peloponnesian hands) (I.35.5, 36.3,
44.2, 68.4), and the usefulness of its location on the sailing-
route (for triremes at least) to and from Sicily and Italy (I.36.2,
44.3). These reasons are, however, the obvious and natural ones
to mention, and he could hardly have avoided mentioning them (particularly since they figured in the speeches and negotiations); but
if he had kept them permanently in mind as important strategic factors, they would have been brought up again at many points in his
account of later events. In fact they are not. The help which
Corcyra gave to Athens, even before the *stasis*, was minimal; and
was unsurprisingly still less after it. But at no point does
Thucydides say anything like 'The Corcyreans did not send ships
to help the Athenians because ...', or even comment on the one
occasion in (431) when they did give naval assistance on a large
scale. Ste. Croix breezily describes the Athenians as 'rarely
even troubling to ask' for Corcyrean contingents; but we do not
know this, and Thucydides says nothing about it. The importance of
the Corcyrean navy to Athens is not in any way followed up. Nor,
though this is perhaps less starkly obvious, is the relevance of
Corcyra's geographical position followed up in his accounts either
of the Sicilian expedition or of the arrival of Sicilian contingents
to join the war in the Aegean.

This is on any account remarkable, particularly if (as I shall try
to show) Corcyra's strategic importance was in fact considerable. But
it may fairly be argued - at greater length than is appropriate here -
that Thucydides was not much interested in - and perhaps not very
perceptive about - strategy at all, in one fairly clear sense of that
term. There is a striking gap between his tactical descriptions of
particular battles and campaigns on the one hand, which are often
given in great detail, and the very broad logistical and political
accounts on the other, which are too general to be of much help to us.
This is, I think, particularly true of the Archidamian War, where there
are many specifically strategic questions which he leaves unanswered.
What was the strategic importance of Acarnania to both sides? What
effect did Phormio's victories have on the naval situation? Why did
Athens choose to make a major attack on Leucas in 426? With what
intentions did she capture Cythera in 424? Did Demosthenes or
Nicias hold a coherent view about what strategy should be used in war?
Thucydides' silence on such matters cannot, as Gomme seems to suggest
(p.21), be explained by saying that he 'assumes a knowledge in his

120

readers', since some of them at least could not have been common knowledge; equally the suggestion (see for instance Wade-Gery, in the *Oxford Classical Dictionary*) that he was stupid about strategy will not account for all or even most cases. We must assume a gap in his interests, a surprising gap for someone who, when all is said said and done, set out to write the history of a war.

One possible reason is that Thucydides accepted Pericles' views on what Athenian strategy ought to be, and felt only a kind of uninterested and cynical despair about the strategy that actually prevailed after (and perhaps sometimes before) Pericles' death in 429. There are, of course, longstanding controversies about 'Periclean strategy'; I shall argue below that Pericles' objectives at the time of the Corcyrean debate in 433 were similar to his objectives for the Peloponnesian War as a whole - keep the navy strong, do not add to the empire, take no risks. Such a policy involved no very specific strategic aims for Corcyra (or perhaps anywhere else) of a kind that required detailed exegesis. When Pericles died, Thucydides saw subsequent Athenian strategy as not much more than a set of *ad hoc* attempts to make piecemeal military gains, attempts often motivated by the desire for self-aggrandizement on the part of inferior politicians; and in some degree, indeed, that picture may be a correct one. In any case, we must accept that his strategic or quasi-strategic interests, so far as the Archidamian War is concerned, seem largely restricted to certain very general features of the political and military position at the outbreak of war, and in particular to certain policies which he attributes to Pericles. This is evident from the fact that his discussion of these features and policies is almost entirely confined to Bks. I and II, and to the period when Pericles was alive; much of it, indeed, is put into Pericles' mouth. Moreover, it is tolerably clear that he thought Pericles' policy (as he reports it) was the right one. (See I.32-44, 66-87, 118-125, 139-146: II.7-11, 13, 60-65.)

2. The Value of Corcyra

I have suggested one reason why Thucydides says little about the strategic importance of Corcyra in the later part of our period; but whether or not I am right, his remarks on that importance are in fact confined to the debate before Sybota (I.36, 44). He mentions two reasons for the Corcyra alliance being valuable to Athens, and mentions them more than once. The first is the Corcyrean navy: this is put in the mouth of the Corcyreans (I.36.3) and of the Corinthians speaking in front of the Spartans (68.4); and also in the minds of the Athenians (44.2). Its position in the text of these passages strongly suggests that this first reason was more important than the second, i.e. the geographical position of Corcyra in relation to the western Greeks (in Italy and Sicily), though this latter is stressed not only by the Corcyrean embassy (36.2) but also by Thucydides in his own person (44.3).

Both advantages are tolerably clear in general terms. The first has different interpretations. There was the negative advantage, which is the one chiefly stressed by Thucydides, of preventing Corcyra's navy being absorbed by Corinth and hence able to fight on the Peloponnesian side; the more positive advantage of having an ally with a powerful fleet (either free or in some sense subject, on the analogy of states like Chios and Lesbos which were subject to Athens and contri-

buted ships rather than money to the Athenian war effort); or, more
positively still, using the unique advantage of the unpaid slave rowers
in the Corcyrean navy for a really aggressive strategy which I shall
describe immediately below. The second, Corcyra's geographical
position, is explained by the Corcyrean ambassador in 36.2: he says
that the Athenians would be able to stop a ναυτικὸν ('naval force',
but essentially triremes: merchantmen, more seaworthy, did not need
to hug the coast) coming from western Greece to the Peloponnese or
vice versa. This too has more than one aspect. There was a real
danger that the western Greek cities would reinforce Sparta (Sparta
did in fact order a large fleet from them, II.7), and that Sparta would
intervene in Athenian attempts upon Sicily (as actually happened: VI.
93, 104ff.). Moreover, the alliance with Corcyra might not only
prevent these dangers but also offer prositive assistance to Athens
in helping Athens' own enterprises towards the west (as in the
Sicilian Expedition: see Diodorus 12.54).

Most of these points have been discussed in the main text; here I
want to pursue the least obvious of them, and see how the Corcyrean
alliance might have given Athens some really positive chances of
victory. The first point to be made must surely be that, on any
plausible reading of the facts, much the most effective blows which
Athens dealt Sparta during the course of the war were in 425-24, re-
sulting from the capture of Pylos and Cythera. Thucydides tells us
why in IV.41: οἱ δὲ Λακεδαιμόνιοι ἀμαθεῖς ὄντες ἐν τῷ πρὶν
χρόνῳ λῃστείας καὶ τοῦ τοιούτου πολέμου, τῶν τε Εἱλώτων
αὐτομολούντων καὶ φοβούμενοι μὴ καὶ ἐπὶ μακρότερον σφίσι
τι νεωτερισθῇ τῶν κατὰ τὴν χώραν, οὐ ῥᾳδίως ἔφερον, ἀλλὰ
καίπερ οὐ βουλόμενοι ἔνδηλοι εἶναι τοῖς Ἀθηναίοις ἐπρεσβεύοντο παρ᾽ αὐτοὺς καὶ ἐπειρῶντο τήν τε Πύλον καὶ τοὺς
ἄνδρας κομίζεσθαι. 'The Lacedaimonians had no previous experience
of raiding and warfare of that kind; the helots were deserting, and they
were frightened that revolutionary behaviour would spread even more
widely in their country. So they were exceedingly disturbed, and
(though not wishing to make this apparent to the Athenians) they
sent embassies to Athens in an attempt to recover Pylos and their
men'. And again in IV.55: Οἱ δὲ Λακεδαιμόνιοι ἰδόντες μὲν᾽τοὺς
Ἀθηναίους τὰ Κύθηρα ἔχοντας, προσδεχόμενοι δὲ καὶ ἐς τὴν
γῆν σφῶν ἀποβάσεις τοιαύτας ποιήσεσθαι, ἀθρόᾳ μὲν οὐδαμοῦ
τῇ δυνάμει ἀντετάξαντο, κατὰ δὲ τὴν χώραν φρουρὰς διέπεμψαν,
ὁπλιτῶν πλῆθος, ὡς ἑκασταχόσε ἔδει, καὶ τὰ ἄλλα ἐν φυλακῇ
πολλῇ ἦσαν, φοβούμενοι μὴ σφίσι νεώτερον τι γένηται τῶν
περὶ τὴν κατάστασιν, γεγενημένου μὲν τοῦ ἐν τῇ νήσῳ πάθους
ἀνελπίστου καὶ μεγάλου, Πύλου δὲ ἐχομένης καὶ Κυθήρων καὶ
πανταχόθεν σφᾶς περιεστῶτος πολέμου ταχέος καὶ ἀπροφυλάκτου.
'The Lacedaimonians saw that the Athenians now held Cythera, and expected that there would be other similar landings in their own territory.
They did not oppose them at any point with their whole force, but sent
out troops to act as garrisons in the country - bodies of hoplites
in whatever numbers were suitable in each case. In general they were
very much on their guard, being frightened that there would be some
revolution against the established order: for they had suffered a great
and unexpected disaster on the island, Pylos and Cythera were occupied,
and they were now surrounded by military attacks from all sides, rapid-
ly mounted and impossible to guard against in advance'.

It is clear from these and other passages (cf. IV.80.2-4, V.14.3,

6.3, 113.2) not only - what we already know on more general grounds - that Sparta's main weakness lay in her need to prevent a helot revolt, but also that Athenian occupation of only two places (Pylos and Cythera) was sufficient to show up that weakness as a serious one.

We are talking here of a strategy which for the sake of brevity may be called ἐπιτείχισις, 'offensive fortification': that is, the occupation and defence of places in or near enemy territory, with aggressive intentions. Whether or not the term ἐπιτείχισις could be used, or used by Thucydides, to include whole cities or city-states - whether Cythera, for instance, could come under this heading - is arguable but here irrelevant; we are now speaking of a policy which includes any such occupation, so long as - for this is obviously a crucial strategic point - it was in or sufficiently near to Spartan-dominated territory (Laconia in the Thucydidean sense, which includes Messenia) to be effective. This policy was not, in my judgement, part of any Periclean strategy, as reported by Thucydides: partly because Pericles did not pursue it even when he might have done (e.g. at Prasiai in 430: II.56.6), and partly because Pericles himself describes this possibility (I.142.2-4) only as a retaliatory option - if the Peloponnesians do it, the Athenians can do it too.

In fact, the Athenians themselves did not pursue the policy to any great extent. We can point only to the occupation of Atlanta (431:II.32) and the walling-off of the Methana promontory (425: IV.45), too far from Sparta to be relevant; and Demosthenes' much later (413) occupation of a headland opposite to Cythera (VII.26), abandoned shortly afterwards because of the expense (VIII.4). Some of the Athenian advantages gained in 425 were admittedly due to the capture of the Spartans on Sphacteria, which can be regarded as in a sense accidental: that is, at least, not something which could be hoped for from ἐπιτείχισις in general. But by no means all: in V.14 Thucydides specifically makes the point that the helots were deserting and that the Spartans continued to fear a revolution, and it is not for nothing that in V.35 the Spartans were prepared to let the Athenians garrison Pylos, so long as the Messenians and helots were withdrawn. Why then was there not a stronger or more seriously-executed policy, since it must have been clear to the Athenians that what they had done - particularly at Pylos - had produced such satisfactory results?

Part of the answer is inherent in what Thucydides tells us about the particular case at Pylos (see Wilson, 1979). Demosthenes' reported thoughts in IV.3 give us an idea of the desirable conditions for a successful ἐπιτείχισις; and some of the difficulties are also there mentioned, in particular the expense (IV.3.3) and the problems of supply (in 27.1 the Athenians are represented as thinking οὐδ᾽ ἐν θέρει οἷοι τ᾽ ὄντες ἱκανὰ περιπέμπειν, 'that they were unable to send round sufficient supplies even in summer').

These are essentially logistic difficulties, concerning money and man-power. Behind them lies a feature of great importance. It was not only the occupation of fortified positions in itself which caused Sparta so much trouble, but this *in combination with* the use of Athenian seapower (the ἀποβάσεις ('landings') of IV.55.1). To make the policy of ἐπιτείχισις really effective, Athens would have to dispose of a fairly substantial fleet operating permanently, or as continuously as possible, in the area. Given such a fleet, the limitations of the Pylos case would mostly disappear: materials for fortification would be transported, there would be not difficulty of supply, and the Peloponnesians would be unable to mount any *ad hoc* attack by sea. Moreover the advantages would be multiplied: troops could be easily and quickly moved from one position to another, and landings constantly made at other points in Laconia. The Spartans would have little chance of putting up any effective defence against this, and no rest or security even during the winter season.

The logistical difficulties of the strategy are not so much concerned with the problems of naval operations during winter (much exaggerated by many authors), which would in any case be minimised by the Athenian possession of harbours at Pylos, Cythera and perhaps elsewhere. They are strictly financial; and the need for a permanent fleet is by far the gravest. Just how large a fleet would be required is speculative: much would depend on how far the Athenians had managed to crush or cow the Peloponnesian navy (hence the import-ance of Sybota and Phormio's battles). But if we take an arbitrary figure of fifty triremes, we have to remember that this would in-volved continuous payment for something like 10,000 men - far more than any number of land troops likely to be used, at least in the early stages. It is sufficiently clear that Athens could not easily execute such a policy without a good deal more logistical or financial support.

The interest of Corcyra to the strategic historian lies in the possibility that Corcyra could have given such support, because of the size and - more important - the nature of her navy. Nearly all the evidence and arguments concerning the Corcyrean navy come from what Thucydides tells us about the battle of Sybota and about the Corcyrean civil war. They are fully treated above: here I give only the brief conclusions. It seems that (1) the navy was in general manned (a) by slave-rowers, not by the free citizens of the *demos* of by hired seamen, and (b) by men of the middle or upper class, serving as *epibatai*; (2) the slave-rowers were trained and in general efficient; (3) the navy could operate effectively at some distance from Corcyra, as it did at Epidamnos, Leucas and Cyllene (I.30.2-3: to set fire to a major Peloponnesian port was no small achievement); and (4) there was a real possibility of some other state taking over the Corcyrean navy, if that state had political control of Corcyra: Athens was frightened of just this (I.44.2), as the Corcyrean envoys had intended (36.3). The fact that the fleet was largely manned by slaves was evidently no impediment to (3) or (4): perhaps even facilitated these possibilities.

From this we may see one obvious advantage for Athenian strategy: though we must also induce less obvious disadvantages. The advantage, of course, is the possibility of a permanent allied fleet of *unpaid rowers*. This might have presented some problems: the slaves may also have been used on the land and elsewhere, and would have to be with-drawn in order to man a permanent fleet. But to the Corcyreans, who boasted of being as rich as any state in Greece (I.25.4), that would not be crippling: particularly in view of the large numbers of slaves at their disposal. A fleet of fifty triremes would need about 8,500 slave-rowers, less than half the force at Sybota. Combined with fifty Athenian triremes with paid crews (perhaps costing about 500 talents a year), that would be enough to realise that strategy under discussion. Moreover, such a combination would allow the Athenians

to train and officer them as best suited, welding the whole into a
permanent and professional fighting force to rival the Spartan
professionalism by land.

The disadvantages were political. To ensure the stability needed
for a permanent fleet, Athens had three main options. (1) She
could back the *demos* (as she commonly did, and as in fact she did
in the *stasis*). But it is likely that many of the slaves were pri-
vately owned by the *oligoi*, so that the destruction of the *oligoi*
might adversely affect the possibility of using trained slave-rowers.
More importantly, the *oligoi* were necessary - as is proved by events
after the *stasis* - for the effective manning of the navy, and no
doubt also for the economic viability of Corcyra in general. (2)
She could back the *oligoi*; but there could have been some possible
political repercussions of such a volte-face in Athenian policy
- although Athens very occasionally backed *oligoi* against *demos*, the
demos of most cities felt that they could rely on Athenian aid
against *oligoi*, an expectation surely useful to Athens. Moreover,
the *demos* in Corcyra seem to have been the more powerful (and
certainly behaved with unbridled ferocity), and perhaps could not
have been kept down for long. In any case the prisoners returned
by Corinth, who were πρῶτοι and at least potential *oligoi*, were
firmly aligned on the Peloponnesian side: in effect, the *oligoi*
were effectively or passively pro-Spartan before Athens had a chance
to do anything about it. A final policy remained (3): Athens
could try to hold the situation together by somehow paying off both
sides. That was not impossible: both *oligoi* and *demos* would gain
in wealth and power from the defeat of Corinth and a possible extension of influence or empire. But it would have required a great
deal of negotiation, and much more firmness and consistency than
Athens actually showed. A permanent Athenian presence (to use the
modern jargon) in Corcyra, however, combined with a clear and tempting programme for the benefit of all Corcyreans (except perhaps the
slaves!), should have been able to pull it off - even in 427.

It was desirable that this diplomacy be put into effect at the
earliest possible moment, and enforced as far as possible: otherwise
- what happened in the event - there would be latitude for party
strife and for an ambiguous policy towards Athens. There was no
very strong pro-Athenian tradition at Corcyra: a strong anti-
Corinthian feeling existed, but chiefly because Corinth was the
most obviously threatening power. The Corcyreans had made no alliances
in the past (I.32), and rejected the appeal by the democrats of
Epidamnos; their passions and power were invoked only after Corinth
had sent settlers and troops to the city (I.24, 26), and even then
they turned first to their Peloponnesian friends. The Corcyrean
prisoners, returned perhaps in 430, as agents for Corinth, tried
to wean Corcyra away from Athens; and it is not very surprising
that the Corcyreans voted for neutrality. (Like many Greek states,
Corcyra may have feared Athenian imperialism.) Judging from the
context in Thucydides (III.7off.), we may take this vote to represent unforced Corcyrean opinion: Peithias, the pro-Athenian leader
of the democratic party, needed to persuade (ἀναπείσειν, 70.6)
the people to make Corcyra a full ally of Athens.

These points were discussed in more detail earlier; and it seems
plain that the Athenians should have opted for a full *symmachy* rather
than a mere *epimachy* right at the start: or if not then, after Sybota,

when the value of Athens to Corcyra should have been very clear.
That they did not may have been partly due to a policy of not
aggravating the situation vis-à-vis the Spartan Alliance; but if
so, such a policy achieved only the worst of both worlds - the
Alliance was aggravated (or certainly Corinth was), and the help
Athens had from Corcyra was minimal. At the beginning, the
Corcyeans were anxious for a *symmachy* (ξυμμαχίας, I.32.2).
Even after Sybota, though the Corinthians gave way, yet they had
not been effectively defeated and still presented a threat: a
symmachy would still have been desirable.

For Corcyra to give proper support to Athens, however, it was necessary
not only that she should be diplomatically nursed in the right way,
but also that the island should be properly defended. This in effect
meant preventing Peloponnesian expeditions designed to conquer or
cripple it, which in turn meant that Athens should control the sea
in that area. But Athenian domination of the sea in the north-west
was a possibility that had to be fought and planned for, not a reality
from the beginning. Nor, in fact, was it ever fully achieved. 'Athens
... was completely dominant at sea as the Peloponnesians were by
land' (Ste.Croix, 1972) is not true for the sea in the north-west.
It is true (a) that, until the technological changes in trireme-
construction (and perhaps sometimes even thereafter), Athenian
squadrons could defeat equal or even greater numbers of other triremes
in open water, because of their greater skill; (b) that, until about
the same time, Athens could generally deploy more ships than any of
her rivals (though not in the north-west); and (c) that, in the actual
battles fought in the north-west, Athens nearly always triumphed. But
against this we must set the facts (d) that Athens could not prevent
quite large Peloponnesian fleets from operating in the area (431,
forty ships from Corinth to Astakos and Cephallenia; 430, 100 ships
against Zacynthos; 429, Cnemus gets 1,000 hoplites to Ambracia by
sea, and there were fleets of forty-seven and seventy-seven triremes
in the Gulfs of Corinth and Patras: 427, fifty-three ships from the
Peloponnese to Corcyra: 425, sixty ships from the Peloponnese to
Corcyra and thence to Pylos); and (e) that the Athenian naval successes
at Naupactos in 429 were in part due to good fortune. If Athens was
ever 'completely dominant at sea' in the north-west, it was after -
certainly not before, and not during - our period; and such dominance
as she then had was in part due to her singular good fortune at Pylos,
where in 425 the lucky accident of the marooned Spartans allowed her
to demand the handing over of the whole Peloponnesian fleet and all
other warships in Laconia (IV.16.1).
  To be dominant 'as the Peloponnesians were by land', Athens had to
be able not only to win any reasonably-matched naval battle, but to
control the seas. Peloponnesian dominance by land would not have
amounted to much if the Spartan Alliance had been unable to prevent
large Athenian armies from campaigning more or less at will every
year in territory which the Peloponnesians were supposed to dominate;
and that is how the Peloponnesian fleet campaigned in the north-west.
Control would have meant, if not an absolute blockade of the area, at
least denying it to the Spartan Alliance. Yet until Phormio's victories in 429, there is little direct evidence even that the Peloponnesians
always thought their expeditions particularly risky, and at least some
indications to the contrary (e.g. the thoughts of the Corinthian com-

manders before Phormio's first battle, II.83); and thereafter, though their fleets characteristically dodged the Athenians, they were nevertheless in operation till 425. (Even the Athenian victory at Pylos in that year was partly due to good luck: see Wilson (1979).)

The only way the Athenians could control the sea in the north-west was by a permanent or at least semi-permanent occupation of the area - in effect a blockade which would prevent any Peloponnesian fleet from operating. They had their base at Naupactos; but it is clear from the numbers of ships in the Corinthian fleet at Sybota, and from those in the Peloponnesian fleet which fought against Phormio in his second battle, that the Peloponnesians could deploy considerable numbers of triremes from sources both to the east of Naupactos (within the Corinthian Gulf) and to the west of it. The Corinthian Gulf states were highly capable in this respect (Corinth alone produced ninety ships for Sybota): and the Spartan Alliance could (and did) draw on large numbers from Ambracia, Leucas, Elis and other states not in the Gulf. In other words, the Alliance could confront the Athenians at Naupactos with a powerful fleet coming either from inside or from outside the Gulf: perhaps with at least 100 ships in either case.

Clearly the blockade of those ships which originated from inside the Gulf was highly desirable (and Phormio seems to have achieved this, if only temporarily). Not only would it effectively diminish - perhaps by as much as half - the Peloponnesian navy, but the Naupactos squadron could prevent a large part of that navy from operating in the north-west whilst itself remaining close to the area. If the squadron were large enough, it might be able to do this whilst also inhibiting, if not actually rendering impossible, Peloponnesian naval expeditions originating from west of the narrows (from Cyllene or elsewhere). But in order to do this, the squadron would have to be a considerable one: large enough, in fact, to cope with the fleets both inside and outside the Gulf - and these might have to be faced simultaneously, if the Peloponnesians could coordinate their plans.

Despite the earlier confidence of Phormio's sailors (II.88.2), it is absurd to suppose that this could have been achieved with twenty or even with thirty ships. Phormio was faced with only seventy-seven Peloponnesians in his second battle, and even then won partly by good fortune: but the Spartan Alliance could more than double that number. Anything much under fifty triremes at Naupactos could not be relied on to do the job, and anything much above that number would be financially impossible; yet Naupactos was an ideal position from which to check or cripple the Peloponnesian navy. Any effective north-west strategy would have to start from there.

It was essential to prevent Peloponnesian expeditions *to* or *through* the north-west: that is, to Corcyra and Acarnania. For it was such expeditions that might nullify the benefits to Athens of alliance with these places. The possession or adherence of Zacynthos, for this pur- pose, and even more of Cephallenia was or could have been extremely useful, though they did not lie directly on the natural Peloponnesian route. This route was from the west Peloponnese (Cyllene) across to the region of Oiniadai, and up the Acarnanian coast to Leucas; if they wished to go further, they could use the Leucadian isthmus, and unite their forces with those of Ambracia (see II.80). The most crucial place for the Athenians to hold, in order to render this route impos- sible or at least risky, was Oiniadai; and hardly less important was

Leucas. Both were no doubt tough nuts to crack; but there is not much evidence that the Athenians tried hard enough to crack them. Given possession of those two places, or even Oiniadai alone, the Athenians could heave sealed off the north-west from Peloponnesian intervention. But, yet again, the effective occupation of these places (if not their capture), with a fleet large enough to keep the Peloponnesians from intervening, demanded more logistic support than Athens could deploy by herself. Athens needed the Corcyrean navy to keep the north-west securely attached to Athens.

What could Athens offer her potential ally? Perhaps the most important point is a negative one: she should make it completely clear that she did *not* intend to incorporate Corcyra within her empire, as with the Aegean subject-states. Fear of Athenian presence was chiefly responsible for the Acarnanians' rejection of Athens in 426, and at least a relevant factor in the Corcyrean *stasis*; those states had not in any case been diplomatically nursed in the right sort of way. Athens had to make it clear, with full honesty and well in advance, what the strategic plan was and what the advantages of it would be to all parties; and a central feature would have to be increased wealth and power for Corcyra. The destruction or reduction of Corinth as a colonial and economic power would be a clear gain; and the fact that Sparta would assist Corinth in the north-west, and was actually assisting her as early as 431, was sufficiently clear for Athens to insist on help in manpower and triremes.

A plausible deal, in fairly specific terms, might look like this: Corcyra was to assist Athens in setting up and operating the strategy for blockade, including the existing base at Naupactos. The Corcyreans could provide a permanent fleet of perhaps fifty triremes (not impossibly onerous, for they need not pay their slave-rowers). This would effectively cripple the Peloponnesian navy, and it might not have proved too difficult (given a concerted effort) to capture Oiniadai and Leucas. This achieved, Athens would continue to be supported by Corcyra in the policy of ἐπιτείχισις and guerilla warfare in the southern Peloponnese, directed specifically against Sparta. In return for this service, the Corcyreans could be offered complete control of all maritime trade and territory from Actium northwards, and permanent freedom from Corinthian attacks. A separate option was also available, in the form of sharing with Athens the profits of any expansion in Sicily and Italy.

Such diplomacy would, of course, have demanded a degree of long-term stability of both sides perhaps unusual among the classical Greeks; but the Athenian Alliance of 377 offers a reasonable model of what might have been attempted (see Hammond (1959), pp.486ff.), and there were solid reasons why it had a good chance of succeeding. The benefits to Corcyra were very real, very clearly visible, and probably attainable in a tolerably short time - with proper cooperation, Corinthian control could have been eliminated within a few years at the most. Moreover the strategy could have been organised, from the diplomatic as well as the military viewpoint, step by step; for instance, bases handed over to the Corcyreans *pari passu* with the deployment of Corcyrean help.

From the actual history of Corcyra in its relation to Athens it may appear that such diplomacy was impossibly fragile. But it must be remembered that much of the trouble was due to the ability of the

Spartan Alliance to interfere. Without the actual and potential presence of the Peloponnesians (or even with it), the Corcyrean *stasis* could have been controlled or prevented altogether, with Athenian help; and if expeditions by the Peloponnesians, such as Cnemos' in 429, had been prevented, the Athenians could have settled down to capturing the Corinthian dependencies at their leisure. For this, the first steps which ensured the blockade were all-important; and that needed only the cooperation of Corcyra for the provision of a permanent fleet - something which the Athenians could have made a condition of the original alliance, and which (after their experience of the necessity for Athenian help at Sybota) the Corcyreans themselves would surely have seen as to their own advantage.

Here we may also note - though only briefly, since the topic merits a full treatment in its own right - the considerable help in this strategy which Athens might have gained from Acarnania, given a sufficiently close alliance on the same lines. It may be sufficient here to observe that, even after the diplomatic slap in the face administered by Demosthenes when he abandoned the siege of Leucas against the will of the Acarnanians in 426 (III.94-95), he was still able to persuade them to send 1,000 hoplites - an impressive contingent - to his assistance at Naupactos shortly afterwards (III.102); that, even when Athens had in effect abandoned the north-west, some Acarnanians still joined the Athenian forces in Sicily out of friendship for Demosthenes and goodwill towards Athens (VII.57); and that the Acarnanians by themselves had succeeded by 424 in forcing the strategically crucial town of Oiniadai to join the Athenian alliance (IV.77). All this, in the general historical context of our period, suggests that a closer alliance with Acarnania would have put the north-west firmly in Athens' grasp without much difficulty. The Acarnanians, unlike the Corcyreans, were a dispersed people; but their fear of Athenian power, as shown after Demosthenes' overwhelming victory against Ambracia (III.113), suggests also that Athenian diplomacy failed in much the same way as it failed with Corcyra.

3. *The Athenian attitude*

I have argued in the last sections that the Corcyrean alliance, if properly handled, would have given Athens the chance of outright victory in the war via an aggressive north-west strategy; but, whether or not this is correct, it is clear that Athens' attitude to the alliance is worth consideration, since on any account there were considerable advantages to Athens at stake.

First, did the Athenians at the outbreak of war have any serious conception of the north-west strategy? The evidence suggests a negative answer to this question. It is remarkable that in I.44.2 all the stress is put on the danger of *not* making some sort of alliance. They had no fear of adding to the risks of war with the Peloponnesians by breaking or appearing to break existing treaties, but great fear that the Corcyrean navy would join Corinth: ἐδόκει γὰρ ὁ πρὸς Πελοποννησίους πόλεμος καὶ ὡς ἔσεσθαι αὐτοῖς, καὶ τὴν Κέρκυραν ἐβούλοντο μὴ προέσθαι τοῖς Κορινθίοις ναυτικὸν ἔχουσαν τοσοῦτον: 'They thought that war with the Peloponnesians would come upon them anyway, and they did not wish Corcyra to be given over to the Corinthians, since it had such a

big navy.' But that they had a centralised and monopolistic view
of Athenian sea-power, sharply contrasted with any possibility of a
genuine alliance, is shown by the words immediately following:
ξυγκρούειν δὲ ὅτι μάλιστα αὐτοὺς ἀλλήλοις, ἵνα ἀσθενεστέροις
οὖσιν, ἤν τι δέῃ, Κορινθίοις τε καὶ τοῖς ἄλλοις ναυτικὸν
ἔχουσιν ἐς πόλεμον καθιστῶνται: '[they wanted] them to come
into conflict with each other as much as possible, so that, if need
arose, they themselves would enter upon a war with the Corinthians
and the other naval powers having been weakened by that conflict'
(*ibid.*). Thucydides speaks here of 'the other naval powers' in
the plural (τοῖς ἄλλοις ναυτικὸν ἔχουσιν); the phrase may
include Corcyra, or the Athenians may be thinking only or chiefly
of Corinth's naval allies. But in any case they were willing, indeed
anxious, to have both navies badly mauled by each other - as in fact
happened.

Why did the Athenians not want a strong Corcyrean navy allied to
them? Such a policy may have been ultimately self-defeating; but there
were reasons behind it. Athens feared above all the rebellion of her
subjects, particularly those who had any kind of effective fleet: a
lesson no doubt first learned from the Samian revolt before the war
(I.115ff.). She wanted all the ships of her subject-allies either
built and manned by Athens (from the tribute they paid) or under fairly direct Athenian control, as in the case of Chios and Lesbos who
retained some ships of their own. It would be hard to enforce that
principle on Corcyra and keep it enforced: Corcyra was both more
powerful and more remote than the Aegean city-states, and even if
she remained loyal to Athens she was still vulnerable to the attacks
of the Spartan Alliance. These difficulties remained much the same,
whether Corcyra was seen as a subject or as an ally. At the same
time, adherence to the principle of centralised Athenian control made
the alliances necessary for an adequate north-west strategy difficult
or impossible.

Nevertheless, the Athenians were certainly aware that the north-
west offered important chances of victory. This emerges clearly in a
passage where Thucydides lists the pre-war preparations: Ἀθηναῖοι
δὲ τήν τε ὑπάρχουσαν ξυμμαχίαν ἐξήταζον καὶ ἐς τὰ περὶ
Πελοπόννησον μᾶλλον χωρία ἐπρεσβεύοντο, Κέρκυραν καὶ
Κεφαλληνίαν καὶ Ἀκαρνᾶνας καὶ Ζάκυνθον, ὁρῶντες, εἰ
σφίσι φίλια ταῦτ' εἴη βεβαίως, πέριξ τὴν Πελοπόννησον
καταπολεμήσοντες (II.7.3). There is some dispute here over the
meaning: in particular the sense of ὁρῶντες ... καταπολεμήσοντες,
which Gomme takes to mean 'seeing that we [?] should be fighting all
round the Peloponnese'. That is surely too weak, and violates the
sense of καταπολεμήσοντες, which normally has the force of 'wear
down by fighting' (see II.90.3). Gomme's alternative, taking
βεβαίως with καταπολεμήσοντες, 'we [?] shall then be waging
war against the Peloponnese, from every direction, with a secure base'
is not much better. It would be awkward to have to understand an
object for καταπολεμήσοντες ('the enemy', for instance), and its
natural object is τὴν Πελοπόννησον : hence πέριξ must be adverb-
ial. We translate: 'The Athenians reviewed their existing system
of alliances; and in particular they sent embassies to the places
round the Peloponnese - Corcyra and Cephallenia and the Acarnanians
and Zacynthos: seeing that, if these places were firmly on their side,

they would wear down the Peloponnese by warfare round about it.'
It is misleading to translate '*from all* round it', which might
carry the (false) implication that these allies were situated all
round the Peloponnese, which they were not - all were in the north-
west. The sense is rather that, given these allies, the Athenians
would then be able to attack ar various points all round the
Peloponnese.

The passage does show that the Athenians had some idea of a north-
west strategy, though a substantially different and fainter one from
our own. Part of their thought was that bases in the north-west
would facilitate their attacks on the Peloponnese: and so of course
they would, since their ships could rest and repair there after a
periplous, instead of having to return to Athens. But that may not
be all: Zacynthos, Cephallenia and Naupactos (or even one of these)
would be sufficient for this purpose, and neither Corcyra nor
Acarnania were suitable candidates for a base used specifically against
the Peloponnese in this context (as opposed to a base of operations in
north-west Greece itself). Some further strategic thought may have
been in the Athenians' heads; it is hard to see their interest in
all four places just as double (or quadruple) insurance, designed to
be certain of having at least one base for ships on a *periplous* -
against the Peloponnese, they never used them as such. They did not,
for instance, descend with a fleet based on Zacynthos or Corcyra
on such Peloponnesian targets as Cyllene, or Messenia, or the Achaean
cities, all within easy range. What they did do was to use some at
least of the bases for operations in north-west Greece itself. These
operations were against the Peloponnesians - in particular, Corinth -
but not in the Peloponnese. This, surely, is part of what the Athenians had in mind. Just as they could operate against the Spartan
Alliance in the Saronic Gulf, so (with these new bases) they could
operate in north-west Greece, thus 'wearing down the Peloponnese' by
military engagements 'round about it'. This is, of course, not only a
long way from our north-west strategy, but importantly different
from it. The aim is not to control the north-west in order to make
use of it and the allies there in a strategy of blockade and
ἐπιτειχισις specifically against Sparta, but (in effect) a policy
of general pressure: the Peloponnesians are to be harried wherever
the Athenians have an opportunity, and thus 'worn down'.

The only other passage which suggests something like our strategy
comes much later, in Alcibiades' speech to the Spartans, (VI.90.3):
εἰ δὲ προχωρήσειε ταῦτα ἢ πάντα ἢ καὶ τὰ πλείω, ἤδη τῇ
Πελοποννήσῳ ἐμέλλομεν ἐπιχειρήσειν, κομίσαντες ξύμπασαν μὲν
τὴν ἐκεῖθεν προσγενομένην δύναμιν τῶν Ἑλλήνων, πολλοὺς δὲ
βαρβάρους μισθωσάμενοι καὶ Ἴβηρας καὶ ἄλλους τῶν ἐκεῖ
ὁμολογουμένων νῦν βαρβάρων μαχιμωτάτους, τριήρεις τε πρὸς
ταῖς ἡμετέραις πολλὰς ναυπηγησάμενοι, ἐχούσης τῆς Ἰταλίας
ξύλα ἄφθονα, οἷς τὴν Πελοπόννησον πέριξ πολιορκοῦντες καὶ
τῷ πεζῷ ἅμα ἐκ γῆς ἐφορμαῖς τῶν πόλεων τὰς μὲν βίᾳ λαβόντες,
τὰς δ' ἐντειχισάμενοι, ῥᾳδίως ἠλπίζομεν καταπολεμήσειν καὶ
μετὰ ταῦτα καὶ τοῦ ξύμπαντος Ἑλληνικοῦ ἄρξειν. 'If all these
plans went well, or even most of them, we already had it in mind to take
on the Peloponnese: we should bring with us all the Greek forces, now
added to our own, which we should have gained from there [sc. Italy and
Sicily], hire many native troops, Iberians and others of the barbarians

131

in those parts now recognised as being the best fighters, and build many triremes to add to our own, since Italy has vast quantities of wood. With all these resources we should set up a blockade round about the Peloponnese, and at the same time make assaults with our army from the land - taking some cities by assault, and building forts in the territory of others. In this way we hoped that we should easily wear you down by war, and afterwards that we should rule the whole of the Greek world.'

We may first raise the question of how seriously to take the passage. It is, admittedly, (1) part of a Thucydidean speech, with all the uncertainties about historicity which some scholars take that to imply; (2) spoken by Alcibiades, a character not noted for accurate and honest reportage; (3) designed to persuade the Spartans into taking certain action, and therefore perhaps likely to exaggerate certain dangers; and (4) reporting 'Athenian intentions' which may not have been in the minds of all or most Athenians, and some of which may seem grandiose or even fantastic (particularly the idea that, after conquering Italy and Sicily that Athens would attack Carthage, VI.90. 2). On some or all of these grounds we should be inclined to view the passage with some suspicion.

On the other hand, the evidence that Thucydides gives us elsewhere strongly rebuts *a priori* doubts. Whatever we may think about Thucydidean speeches, Alcibiades would not have discredited himself with the normally sceptical Spartans by excessive exaggeration or fantasy. They were in fact persuaded by what he said, νομίσαντες παρὰ τοῦ σαφέστατα εἰδότος ἀκηκοέναι (VI.93.1), 'thinking that they had heard from the man who had the clearest knowledge'. The Athenians certainly intended to conquer the whole of Sicily (VI.1.1, 61): Alcibiades believed, or at least is quoted as saying, that Sicilian gains would enable them to rule all Greece (VI.18.4), and his speech was persuasive (19.1): even the Carthaginian idea was not an *ad hoc* invention for the Spartans' benefit (15.2). The motives and beliefs on which the Sicilian Expedition was based are not all perspicuous; but the hope of increased revenues, allies and other resources must have played a major part - and it is just these factors, deployed futuristically in his speech, that Alcibiades stresses. There seems no doubt that, if the Athenians had in fact been successful in Sicily, this is at least the sort of way they would have used them against the Peloponnese. The Spartans at least believed in 4.3 that the additional resources would have been extremely dangerous to them, just as they believed that those resources on the Spartan side would be decisive (VIII.2.3-4); both sides may have had an exaggerated idea of Sicilian power or participation, but that does not invalidate what Alcibiades (or Thucydides) tells us of their intentions.

There is some doubt about the exact meaning of the crucial lines, 21-24. (a) The Mss read οἷς: this would suggest that both the Ἑλλήνων in line 18, and the barbarian troops in line 18-20, are to take part in πολιορκοῦντες, as well as the triremes in lines 20-21. There seems nothing strange in this: the well-known shortage of Athenian man-power is to be supplemented by these troops, who (presumably) are to make descents on the Peloponnesian coast from the triremes in the way that had been constant Athenian practice ever since the beginning of the war. Andrewes and Dover say (p.363) that the emendation to αἷς, 'referring to the triremes alone, is necessary, as καὶ τῷ πεζῷ ἅμα shows'; but this is somewhat too blithe. For τῷ πεξῷ most naturally refers to *other* land forces, which are not sea-borne (not engaged in πολιορκοῦντες) but start ἐκ γῆς: that is, presumably, from Athens itself or other land-bases on Athens' side in the Peloponnese. Since some land forces must be carried in the triremes, οἷς (which allows the forces from Sicily to be πολιορκοῦντες) makes more sense than αἷς. (b) ἐντειχισάμενοι must, as Andrewes and Dover say (p.364), mean 'building forts in their territory' (πόλεων referring, as commonly, to city-states rather than to what we should normally mean in English by 'cities'), the idea being to cow or check the city by means of a fortification close to it. This is in substance the same as ἐπιτείχισις (fortification 'against' or, as it were, 'on top of' someone). But Alcibiades is hardly talking about the policy discussed earlier under that description. For (see (a) above) he clearly has the idea that the Athenians will also be working with a large land-based army (τῷ πεζῷ); it is these troops, not the ones engaged in πολιορκοῦντες in the earlier clause, who will be capturing cities by force and ἐντειχισάμενοι. He is not describing sea-borne descents for the purpose of securing bases defensible by sea, as at Pylos, Cythera and elsewhere. (c) καταπολεμήσειν presents a problem. We can take it, as is natural in this context, to have the force of 'overcome' - that is, they hoped that the Peloponnesians would not just be worn down by war but (as it were) worn down and out. But that makes καταπολεμήσοντες in II.7.3 impossible: we should have to translate 'realising that then [sc. with the Ionian islands on their side] they would overcome (wear out) the Peloponnese' - but that is simply not true, nor would the Athenians have thought it to be true in 431. καταπολεμήσοντες must there mean simply 'wear down', not 'wear out'. Are we then to say that the word has two distinct meanings? That is, I think, too strong: it is better to maintain that it has (as philosophers used to say) both a 'task' and an 'achievement' use. It *means* simply 'wear down'; the *context* then determines whether that process is conceived as achieving an end result or not. In II.7.3 the Athenians see that they will be able to engage in the process of wearing the Peloponnese down, without the implication that they will necessarily wear it out; in VI.90.3 that implication is present.

This interpretation, if correct, shows fairly clearly that those Athenians who shared Alcibiades' ideas appreciated the need for more resources in order to defeat the Peloponnesians, and had some notion - no doubt a fairly vague one - of how this was to be done: roughly, by simultaneous attack from the sea and from Athens' land-bases in the Peloponnese. But it also shows (see (b) above) that they had no policy of sea-based ἐπιτείχισις as we described it earlier, even given such additional resources. The idea inherent in πολιορκοῦντες is essentially the same as that in II.7.3, only this time more optimistic because of their extra strength; if it is a coherent policy at all, it is a sort of saturation policy, not a specific plan to multiply the cases of Pylos and Cythera, encourage a helot revolt, and thus subvert the Spartan state by internal conflict and guerilla warfare. In particular there is no indication (as there is in II.7.3) that Corcyra and the Ionian islands have an important strategic role.

Part of the difficulty in assessing Athenian strategic ideas is uncertainty about whether their efforts were directed (at any one time) to (a) the Peloponnesians in general, or (b) Sparta in particular. Alcibiades, in the passage above, looks forward to a time when greatly increased resources would enable Athens actually to conquer and rule the whole of the Peloponnese (indded the whole of Greece). But in practice Athens came nowhere near being able to do this. She had the options of (a) trying to crush the allies of Sparta, or seduce them from the Spartan Alliance, or in some other way discourage them from continuing the war; or (b) launching some kind of effective military attack against Sparta herself. It is (a) that seems to be behind most of what Thucydides represents the Athenians (including Pericles) as saying or thinking (e.g. in II.7 and the speech of I.140) and doing (e.g. the expeditions of 431 and 430, II.23 and 56: directed as much against Sparta's allies as against Sparta). I can see no evidence that the policy of sea-based ἐπιτειχίσις aimed specifically at Sparta was seriously entertained before 425, except perhaps by Demosthenes and a few others. (Demosthenes' colleagues regarded his plan to fortify Pylos as a waste of money: IV.3.) Even then the evidence is indirect: the (unpredicted) success of Pylos led to the occupation of Cythera in 424, but to little more than that. As has been argued earlier, the reasons for not pursuing such a policy were probably logistic and financial. A *fortiori* there was no Athenian policy to use the Corcyrean navy for such a strategy.

There is only one piece of evidence that might be quoted on the other side, and that of a very dubious nature. In his speech, just before the war, Pericles anticipates that the Peloponnesian navy will be inactive because the Athenian fleet, in large numbers, will be constantly on guard against it and hemming it in: διὰ τὸ ὑφ' ἡμῶν πολλαῖς ναυσὶν αἰεὶ ἐφορμεῖσθαι ... πρὸς μὲν γὰρ ὀλίγας ἐφορμούσας κἂν διακινδυνεύσειαν ... πολλαῖς δὲ εἰργόμενοι ἡσυχάσουσι (I. 142.7-8). ἐφορμεῖσθαι is usually translated (unthinkingly) as 'blockade', with the result that most scholars, aware of the impossibility of blockading the Peloponnese permanently (αἰεὶ) with unseaworthy triremes, have not taken the passage seriously as a piece of strategy. However, as we had occasion to notice when commenting on III.76, ἐφορμεῖσθαι (and its associated forms) does not always refer to anything so tight as a blockade, in the usual sense of the term: it can mean something looser, more like 'anchored over against', 'on the watch against', 'on guard against' (like the Peloponnesian ships at Cyllene with reference to Corcyra in III.76). That suggests at least a possible strategy: if we translate 'blockade', the passage saddles Pericles (or Thucydides) with both an impracticable plan and a forecast of Peloponnesian inactivity which was quite false - for the Peloponnesians operated constantly with large fleets during the early years of the war, at least in the north-west.

Nevertheless the passage must mean more than just that Athenian ships from Piraeus, or even when conducting a *periplous* of the Peloponnese, would always engage Peloponnesian fleets: εἰργόμενοι, 'hemmed in', suggests something *like* a loose form of blockade. That would be possible if Pericles anticipated the use of large fleets based in the north-west: at Naupactos, Zacynthos, Cephallenia or Corcyra - as II.7.3 suggests. From this we may go on to surmise that, as we have said, the expense of maintaining such fleets - and they would have to be both substantial and permanent if their operations were to have the effect described in I.142 by Pericles - would be out of the question, and that therefore Pericles must have had in mind the use of the Corcyrean navy along the lines already discussed.

But that is no more than guesswork: it is contradicted by I.44.2 and by Thucydides' silence about such a strategy. More probably, Pericles hoped for a naval offensive which (even without reliable, large and permanent Corcyrean contributions) would keep the Peloponnesian fleet inactive and in a sense 'hem them in', but was prevented by the expense of the Potidaian siege and the much worse effects of the plague. Without those, he might have been able to base sufficiently large squadrons in the north-west to justify his remarks in I.142.

That the Athenians did not conceive of the north-west strategy does not mean that they lacked all strategic insight or interest in this area. But even if they saw clearly (which I doubt), they certainly did not act wholeheartedly or even consistently. Oiniadai was not assailed in the war until 428, and then without success - Asopios brought only thirty ships against it. The town of Leucas itself was not attacked until 426, again only with thirty ships; and Demosthenes was persuaded to abandon the attack rather than organise an effective siege. Anaktorion, admittedly of peripheral interest, was left unscathed until 425.

Only Naupactos suggests a serious and consistently-maintained strategic policy: and even this is doubtful. Phormio was sent there with twenty ships in the winter of 430/29, and set up a complete blockade (φυλακὴν εἶχε μήτ᾽ ἐκπλεῖν ἐκ Κορίνθου καὶ τοῦ Κρισαίου κόλπου μηδένα, μήτ᾽ ἐσπλεῖν; 'he kept guard so that no one should sail from Corinth and the Krisaian Gulf or into it', (II.69.1); but the fleet returned with him to Athens in the spring of 428 (II.103.1). His son Asopios took twelve ships out of thirty to Naupactos in the summer of that year, but apparently used them primarily for the abortive attack on Oeniadai; after that the Athenians are described simply as 'sailing away' (ἀπο-πλεύσαντες, III.7.4): perhaps back to Naupactos, perhaps not. In 427 Nicostratus comes to Corcyra from Naupactos with twelve ships (perhaps the same twelve): his departure is not mentioned. Demosthenes' unsuccessful army retreated to Naupactos in 426 (III.99.5); and at the end of the summer 'the Athenians in Naupactos' (οἱ ἐν τῇ Ναυπάκτῳ ᾿Αθηναῖοι, IV.49.1) join the Acarnanians in an expedition which captures Anaktorion. That, in our period, includes virtually all we are told about the place: and we are told precious little after 425.

We cannot conclude from this that the Athenians kept a permanent fleet of any size at Naupactos; indeed the indications - particularly the return of Phormio's squadron in 428 - are all the other way. Nor can we even conclude that the fleet's job was to blockade; that is mentioned only in reference to Phormio, and the subsequent silence is significant. The commanders there had, perhaps, a 'watching brief' in a fairly literal sense of the phrase: not, I think, strict orders to blockade - something which may, in fact, have been just Phormio's idea. In later years, moreover, there is some evidence that Naupactos was not permanently manned, and the same is likely to be true throughout the war.

4. A note on Pericles

I have spoken in the last section and elsewhere of the 'Athenian attitude', and talked about what 'the Athenians' or 'Athens' did or intended. That is misleading insofar as it may convey the impression of a consistent and generally agreed strategy or foreign policy shared by all or most Athenians; whereas the truth is likely to be that - at least on some occasions - there were sharply divided opinions. Some scholars, for instance, have spoken of a 'peace party' and a 'war party' at Athens which were constantly at loggerheads with each other. I have also made some references to Pericles, and perhaps spoken as if what 'the Athenians' did was identical with what Pericles did. Thucydides himself, indeed, seems sometimes to make no clear distinctions here: he talks now of an Athenian expedition 'under Pericles' command' (e.g. II.31.1), now of 'Pericles' doing such-and-such (e.g. II.22.2), now of 'the Athenians' doing it (e.g. II.24.1).

There is, in my judgement, little hope of our achieving any very detailed knowledge of the relationship of Athenian interal politics to Athenian strategy, even though Thucydides does give us some interesting information at certain points (notably the debate about the Sicilian Expedition in VI.8ff.). Discussion about Pericles, of whom we know more than we know of any other figure, may be more fruitful; but a whole book would be needed to give adequate answers to such questions as whether Pericles had a consistent foreign policy and set of strategic aims, and whether he was always able to obtain the support of his fellow-citizens in implementing them. Certainly positive answers to these questions cannot be taken for granted: both internal politics and unpredictable external events may make it fruitless to search for consistency in either Periclean or Athenian policy or practice. That view, however, may be unduly pessimistic; and I shall try to say a few things about Pericles in relation to Corcyra which may shed some light on our special interest.

The first thing to be done is surely to distinguish Periclean strategy before and after the outbreak of the Peloponnesian War. There is a good deal of evidence (for the arguments and sources see Hammond, 1959, pp.313ff.) that before the war Pericles was associated with a policy which was designed to expand the Athenian empire, perhaps particularly in the west - which could, of course, have included an interest in Corcyra as lying in a key position on the coastal route. Thucydides himself first mentioned Pericles as leading an attack, with Achaean help, on Oiniadai (I.111.3), which we have seen was strategically crucial to the whole north-west. His initiative in the founding of Thurii in particular (Hammond, *ibid.*) shows that he had some interest in Italy and Sicily as targets for Athenian imperialism.

This certainly contrasts which what I shall claim to be Pericles' strategy from 431 onwards; the reasons for the change are more doubtful, particularly since we cannot be certain which Athenian moves in the few decades before the war - roughly, from 461-31, when Athens and the Peloponnese were often in conflict - were initiated or backed by Pericles. It may be that, as a young man, he was more optimistic about an expansionist policy and more willing to take risks; perhaps he needed to take such risks in order to achieve successes necessary to gain and keep popularity; more importantly than either, the risks were less before 431 because the Spartan Alliance had not yet decided

on a fight to the death against Athens, and its members were not
always united. But in any case the contrast is there. My own view
is a simple one: that Pericles wanted to expand and increase Athens'
power insofar as that was consistent with her safety, and that in
431 he appreciated that it was no longer consistent.

For - unless we convict Thucydides of gross falsehood - there is
no doubt that the speeches of 431 and 430 (I.140ff., II.60ff.)
advocate no expansion of empire. As Thucydides himself says,
ὁ μὲν γὰρ ἡσυχάζοντάς τε καὶ τὸ ναυτικὸν θεραπεύοντας καὶ
ἀρχὴν μὴ ἐπικτωμένους ἐν τῷ πολέμῳ μηδὲ τῇ πόλει
κινδυνεύοντας ἔφη περιέσεσθαι, 'for he said they would win
through if they kept quiet, looked after their navy, did not add to
their empire in the war, and took no risks with the city' (II.65.7):
in the words of Pericles' own speech, ἀρχήν ... μὴ ἐπικτᾶσθαι,
'and not add to the empire' (I.144.1).

Some scholars have doubted how far Thucydides' speeches represent
what was actually said. I take the view that he at least attempted
to do so. Further, it would be odd if he deceived us about what
Pericles said on these occasions. There would have been plenty of
people who remembered what he said well enough; and the speeches
have all the more claim to accuracy in that they contain some predictions which were not verified by events (the 'blockade' of the
Peloponnesian navy discussed above, the impossibility of the Spartan
Alliance matching Athens by sea, etc.: see I.142-43) - predictions
Thucydides would not have put in the mouth of his most admired states-
man had they not actually been spoken. Moreover, Pericles was surely
saying what he actually believed throughout the speeches: as Thucydides tells us, he had such esteem in Athens that he had no need
πρὸς ἡδονήν τι λέγειν, 'to say anything just to keep people
happy', but could even 'contradict them in anger' (πρὸς ὀργήν τι
ἀντειπεῖν, II.65.8). We have, then, to accept that Pericles'
strategic policy was one of quietism and non-expansionism, so far
as extension of empire was concerned, from 431 onwards.

One (only one) difficulty about applying all this to the case of
Corcyra is that we want to know how Pericles stood in respect of the
Corcyrean alliance debated in 433 - a date which might equally be
taken as early enough to fall within Pericles' pre-war expansionist
policy, or as late enough to fall within his post-war quietism. The
view taken here is that his policy with regard to Corcyra at that
time was, in fact, a sort of compromise between the two: but tending more towards the war-time policy, since it was clear (as
Thucydides tells us, I.44.2) to Athens, and to Pericles, that war
was bound to come. I also believe that, as Plutarch tells us
(*Pericles* 29), it was in fact Pericles who persuaded the Athenians
to send help to Corcyra in 433: though Thucydides does not mention
Pericles in this connection, speaking only of 'Athens' and 'the
Athenians' (I.44.1, 50.5). Let us see how this fits the facts.

Pericles' motives would have been those ascribed by Thucydides
to 'the Athenians' in I.44: fear that Corcyra's navy would fall into
Peloponnesian hands, and the usefulness of Corcyra's geographical
position. Both these can be interpreted along fairly quietist lines.
The former does not imply any positive policy as regards the Corcyrean
navy, or hope that it would play a big part in Athenian strategy;
and the latter may have been seen as important for the negative task
of preventing reinforcements to the Peloponnese from the western

Greeks, not (or not so much) for the positive enterprises that might
be undertaken by Athens (like the Sicilian Expedition, criticised by
Thucydides in II.65, and certainly not in line with Periclean war-
time policy). At least there would have been no question of adding
Corcyra to the empire; and in that sense Pericles was already adopt-
ing, in 433, his war-time policy.

There were two debates at Athens about the matter. At the first,
the Athenians favoured a policy of non-intervention, but at the second they changed their minds (I.44). Further uncertainty is shown
by the sending of only ten ships to start with - just a token force,
and commanded by a man whose family was pro-Spartan (Lacedaimonios
son of Cimon) - and the addition of a further twenty ships soon
afterwards (I.45, 50). The probability is that Pericles lent his
weight to a more interventionist policy than the Athenians might
otherwise have adopted, in other words, that he helped them to change
their minds in the second debate, and was in favour of increasing the
number of ships sent. This latter, at least, can reasonably be seen
as realistic rather than aggressive: he realised that ten ships would
not be enough to do the job (Thucydides makes this point, but of 'the
Athenians' rather than Pericles (I.50.5)).

The whole style (so to speak) of Athens' intervention in Corcyra,
and the way in which the ships were actually used at Sybota, is
thoroughly in line with the general tone of Pericles' war-policy as
he stated it in 431 (I.140ff.). That tone takes a middle path
between aggression and backing down: nearly all the strategic points
he makes are *conditional*: 'If they build forts on our land, so can
we on theirs', 'If they invade us by land, we can attack them by sea'
(I.142). His line is not to take the initiative in starting the
war, but equally not to give in to Spartan demands. In just such a
spirit the Athenians at Sybota tell the Corinthians that they are
not starting a war and not breaking the treaty, but that they will
not retreat from their commitment to defend Corcyra (I.53). However
strong Pericles' influence on the Athenians about Corcya - and it could
not have been overwhelming, in view of their changes of mind - the
actual events are in line with his war-time policy.

That may also account, at least in part, for Athens' failure to
make a proper alliance with Corcyra (or to use her alliance to the
full), which has been a principal theme of this book. If from 433
onwards Pericles regarded Athenian policy as being on a war-time
basis, he would not have wished to take the risk of adding Corcyra
to the empire - and that piece of expansionism might have been necessary for a full use of the alliance. Of course there were other
factors, in particular the political changes that occurred between
433 and 430, perhaps owing to the influence of the prisoners returned by Corinth, which swung Corcyrean feeling away from Athens. But
Pericles, who had been in command during the revolts both of Euboea
and of Samos I.114-17), would have been particularly convinced of
the supreme importance of not allowing Athens' allies to have independent navies. In view of Corcyra's potential importance to
Athenian strategy, as we have argued above, this is perhaps one of
the few cases where Pericles' caution - praised so highly by
Thucydides in II.65 - was not justified.

MAPS

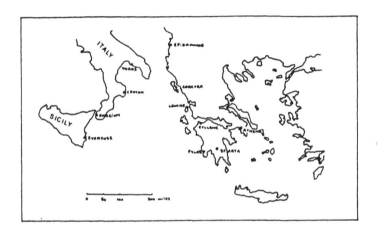

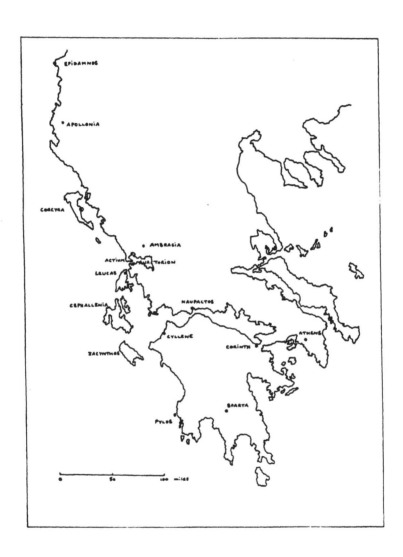

EPIDAMNOS

APOLLONIA

CORCYRA

AMBRACIA

ACTIUM ANAKTORION

LEUCAS

CEPHALLENIA

NAUPACTOS

CYLLENE

CORINTH

ATHENS

ZACYNTHOS

SPARTA

PYLOS

0   50   100 miles

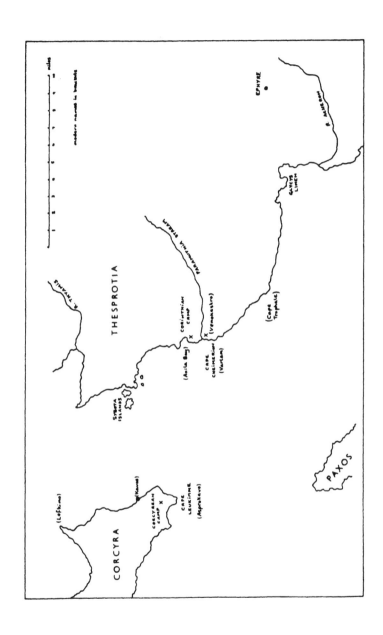

CORCYRA

(Lefkimo)

(Kavos)

CORCYRAEAN
CAMP X

CAPE
LEUKIMNE
(/Aprotsva)

PAXOS

THESPROTIA

SIVANAS

SYBOTA
ISLANDS

(Avila Bay)

CORINTHIAN
CAMP X

X CAPE
CHEIMERIUM
(Varlam) (Vrachonisi)

PARAMYTHIA STREAM

Cape
Trophalus)

GLYCYS
LIMEN

EPHYRE
●

R. ACHERON

miles

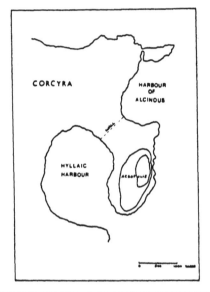

142

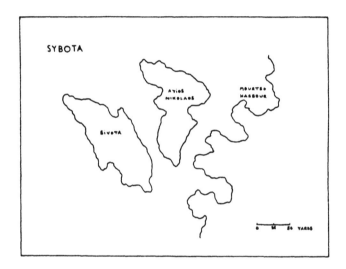

SYBOTA

SIVOTA

AγιοS
NIKOLAOS

MOURTOS
HASSOUR

0   M   50 YARDS

SELECT BIBLIOGRAPHY

(1) Works which bear directly on the problems discussed in the text.

A.W. Gomme   *A Historical Commentary on Thucydides* (Oxford, 1956 onwards) Vols. I-III, continued in Vol. IV with A. Andrewes and K.J. Dover (1970).

N.G.L. Hammond   'Naval operations in the South Channel of Corcyra, 435-33 B.C.', in *Journal of Hellenic Studies*, Vol. 65 (1945), pp.26ff. *Epirus* (Oxford, 1967).

G.E.M.de Ste Croix   *The Origins of the Peloponnesian War* (Duckworth, 1972).

(2) A selection of editions of Thucydides and other useful background works

M. Amit   *Athens and the Sea* (Collections Latomus, Brussels, 1965).

T. Arnold   Thucydides (edition) (Oxford, 1847).

G. Busolt   *Griechische Geschichte* (Gotha, 1893-1904).

Sir R. Custance   *War at Sea* (Blackwood, Edinburgh & London, 1919).

G. Grote   *History of Greece* (London, 1888).

N.G.L. Hammond   *History of Greece* (Oxford, 1959).

D. Kagan   *The Archidamian War* (Cornell, 1974).

A. Philipson   *Die Griechischen Landschaften*: edited by E. Kirsten (Frankfurt am M., 1950-59).

J.M. Stahl   Thucydides (edition: edited by E.F. Poppo) (Leipzig, 1882-88).

J. Steup   Thucydides (edition: edited by J. Classen) (Berlin, 1900-22).

J.B. Wilson   *Pylos* (Aris and Phillips, U.K., 1979).

Cambridge Ancient History, 3rd edition (Cambridge, 1970 onwards).

www.ingramcontent.com/pod-product-compliance
Ingram Content Group UK Ltd.
Pitfield, Milton Keynes, MK11 3LW, UK
UKHW020737280225
455688UK00012B/717